C000078341

Previous books by Peter Harclerode and David Reynolds:
Commando – The Illustrated History of Britain's Green Berets

Previous books by Peter Harclerode:
Go To It! The Illustrated History of The 6th Airborne Division
Unholy Babylon – The Secrets of Saddam's War (as Gregory Alexander with
Adel Darwish)
PARA! Fifty Years of The Parachute Regiment
Arnhem – A Tragedy of Errors
The Lost Masters – The Looting of Europe's Treasurehouses
Warfare
Secret Soldiers – Special Forces In The War Against Terrorism
*Fighting Dirty – The Story of Covert Operations From Ho Chi Minh to Osama
bin Laden*

Previous books by David Reynolds:
Paras – The Illustrated History of Britain's Airborne Forces
Task Force – The Illustrated History of the Falklands War

GURKHA

'As I write these last words, my thoughts return to you who are my comrades, the stubborn and indomitable peasants of Nepal. Once more I hear the laughter with which you greeted every hardship. Once more I see you in your bivouacs or about your fires on forced march or in the trenches, now shivering with wet and cold, now scorched by a pitiless and burning sun. Uncomplaining you endure hunger and thirst and wounds; and at the last your unwavering lines disappear into the smoke and wrath of battle. Bravest of the brave, most generous of the generous, never had a country more faithful friends than you.'

Professor Sir Ralph Turner MC, who served with the 3rd Queen Alexandra's Own Gurkha Rifles in the First World War

GURKHA

The Illustrated History

PETER HARCLERODE &
DAVID REYNOLDS

SUTTON PUBLISHING

This book is dedicated to the officers and soldiers of
The Gurkha Brigade and The Brigade of Gurkhas,
and to the memory of those who fell in action.

First published in 2003 by
Sutton Publishing Limited · Phoenix Mill
Thrupp · Stroud · Gloucestershire · GL5 2BU

Copyright © Peter Harclerode and David Reynolds, 2003

All rights reserved. No part of this publication may be reproduced, stored in a retrieval system, or transmitted, in any form, or by any means, electronic, mechanical, photocopying, recording or otherwise, without the prior permission of the publisher and copyright holders.

Peter Harclerode and David Reynolds have asserted their moral right to be identified as the authors of this work.

British Library Cataloguing in Publication Data
A catalogue record for this book is available from the British Library.

ISBN 0 7509 2844 1

Endpapers: *Front*: Gurkhas of 1 RGR pictured in Pristina as houses burn just hours after the coalition force had entered Kosovo.
Back: Gurkha recruits train with the kukri.
Half-title page photograph: Gurkhas armed with rifles and kukris taking part in a dawn attack in Tunisia during the Second World War.
Title page photograph: Gurkha soldiers pictured during their attachment to 2 PARA.
Frontispiece: The Queen's Truncheon on being brought back into service with The Royal Gurkha Rifles in 1997.

Typeset in Sabon 11/14pt.
Typesetting and origination by
Sutton Publishing Limited.
Printed and bound in England by
J.H. Haynes & Co. Ltd, Sparkford.

Contents

Acknowledgements   vi
Authors' Foreword   vii

1. Origins and Early Years   1
2. The First World War   15
3. The Second World War   24
4. The War in Burma   42
5. Partition and The Malayan Emergency   77
6. The Brunei Rebellion   99
7. The Borneo Confrontation   113
8. Gurkha Airborne Troops   148
9. The Gurkha Corps Units   176
10. The Modern Brigade   213
11. Recruitment and Training   234

Further Reading   251
Index   252

Acknowledgements

The authors would like to express their sincere thanks to the following for their great kindness in providing considerable assistance during the research for this book: Brig Christopher Bullock, Curator, the Gurkha Museum; Brig Bruce Jackman, Honorary Secretary, the Sirmoor Club/2nd King Edward VII's Own Gurkha Rifles Association; Col Dennis Wood, Historian, 2nd King Edward VII's Own Gurkha Rifles; Lt Col Digby Willoughby, former Commandant 1st/2nd King Edward VII's Own Gurkha Rifles; Maj Martin Fuller, Honorary Secretary, 4th Prince of Wales's Own Gurkha Rifles Association; Maj Patrick Robeson, Honorary Secretary, 6th Queen Elizabeth's Own Gurkha Rifles Association; Lt Col Keith Robinson, Honorary Secretary, 7th Duke of Edinburgh's Own Gurkha Rifles Association; Col A.G. Watson, Honorary Secretary, 9th Gurkha Rifles Association; Maj Andrew Watt, Honorary Secretary, 10th Princess Mary's Own Gurkha Rifles Association; Lt Col Bill Dawson, Regimental Secretary, the Royal Gurkha Rifles; Col James Stuart, Honorary Secretary, The Queen's Gurkha Engineers Association; Lt Col Mike Barrett, Honorary Secretary, The Queen's Gurkha Signals Association; Col Richard Cawthorn, Historian, The Queen's Own Gurkha Transport Regiment/The Queen's Own Gurkha Logistics Regiment; Lt Col Angus Fairlie, Curator, Regimental Museum, The Highlanders.

PHOTOGRAPHS

The Gurkha Museum at Winchester supplied a number of important photographs which are the copyright of the museum and offer a unique insight into the early years of Gurkha history. Andrew Chittock and Dilip Banerjee photographed members of The Brigade of Gurkhas in Bosnia, Kosovo, Macedonia, Sierra Leone and East Timor. Carl Schulze, one of Germany's leading military photographers, supplied an excellent collection of images featuring Gurkhas, while Robert Morrison provided others taken in the early 1980s. Thanks must also go to Terry Champion at the Land Command picture desk, and to Dick Goodwin, Tom Ross, Bob Morrison, Teddy Neville and Yves Debay.

AUTHORS' FOREWORD

During the last two centuries, the doughty hillmen of Nepal have served the British Crown with unswerving loyalty. In 1814, following a series of conflicts between the mountain kingdom of Nepal and the forces of the Honourable East India Company, the first Gurkhas were recruited into British service. During the ensuing years, they soon distinguished themselves as fearless fighters in wars in Afghanistan and on India's North East and North West Frontiers, where they took part in operations against rebellious tribesmen.

The year 1914 saw the start of the First World War and battalions of Gurkhas were among those troops despatched by India to fight in France. Others took part in campaigns in the Gallipoli Peninsula, Egypt and Mesopotamia, and by the end of the

Gurkhas deploy from a Royal Navy Sea King helicopter during their deployment in Bosnia as part of the Stabilisation Force (SFOR) in the early 1990s.

war a total of 114,000 Gurkhas had served in the ranks of the Indian Army's Gurkha Brigade, with over 20,000 losing their lives. By then they had established a reputation as fighting men that was second to none.

The period following the First World War saw Gurkha battalions serving on the North West Frontier where once again they were engaged in campaigns against tribesmen who were a worthy foe.

Following the start of the Second World War, in 1940 the Gurkha Brigade underwent a major expansion and the number of its battalions eventually increased to 52. Once again, India despatched troops to the aid of Britain and Gurkhas found themselves serving in North Africa, Italy and Greece. Others served in Asia and South East Asia, taking part in the campaigns against the Japanese in Malaya and Burma. By the end of the war in 1945, over 120,000 Gurkhas had served in the ranks of the Gurkha Brigade, suffering some 20,000 casualties.

In India, the period following the Second World War was one of considerable unrest, culminating in 1947 with Partition, the creation of the state of Pakistan and the withdrawal from India of the British who took with them four Gurkha regiments. These were incorporated into a new body, The Brigade of Gurkhas, which henceforth formed part of the British Army. Based in Malaya, it was soon committed to action with the onset of the Malayan Emergency in 1948 which lasted for twelve years. During this time, Gurkha battalions and the newly formed corps units of The Brigade of Gurkhas were continuously deployed on operations against Communist Terrorists. In this period, Gurkha units frequently took the war to the enemy, hunting them down in the deepest areas of jungle hitherto regarded as sanctuaries by the terrorists.

The mid-1960s found The Brigade of Gurkhas heavily involved in the Borneo Confrontation, eventually taking part in operations across the border into Kalimantan where companies carried out reconnaissance missions and punitive strikes against Indonesian forces.

Despite its successes, The Brigade of Gurkhas saw a gradual erosion of its strength during the 1970s and 1980s as a seemingly endless series of defence cuts reduced the number of units. In 1994, these culminated in the amalgamation of the brigade's four infantry regiments into The Royal Gurkha Rifles whose three battalions were soon reduced to two plus three reinforcement companies and two demonstration companies; at the same time, the corps units were reduced to one squadron each.

The 1990s, however, saw Gurkha units participating in operations in the Gulf War of 1991 and in the Balkans. The beginning of the twenty-first century found them playing leading roles in intervention operations in Kosovo, Macedonia, Sierra Leone, East Timor and Afghanistan. In 2003, Gurkhas were among the British forces despatched to the Middle East to depose the Iraqi dictator, Saddam Hussein. As always, they proved to be as much an asset to the British Army as their forefathers 60 years earlier on the battlefields of North Africa. Once again, the desert echoed to the war cry of 'Gurkhali Ayo!' – 'The Gurkhas are upon you!'.

Chapter 1
Origins and Early Years

For nearly two centuries, the Gurkha regiments of the Indian and British armies have rendered sterling service to the British crown. Their story begins in the hill kingdom of Gorkha in the eighteenth century, during which the country's leader, Prithwai Narian, laid the basis of the present-day nation of Nepal. He was also responsible for creating a highly efficient fighting force which, following his death in 1774, was used to conquer Sikkim and areas of Tibet, as well as Garwhal and Kumaon to the west. The Nepalese then strayed further, sallying forth over their borders into territories that were the preserve of the British Honourable East India Company.

One of those who advocated a policy of aggression against the British was a maharajah called Bhim Sen Thapa who, holding the office of Prime Minister, was behind the infiltration by Gurkha troops into an area called the Terai, a narrow area of plain separating the mountains of Nepal from the plains of India. A number of raids were carried out and during one such raid in May 1814 Gurkhas attacked three East India Company frontier posts, killing eighteen policemen and a local village headman. Earl Moira, the Governor General of Bengal, responded by sending an ultimatum to Bhim Sen Thapa, who answered: 'If the English want war against the Gurkha conquerors, they can have it.'

By this time British forbearance was exhausted and Moira despatched four columns of troops from Dinapore, Benares, Meerut and Ludhiana. The entire force numbered approximately 30,000 men with 60 guns, while Bhim Sen's army comprised only some 12,000 men, including Nepal's crack 600-strong Purana Gorakh Regiment. In addition to far outnumbering its opponents, the East India Company force possessed good lines of communications and resupply across the Indian plains. Bhim Sen Thapa's, on the other hand, stretched over the mountains along narrow tracks with the Nepalese capital Kathmandu being two months' walk away. The Gurkhas, however, were fighting on their own territory, the steep mountains and deep valleys of which they knew intimately.

The British aimed their initial moves at Bhim Sen Thapa's supply routes, with one column of 4,000 troops, commanded by Maj Gen Rollo Gillespie, being tasked with taking the Doon Valley and then advancing on Srinagar, the capital of Garwhal. The aim was to force the Gurkhas to withdraw eastwards where they would be attacked by a second column of 6,000 men and 12 guns under Maj Gen David Ochterlony, a

Members of C (Gurkha) Company 2 PARA among a group paying its respects at a monument to British dead of the Afghan Wars during Operation Fingal in February 2002.

highly experienced and aggressive soldier, who by then would have advanced up the River Sutlej to engage the main Gurkha forces, under their commander Gen Amarsing Thapa, at Malaun. To the east, meanwhile, two other columns under Gen Marley and Gen Wood were to advance on Kathmandu.

The four columns set off towards their respective objectives in late autumn 1814. Gen Wood's column encountered a Gurkha force at Bhutwal and suffered casualties. Wood withdrew his force just as the Gurkhas themselves were beginning to withdraw and the latter, seeing their chance, followed up and harassed the column mercilessly. Meanwhile, Marley's column was faring little better, retreating in the face of Gurkha attacks pressed home with ferocity and vigour. Marley, like Wood an elderly officer well past the age of retirement, eventually could stomach the fighting no longer and, without informing any of his staff, departed under cover of darkness and disappeared.

Gillespie, meanwhile, had seized Dehra Dun, cutting off Amarsing Thapa from his main forces. In the fighting which followed, the principal battle took place at Kalunga which was held by the Purana Gorakh Regiment, commanded by Amarsing's nephew Balbahadur Thapa. Its positions centred on a small fort sited on a tree-clad hill guarding the route to Garwhal and dominating the surrounding area. On the night of 29 October Gillespie sent the Nepalese commander an offer of terms for surrender but the latter declined. Before dawn on the following day Gillespie's artillery opened fire on the fort while his British and Indian troops formed up for an assault. Launched prematurely and in piecemeal fashion, this was repulsed by the Gurkhas, a second attempt suffering the same fate.

Placing himself at the head of his own regiment, the Royal Irish Dragoons, Gillespie personally led a third attack. Accompanying him was a subaltern commanding a company of the 13th Bengal Native Infantry, Lt Frederick Young. Charging the gate of the fort, Maj Gen Gillespie was shot and fatally wounded some 30 yards from the objective, dying soon afterwards in Young's arms. Meanwhile, the Gurkhas beat off the assault and the attacking force withdrew to await the arrival of a siege train from Delhi.

The next attack on the fort was mounted a month later but met with a similar lack of success. The defenders, however, had suffered heavy casualties and their supplies of ammunition, food and water were running low. After agonising at length, Balbahadur decided to save the remnants of his force by withdrawing under cover of darkness, leaving his wounded to the mercy of the British. On the night of 1 December he and his remaining 70 men slipped away unseen, and when the British eventually entered the fort they found only seriously wounded Gurkhas, women and children. Balbahadur's losses at Kalunga numbered 520 out of a total force of 600 but the Purana Gorakh had killed 781 members of Gillespie's force, 31 of them officers.

Meanwhile, Maj Gen David Ochterlony was steadily pushing back the forces of Amarsing Thapa, using his artillery to batter the latter's defences at Ramgarh. Eventually Amarsing had no choice but to withdraw towards Malaun. In April 1815 Ochterlony succeeded in splitting the Gurkha force by occupying two mountain peaks in the centre of its positions. Amarsing launched a counter-attack against one of them but it failed. Having lost 500 of his men killed, he then withdrew the remainder of his force to Malaun where he intended to make a last stand. By this time, however, Ochterlony had caught up with the Gurkhas and surrounded them. Realising his position was hopeless, Amarsing requested terms of surrender.

Ochterlony agreed that the Gurkhas should be allowed to march out with their arms and colours but demanded that Nepal cede the Terai to the British and return captured areas including Kumaon, Garwhal and Simla. In addition, the Nepalese were to withdraw from Sikkim and to accept the establishment of a British Resident in Kathmandu.

Amarsing had no option but to agree to these terms but Prime Minister Bhim Sen Thapa objected to doing so. Negotiations broke down and the war was resumed in January 1816 with Ochterlony leading a force of 14,000 regular troops, an unknown number of irregulars and 83 guns in an expedition to take Kathmandu. A bitter battle took place at Makwanpore with the British and Indian troops suffering some 250 killed while the Gurkhas lost approximately 500.

In March 1816 the war came to an end with the Treaty of Segouli which was signed by Bhim Sen Thapa and Ochterlony, the latter having given the Nepalese the ultimatum: 'You either take a Resident or War.'

During the fighting Ochterlony had come to admire the Gurkhas' prowess as fighting troops and recommended that they be recruited into British service. The decision was thus taken to raise four irregular Nepalese corps, the first comprising two units formed at Subathu, near Simla, and designated the 1st and 2nd Nasiri Gurkha Battalions respectively, the second of which was later absorbed by the first. In 1849 the Nasiri Battalion took part in an operation against mutinous troops of the 66th Bengal

A very early photograph of the Nasiri Battalion, later designated the 1st Gurkha Regiment, taken *circa* 1857.

Native Infantry and distinguished itself sufficiently that it was given the name, colours and accoutrements of the disloyal unit, which was disbanded. Following the Indian Mutiny of 1857–8, the regiment was renamed the 1st Gurkha Regiment and was classed as light infantry, being given a new regimental centre at Dharamsala in the Kangra Valley of the Punjab. Thereafter the regiment saw extensive service on the North West Frontier against the Pakhtuns and at the end of 1875 was deployed as part of a force sent from India to the Malay States following the murder of the British Resident in Perak. One particularly fierce action at Bukit Putoos, during which troops of the regiment stormed an enemy-held stockade, resulted in the award of the Victoria Cross to Capt N.M. Channer.

The regiment subsequently formed its 2nd Battalion, which was first deployed on active service in the latter part of 1888, when it took part in an expedition to Sikkim, whose ruler had infringed the terms of a treaty with India. In 1894 the 1st Battalion also saw action while escorting a commission tasked with delineating the Afghan boundary of Waziristan. In 1897 the 2nd Battalion returned to the North West Frontier for operations which lasted throughout the following year.

In 1906 the Prince of Wales became Colonel-in-Chief of the regiment. In 1910, following his coronation as King George V, the regiment's name was changed to the 1st King George V's Own Gurkha Rifles (The Malaun Regiment), the sub-title denoting the regiment's origin having been granted in 1903.

The second Gurkha corps raised in 1815 was the Sirmoor Battalion, formed at Nahun in the area of Sirmoor but based thereafter at Dehra Dun in northern India, which became its permanent centre. The task of raising this corps was given to Lt Frederick Young who, as mentioned earlier, had been present at the battle of Kalunga. During the autumn of 1814 he had been commanding a unit of irregular troops when he was attacked by a strong force of Gurkhas. His own men fled, leaving Young and his officers to face the enemy alone. The latter asked why he had not also fled, to which Young replied: 'I have not come so far in order to run away. I came to stay.' Thereafter he sat down. Impressed by such cool aplomb, the Gurkhas replied: 'We could serve under men like you.'

Young subsequently came to be held in much esteem by his captors, who treated him well. He in turn developed a great affection for them and, following his release, raised the Sirmoor Battalion, a unit of 3,000 men. Within six months he was able to report it as ready for active service. Two years later the battalion saw action for the first time during a campaign against the Mahrattas and Pindaris in which it distinguished itself. In 1824 a detachment of 200 men was deployed under Young's command from Dehra Dun, marching 36 miles to Koonja in the area of Eastern Doon, where it faced a force of 800 Goojar rebels who had seized a mud fort in which they had subsequently established themselves. Despite the overwhelming odds and under heavy fire, Young mounted an attack and succeeded in forcing open the fort's gates with the aid of a battering ram fashioned from a cut-down tree. Heavy hand-to-hand fighting ensued, during which 150 Goojars were killed and the remainder of the enemy routed.

Thereafter the battalion was permitted to include the design of a ram's head on its accoutrements in commemoration of this action.

A year later three companies of the Sirmoor Battalion under Capt Fisher and elements of the Nasiri Battalion were included in an expeditionary force despatched to the state of Bhurtpore which had been usurped by an individual named Doorjan Sal whose forces comprised 25,000 Jats, Pakhtuns and Rajputs. The city of Bhurtpore itself was heavily fortified, being surrounded by tall earthen walls and a moat, albeit that the latter was not filled with water. Such was the strength and thickness of the walls that siege artillery made little impression on them and the attacking force was obliged to resort to mining, with two large mines being dug and filled with explosives. These were blown at dawn on 18 January 1826 with an assault on the city taking place immediately afterwards. Heavy fighting took place during which the three Sirmoor companies distinguished themselves at the cost of only light casualties.

The Sirmoor Battalion saw no further active service until the First Sikh War, when in January and February 1846, together with the Nasiri Battalion, it took part in a series of fierce battles against a large force of Sikhs under their leader Sirdar Ranjore Singh. Both Gurkha units distinguished themselves during the fighting in which the Commandant of the Sirmoor Battalion, Maj Fisher, was killed at the head of his troops.

It was during the Indian Mutiny of 1857–8, however, that the Sirmoor Battalion rose to prominence. The mutiny followed the introduction of the new Enfield rifle, the ammunition for which comprised greased paper cartridges containing powder and ball. Users of the rifle were required to bite off the end of cartridge and extract the ball before pouring the powder charge down the barrel. This was followed by the ball, which was rammed down on to the powder, the greased paper from the cartridge then being used as a wad to secure the entire load. As part of their efforts to foment unrest in the East India Company's Bengal Army, Indian nationalists spread rumours that the cartridges were greased with a mixture of pig and cow fat. For Muslims contact with pig fat was defiling while Hindus regarded the cow as sacred. In April 1857 Indian troops at Meerut refused to handle the cartridges and were punished severely. This incensed their comrades, who mutinied on 10 May, killing their British officers and marching on the city of Delhi where they were joined by the garrison there. Thereafter the mutiny spread throughout northern India.

On 14 May the Sirmoor Battalion marched from Dehra Dun to Meerut, encountering en route some mutineers who were summarily tried and executed. On 31 May the Commandant, Maj Charles Reid, learning that a force under Maj Gen Archdale Wilson, marching towards Delhi, was in danger of being attacked, force-marched his men 27 miles overnight to reach Wilson on the following day. There the battalion met the 60th Rifles (King's Royal Rifle Corps) with which it occupied a large mansion called Hindu Rao's House. Of solid construction and capable of accommodating a sizeable force, it became the key position in the British defences on the right flank of the Delhi Ridge.

In the Indian Mutiny of 1857–8 the 2nd Gurkhas showed striking proof of their loyalty at Delhi where, together with the 60th Rifles (now part of The Royal Green Jackets), they held Hindu Rao's House, the key to the British position which was under continuous fire from the mutineers, for over three months.

Together with the Guides Infantry, the Sirmoor Battalion and 60th Rifles held Hindu Rao's House for a period of three months and eight days against constant attacks by the rebels, and it was not until 12 August that reinforcements arrived under Brig Gen John Nicholson. For this feat of arms the Sirmoor Battalion was accorded the privilege of wearing the scarlet-faced green uniform of the 60th Rifles and was subsequently awarded the status of a rifle regiment, its name being changed to the Sirmoor Rifle Regiment. In being accorded the honour of becoming such, however, it had to forfeit its colours, which were replaced by a truncheon to be carried instead. Named the Queen's Truncheon and unique throughout the world, it is made of bronze and measures 6 feet in height, being surmounted by three figures of Gurkha riflemen supporting a silver imperial crown. From this time on all recruits to the regiment swore allegiance to the British sovereign before the Queen's Truncheon during an attestation parade.

Thereafter the regiment was renamed the 2nd Prince of Wales's Own Gurkha Rifles (The Sirmoor Rifles), with the Prince of Wales (the future King Edward VII) appointed

as Colonel of the Regiment. In 1878 the regiment became the first Gurkha unit to serve in Europe when it was deployed to the Mediterranean during the Russo-Turkish War. Thereafter it returned to the North West Frontier to take part in the Afghan War of 1878–80, the second of three conflicts which took place between 1839 and 1919 in which the British in India attempted to exert control over neighbouring Afghanistan and oppose increasing Russian influence there.

In 1886 the regiment formed a second battalion, which took part in an expeditionary force to northern Burma in 1888–90. In 1901, following the accession of the Prince of Wales to the throne as Edward VII, the regiment's title was changed to the 2nd King Edward VII's Own Gurkha Rifles (The Sirmoor Rifles).

The third Gurkha corps to be raised in 1815 was the Kumaon Battalion, so named as it recruited from the district of that name as well as from Garwhal. With its centre at Almora, the battalion was employed for the first 41 years of its existence in policing the border with Nepal. In 1857, however, by which time it had moved to Rawalpindi, it was despatched to Delhi to take part in operations against the mutineers. It arrived on 1 August and subsequently took part in heavy fighting which culminated in the storming of Ludlow Castle on 12 August. Following the end of the mutiny in 1858, the battalion was despatched to the Himalayas where it remained until the start of the Afghan War in 1878, by which time it had been redesignated the 3rd Gurkha Rifles. In 1891 a second battalion was raised and the 1890s saw both the regiment's battalions serving on the North West Frontier, remaining there into the beginning of the following century. In 1907, as a mark of King Edward VII's appreciation of the regiment and its service, the regiment's title was changed to the 3rd Queen Alexandra's Own Gurkha Rifles, with Her Majesty's personal cypher thereafter being incorporated into the regiment's badge.

Meanwhile, 1850 had seen the raising of a fourth Gurkha unit from a cadre of the Nasiri Battalion. Designated the Extra Gurkha Regiment, its first task was to hold the Kumaon Hills following the outbreak of the Indian Mutiny in 1857. Thereafter, it saw service on the North West Frontier during the late 1860s and in Burma in the early 1870s. By then redesignated the 4th Gurkha Rifles, the regiment took part in the Second Afghan War, taking part in operations around Jalalabad and Kabul before marching, together with the 2nd KEO Gurkha Rifles, 320 miles to the city of Kandahar which was captured. Thereafter it marched on to Baluchistan to deal with the recalcitrant Marris tribes.

In 1886 the 4th Gurkha Rifles raised a second battalion at the regimental centre at Bakloh, this first seeing action in 1889–90 on India's eastern borders with Burma and in the Chin Hills during the following winter. During 1895 both battalions took part in operations on the North West Frontier. In 1900 the 1st Battalion sailed for China where it formed part of the forces sent by the United States, Britain, France, Germany, Italy, India, Australia and Japan to put down the Boxer Rebellion, which broke out in northern China and the Yangtse Valley between June and December 1900.

* * *

(*Opposite*): Riflemen of the 2nd Battalion King Edward VII's Own Gurkha Rifles swear allegiance to the Sovereign on the Queen's Truncheon.

A section of the 4th Gurkha Rifles pictured in Kabul. The picture is thought to have been taken in about 1880.

Forty-two years earlier, in 1858, the 5th Gurkha Rifles had been formed by transferring Nepalese hillmen from irregular units into the 25th Punjab Infantry (Hazara Goorkha Battalion). Raised at Abbotabad to hold the Hazara frontier with Afghanistan, this unit was redesignated the 5th Gurkha Regiment in 1861 (also being known as the Hazara Gurkha Battalion) and first saw active service during the Second Afghan War which came about as a result of Russia establishing a mission in Kabul. The British responded by despatching Gen Sir Neville Chamberlain to the Afghan capital with the task of doing likewise but he was forced to turn back at the border after encountering a strong Afghan force. War broke out, with the Afghans laying siege to the British garrisons in Kabul and Kandahar.

Britain then despatched the Kurram Field Force, under Maj Gen (later Field Marshal) Frederick Roberts VC, into Afghanistan. This formation comprised two brigades consisting of six battalions, including the 5th Gurkha Rifles, who subsequently distinguished themselves in a number of actions fighting alongside the 72nd Highlanders (later The Seaforth Highlanders) with whom they were brigaded throughout the campaign. It was during one of these actions that a 5th Gurkha officer, Capt John Cook, led a charge under heavy fire, his gallantry subsequently being recognised by the award of the Victoria Cross and that of his Gurkhas with seven Indian Orders of Merit.

The campaign eventually culminated in the relief of the garrison at Kandahar following a forced march by troops who, under Maj Gen Roberts, covered 305 miles from Kabul in 23 days over difficult terrain. In addition to the 5th Gurkha Rifles and the 72nd Highlanders, the 2nd KEO Gurkha Rifles and the 92nd Highlanders (later The Gordon Highlanders) formed part of this force, which arrived at Kandahar on 31 August. On the following day the battle of Kandahar commenced with the capture of a village called Sahibad, following which the 2nd KEO Gurkha Rifles and the 92nd Highlanders were confronted by an enemy force of several thousand Afghans supported by two guns. Undaunted, both battalions charged the enemy, routing them completely and capturing the guns. One of these was immediately appropriated by a Gurkha rifleman, who thrust his kilmarnock cap down its muzzle and loudly declared, 'This gun belongs to my regiment, the 2nd Gurkhas!' Thereafter, until the amalgamation of the two battalions of the 2nd KEO Gurkha Rifles in 1994, the 'Kandahar Gun' was always positioned outside the entrance to the officers' mess of the 1st Battalion.

The year 1886 saw the formation of the 2nd Battalion 5th Gurkha Rifles which, five years later, took part in a major operation in Afghanistan known as the Hazara Black Mountain Expedition. During the same year a detachment of the 1st Battalion was carrying out operations amid the snow and glaciers of the far northern reaches of Kashmir where two tribes, the Nagirs and Hunzas, were proving troublesome. These operations involved the storming of fortified positions situated on the top of precipitous cliffs and resulted in the Victoria Cross being awarded to two officers, Lt G. Boisragon and Lt J. Manners-Smith.

The years 1897–8 were a time of turbulence along the North West Frontier and it was during this period that the 5th Gurkha Rifles produced a sub-unit of soldiers specially trained as scouts, all of whom were expert marksmen equipped with special rifles. Highly skilled in fieldcraft, they beat even the Pakhtun tribesmen at their own game and such was their success by the end of the campaign that, augmented by men from the 1st KGO and 3rd QAO Gurkha Rifles, they were formed into a scout battalion.

In 1817, two years after the raising of the first four Nepalese corps, another body had been raised at Orissa as the Cuttack Legion. In 1821 it was transferred to Northern Bengal and its name changed to the Rangpur Light Infantry; five years later it was redesignated the Assam Light Infantry. During this period the rank and file of the regiment comprised plainsmen and it was not until 1828 that Nepalese were enlisted into the regiment. Their number gradually increased until 1886 by which time recruits to the regiment comprised only hillmen from Nepal.

Based in Assam, the regiment served continually on the north-east frontier of India on operations against the warlike local tribes of Nagas, Daphlas, Abors, Chins, Lushais and Manipuris. In addition, it took part in the Second Burmese War of 1852, the second of three conflicts between Britain and Burma. In July of that year, twenty-six years after the first war of 1824–6, hostilities broke out again after a ship

Gun teams of the Assam Light Infantry (later 6th Gurkha Rifles) pictured in 1890.

belonging to the Burmese king was seized by a Royal Navy officer, Commodore Lambert, who had been sent to Rangoon to investigate complaints by British merchants about extortion on the part of the Burmese. Britain despatched forces, including the Assam Light Infantry, from India into Burma and these captured the ports of Lower Burma before advancing on Rangoon. Having occupied all of Lower Burma, the British decided against occupying the rest of the country and the fighting eventually ceased.

In 1899, by which time it had been renamed the 42nd Gurkha Rifle Regiment of Bengal Infantry, the regiment was transferred to the North West Frontier. A second battalion was raised during the following year and three years later the regiment was renamed the 6th Gurkha Rifles.

Next in the corps to be formed was the Mainpuri Levy which was raised in 1823, being renamed the 63rd Bengal Native Infantry during the following year. Some of its companies took part in the First Burmese War of 1824–6 but the entire corps did not see action until 1826, when it participated in the siege and storming of Bhurtpore, whose fortress had resisted all attempts by the East India Company to capture it during the Mahratta War and continued to do so until 1826. In 1861 the regiment was renumbered as the 9th Bengal Native Infantry and its composition altered so that one of its eight companies comprised hillmen from Nepal, the only infantry corps other than the Gurkha regiments already in existence permitted to recruit them. Thereafter it took part in a campaign in Bhutan during 1864–6 and in the Second Afghan War but saw little action in both.

From 1880 to 1890 there were no Gurkhas on the strength of the regiment but from 1893 onwards the 9th Bengal Native Infantry recruited Nepalese hillmen of the Khas caste who, unlike other Gurkhas, were of Rajput rather than Mongol origin and hitherto had not been enlisted in the Indian Army. In addition, it also recruited Thakurs, the caste of highest social standing in Nepal. In 1894 the regiment was renamed the 9th (Gurkha Rifle) Regiment of Bengal Infantry and first saw active service in the Mohmand region of India in 1897–8. A second battalion was raised at the end of 1904, by which time the regimental centre was based at Dehra Dun together with that of the 2nd KEO Gurkha Rifles.

The 1820s also saw the formation of another corps that ultimately became a Gurkha regiment. In 1824 two battalions of troops were raised at Gauhati and Sylheyt in Assam as a frontier guard force, their compositions including mounted and artillery sections. Both took part in the war in Bhutan of 1864–5 and throughout the greater part of the nineteenth century were deployed along India's north-east frontier. In 1879, during operations against the Naga tribes, Lt R.K. Ridgeway was awarded the Victoria Cross for his great gallantry during an attack on the Naga stronghold of Konoma.

Initially only a few Gurkhas were recruited into both battalions but in 1832 entire companies from the 1st KGO and 2nd KEO Gurkha Rifles were transferred to the 1st Battalion, while from 1886 onwards only Nepalese hillmen of the Magar and Gurung jhats (tribes) were recruited into the 1st and 2nd Battalions respectively. In 1861 both battalions had been incorporated into the Bengal Army as the 43rd and 44th Native Infantry respectively, retaining these titles until 1902 when the regiment was split into two new regiments named the 7th and 8th Gurkha Rifles. Shortly afterwards, however, as a result of a decision that all Gurkha regiments were to have an establishment of two battalions, the 7th Gurkha Rifles were redesignated as the 2nd Battalion 8th Gurkha Rifles.

During 1904 the 1st Battalion 8th Gurkha Rifles took part in operations in Tibet during which Lt J.D. Grant won a Victoria Cross for his part in an attack on the fortress at Gyantse in July. In 1911 the battalion conducted a punitive expedition against the Abor tribes on the Assam border following the massacre of a party of civilians. The operation lasted seven months, at the end of which the murderers were apprehended and brought to trial.

The year 1887 had seen an outbreak of lawlessness in certain areas of Burma and a number of military police battalions were formed to counter it. One such unit was the Kubo Valley Military Police Battalion recruited from volunteers, principally Gurkhas, from throughout the Indian Army. The Kubo Valley was a peaceful area in western Burma that was, however, prone to raiding from the hills to the east. Subsequently renamed the 10th Madras Infantry, the battalion's uniform and equipment was that of a regular Gurkha battalion of the Bengal Army. In due course its name was changed again to the 10th Regiment (1st Burma Gurkha Rifles) Madras Infantry and it was as such that it first saw active service during an expedition beginning in 1890 to suppress and subjugate the Chin and Lushai tribes on Burma's eastern borders, remaining assigned to this task until 1894.

In 1903 the battalion was redesignated the 10th Gurkha Rifles and became part of the Indian Army's Gurkha Brigade. Five years later it was split to form the 1st and 2nd Battalions, the regiment's centre being located at Maymo.

In 1907 the 7th Gurkha Rifles were resurrected, their previous existence having been all too brief. Following the battalion's redesignation as the 2nd Battalion 8th Gurkha Rifles in 1902, it became the 2nd Battalion 10th Gurkha Rifles in 1903. Five years later, following agreement between India and Nepal over an increase in the number of Gurkha units, the 2nd/10th was divided to form the 1st and 2nd Battalions 7th Gurkha Rifles. Like the 10th, the 7th recruited from the Rai and Limbu jhats of East Nepal.

Chapter 2

The First World War

The year 1914 saw the outbreak of the First World War, with the British Expeditionary Force in France facing a better-trained and better-equipped enemy in far greater numbers. It was not long before India was requested to provide assistance, her response being to despatch the Indian Corps comprising two divisions, the 3rd (Lahore) and 17th (Meerut), each of which included three Gurkha battalions among its brigades. Accustomed to operations against tribesmen in the mountains and valleys of the North West Frontier and Afghanistan, however, none was trained or properly equipped for the appalling conditions, heavy artillery bombardments and massed machine-gun fire they would meet in the trenches of France.

The first Gurkha unit to arrive on the Western Front was the 2nd Battalion 8th Gurkha Rifles, which was deployed into the front line near Festubert, south of the Ypres Salient, on 29 October. The stocky but short hillmen soon found that the trenches dug by British troops were too deep for them and it was with some difficulty that they beat off a German attack shortly after their arrival. Within 24 hours six of the battalion's British officers had been killed and three wounded. This was due to the fact that at this early stage in the war it was essential for officers to make themselves prominent in setting an example while their soldiers accustomed themselves to conditions very different from those of the North West Frontier.

During November the 2nd/8th were joined in France by the 1st/1st KGO, 2nd/2nd KEO, 2nd/3rd QAO, 1st/4th and 1st/9th Gurkha Rifles, all of which went into the line on arrival and suffered heavy losses during the following weeks. Seven days after going into the trenches at Givenchy with a total strength of 736, the 1st/4th had been reduced to 423 in number. During December further losses were incurred by the Indian Corps when it carried out a series of diversionary attacks as part of a major offensive. By the time it was withdrawn at the end of the month, it had suffered 1,397 killed, 5,860 wounded and 2,322 missing. Following the arrival of reinforcements from India and having refitted, both its divisions returned to the front line on 15 January 1915. Weather conditions were appalling with heavy rain, snow and driving winds, but fortunately there was little fighting, allowing the newly arrived troops time to learn the skills of trench warfare while not under pressure.

In the spring of 1915 a major attack was mounted by the 7th (Meerut) Division's Dehra Dun Brigade against the German lines in the area of a village called Neuve

2nd/3rd QAO Gurkha Rifles being inspected in France in 1915, having been issued with serge uniforms.

Chapelle. On the morning of 10 March two companies of the 2nd/2nd KEO Gurkha Rifles took the Bois de Biez without encountering resistance while the 2nd/3rd, in the left-centre, succeeded in reaching the forward German positions. On approaching the village, however, its companies came under heavy fire. The situation was saved by Havildar (Sgt) Bahadur Thapa, who led his platoon in an attack on a house, wiping out the sixteen enemy inside and capturing two machine-guns, a feat for which he was awarded the Indian Order of Merit.

By this time the 1st/9th had taken up positions on the south-west corner of the Bois de Biez and had begun to dig in. Meanwhile, however, the two divisions on the flanks of the Dehra Dun Brigade had been held up by stiff resistance and thus it was at risk of being cut off. The 2nd/3rd QAO and 1st/9th Gurkha Rifles were ordered to withdraw, allowing the enemy to reoccupy the positions lost earlier and to fortify the Bois de Biez.

The entire brigade was withdrawn on the night of 11 March, being replaced by the Sirhind Brigade of the 3rd (Lahore) Division. Unfortunately, owing to lack of proper coordination on the part of the two brigade headquarters, the relief-in-the-line degenerated into confusion, made worse by constant enemy shelling. This resulted in a delay in the Sirhind Brigade's two leading battalions, the 1st/1st KGO Gurkha Rifles and the 15th Sikhs, being ready for a planned attack at first light. As a result the Allied offensive was postponed and the Germans, whose front lines were no more than 60 yards from those of the British, were able to mount a massive counter-attack, which was beaten off with large numbers of enemy being killed. An attack was mounted later in the day by the Sirhind Brigade but failed despite magnificent efforts by the 1st/1st KGO and 1st/4th Gurkha Rifles. On 20 March the brigade withdrew, being replaced by the Jullundur Brigade.

In September 1915 the first Victoria Cross was awarded to a Gurkha soldier. Rifleman Kulbir Thapa of the 2nd/3rd QAO Gurkha Rifles was trapped behind the forwardmost German line, where he discovered a severely wounded member of the 2nd Battalion The Royal Leicestershire Regiment. Despite being wounded himself, Kulbir carried him out through the German lines in the early hours of 26 September and placed him in a safe position. Thereafter he returned twice through the German positions to collect two other wounded Gurkhas whom he carried all the way to the British lines before returning for the Leicestershire soldier.

In December 1915 the Indian Corps was withdrawn from France and its battalions despatched to other theatres. It had suffered grievously, losing 21,000 officers and men, but its Gurkha battalions had established a reputation second to none during thirteen months of fighting in the trenches.

Meanwhile, three other Gurkha battalions had been deployed to the Gallipoli Peninsula following a request for Gurkha troops from Gen Sir Ian Hamilton to the Secretary of State for War, Lord Kitchener. The 1st/5th, 1st/6th and 2nd/10th Gurkha Rifles arrived as part of 29 Indian Infantry Brigade, whose two other units were Punjabi battalions, later being augmented by the 1st/4th Gurkha Rifles following the withdrawal of the Indian Corps from France.

The first to arrive were the 1st/6th Gurkha Rifles, who landed near Cape Helles on 30 April 1915, taking up a position on the extreme left of the Allied line in that sector. Three days later, supported by the guns of Royal Navy warships, the battalion attacked a Turkish strongpoint on a steep-sided bluff. Despite the major difficulties facing them, its companies succeeded in carrying out their tasks, losing 18 men killed and 42 wounded. Thereafter, at the direction of Gen Hamilton, the feature was christened 'Gurkha Bluff' and was marked as such on all maps and charts.

The 1st/5th and 2nd/10th Gurkha Rifles arrived at the beginning of June to replace 29 Indian Infantry Brigade's two Punjabi battalions. Not long afterwards an attack was mounted on a 700ft-high feature called Achi Baba which dominated the Cape Helles beachhead and the entrance to the Dardanelles. Following a heavy artillery bombardment the 1st/6th Gurkha Rifles, together with the 14th Sikhs and a battalion of The Lancashire Fusiliers, attacked but suffered heavy casualties after being held up by Turkish barbed wire defences that had survived the shelling. Another assault was mounted later in the day by the 1st/5th Gurkha Rifles who, despite attempting more than once to press home their attack, suffered a similar fate, losing 7 British officers and 130 soldiers to the withering fire of 40 machine-guns. Among the wounded was the Commandant, Lt Col G.H. Boisragon VC.

On 28 June three brigades, including 29 Indian Infantry Brigade, mounted an attack designed to push the Turks back 1,000 yards from their positions north-west of Gurkha Bluff. Following a two-hour-long heavy artillery bombardment, the 2nd/10th Gurkha Rifles attacked the enemy clifftop positions, capturing five lines of enemy trenches. They were joined by the 1st/6th who succeeded in extending the line before the Turks launched a number of counter-attacks during which they suffered heavy casualties at the hands of the Gurkhas. Much of the fighting took place at close quarters with the Gurkhas making good use of their kukris. The 2nd/10th, however, suffered heavily, losing all but three of its British officers, all of whom were subalterns, and 40 per cent of its strength.

Following this operation 29 Indian Infantry Brigade was withdrawn to the island of Imbros (now Imroz) where it rested and refitted, being reinforced by drafts sent from India. Early August, however, found it back on the Gallipoli Peninsula, this time taking part in a landing at Anzac Cove. This was in support of an attack to capture the Sari Bair Ridge in an effort to outflank the Turkish positions facing the Allied beachhead at Suvla Bay and to cut off and dominate those on the tip of the peninsula at Cape Helles.

The brigade was allocated the task of leading the attack against a feature called Hill Q in the centre of the Sari Bair Ridge. The advance began on the night of 6 August with the brigade's battalions climbing up steep, rugged terrain. Navigation was difficult, inaccurate maps exacerbating the problem, as the Gurkhas advanced on their initial objective, a peak called Chunuk Bair, which was to be seized before daylight. By dawn on 7 August, however, enemy resistance had increased and the advance slowed to a halt. By the time the leading battalion, the 1st/6th Gurkha Rifles, had fought its way to within 500 yards from Chunuk Bair, it had lost 76 men. At that juncture it was reinforced by two battalions of The South Lancashire and The Royal Warwickshire Regiments, which also suffered heavy losses.

Finally, on 9 August, with the support of heavy naval gunfire, the 1st/6th succeeded in reaching the ridge and closed with the enemy. Following some ten minutes of close-quarter fighting, the Turks broke and fled with some of the battalion in hot pursuit. Tragically, however, at that time six shells (thought by some to be from the warships offshore) landed among the pursuing Gurkhas, causing several casualties and forcing the remainder to withdraw to positions just below the ridge. Together with the remnants of the 2nd/10th Gurkha Rifles, who had also suffered heavy casualties, and the two British battalions, the 1st/6th remained there until the order to withdraw was given on the following day. The attack had failed and the Sari Bair Ridge was still in Turkish hands. British and Imperial casualties numbered approximately 12,000, as did those of the Turks.

This was the last major action of the Gallipoli campaign. In due course the 1st/4th Gurkha Rifles arrived to reinforce 29 Indian Infantry Brigade, their experience of trench warfare in France subsequently being put to good effect. Conditions in the trenches on the peninsula were grim, with constant small arms and artillery fire adding to the problems caused by the heat, flies, inadequate food and contaminated water which inevitably resulted in the appearance of dysentery. With the arrival of winter in November came bad weather and severe storms that added to the troops' misery.

Fortunately, following a visit to the Dardanelles by Lord Kitchener, the decision was made to withdraw from the peninsula and on the night of 19/20 December the final elements of 29 Indian Infantry Brigade withdrew, slipping away silently under cover of darkness without alerting the Turks, who were unaware of the withdrawal until the following morning. The six Gurkha battalions left behind them 25 British officers and 730 Gurkha officers and soldiers killed in action. Some 1,500 Gurkhas had been wounded, while many more were permanently disabled by disease and frostbite.

Gallipoli was not the only theatre in which Gurkhas encountered the Turks. In February 1915, while en route to France with the Indian Corps, the 1st/6th and 2nd/10th Gurkha Rifles had been detached in Egypt to take part in operations to counter a Turkish attempt to capture the Suez Canal. On 3 February, supported by gunfire from British warships, they were part of an Indian force that repelled an attack across the canal from the east. Further attempts that day suffered a similar fate and the Turks withdrew that night.

Meanwhile, in November 1914 another campaign had begun in Mesopotamia (now Iraq) where British Imperial forces had secured Basra in order to prevent any attempts by Turkey to disrupt the oilfields of the Persian Gulf. Responsibility for the campaign had been invested in the government of India, which had despatched forces under Gen Sir John Nixon, who had been charged with occupying and holding all of Lower Mesopotamia. A battle took place at Shaiba, the Turks being defeated and withdrawing up the River Tigris, pursued by a small force of the 6th Indian Division under its commander Maj Gen Charles Townshend.

The first Gurkha unit to arrive in Mesopotamia was the 2nd Battalion 7th Gurkha Rifles, part of a force sent to capture Nasiriyeh on the River Euphrates, which Gen Nixon believed to be a possible base from which the Turks could mount a counter-attack against Basra. Having encountered and driven back Turkish outposts along the river, the force came upon the main Turkish position approximately 5 miles downriver from Nasiriyeh. A fierce battle took place on 24 July, with the 2nd/7th eventually overrunning the Turkish positions and winning their first battle honour.

Following this success Gen Nixon decided to capture the small but strategically important town of Kut, located on the Kut-al-Amara peninsula at the junction of the waterway joining the Tigris and the Euphrates. Advancing upstream, Nixon's forces met little opposition and the town was occupied on 6 October, the enemy having withdrawn upstream to strong positions astride the Tigris at Ctesiphon.

Nixon's ultimate objective was Baghdad and he pressed on upriver, buoyed by the easy victories so far and reinforced by the 3rd (Lahore) and 7th (Meerut) Divisions which had arrived from France. His forces comprised 13,000 men in four columns under Maj Gen Townshend. Opposing them was a strong Turkish force commanded

The 3rd QAO Gurkha Rifles in action in Mesopotamia in 1917.

by Gen Nur-ud-Din, consisting of 18,000 men supported by 52 guns. Its positions on the left bank of the river followed a line of low mounds and consisted of fifteen strongpoints, with the two northernmost being very heavily defended. Unknown to Townshend, the Turkish 35th Division was in reserve nearby.

Battle was joined on the night of 21 November when one of Townshend's four columns, commanded by Maj Gen Delamain, launched an attack on the two northernmost redoubts dubbed 'Vital Point'. The column had to cross 5,000 yards of open desert before reaching its objective and all went well until the leading elements encountered the Turkish barbed wire defences. Casualties mounted as the wire was cut and fierce fighting ensued, with both sides mounting attacks and counter-attacks. Dawn on 22 November found 300 men of the 2nd/7th Gurkha Rifles and 100 of the 21st Punjab Regiment defending a position against the entire Turkish 35th Division.

This small force repelled a number of attacks throughout the day and such was its ferocious defence of its position that the Turks withdrew that evening.

By now Townshend's 6th Indian Division had suffered heavy casualties and he had no choice but to order a withdrawal to Kut, 80 miles away. This commenced on 25 November and lasted seven and a half days, during which the retreating troops were continually harassed by the Turks. On arrival at Kut, Townshend put the town into a state of defence while awaiting the arrival of a relief force under Lt Gen Sir Fenton Aylmer VC, then advancing up the Tigris.

Aylmer, whose force included the 1st/2nd KEO and 1st/9th Gurkha Rifles, had decided to head across country south of the Tigris towards a strong Turkish position called the Dujaila Redoubt, some 8 miles east of Kut. There he intended to cut the Turkish line of communications while part of his force advanced on Kut itself. Initially all progressed smoothly and it appeared that he would be successful. However, he paused to wait for his artillery to come up, and by the time he launched his attack on the Dujaila Redoubt on 8 March the Turks had been alerted and reinforcements brought up.

The 1st/2nd KEO and 1st/9th Gurkha Rifles led the attack and there was fierce close-quarter fighting. Eventually, however, the Turks' superior numbers and their well-sited positions swung the tide of battle in their favour. The 1st/2nd suffered 80 killed and 100 wounded while the 1st/9th also incurred heavy losses, particularly among its British and Gurkha officers. On the following day Aylmer's force withdrew.

The 10,000 men of the hard-pressed garrison in Kut were by now suffering from lack of food and water. Attempts to drop supplies from aircraft failed, as did a bid using a steamer crewed by Royal Navy personnel. A further effort to relieve the garrison was made in April 1916 by a force under Lt Gen Sir G.F. Gorringe, which encountered a strong Turkish force at Bait Isa. A major action took place with two Gurkha battalions, the 1st/8th and 1st/9th Gurkha Rifles, leading the British attack. Despite their best endeavours, however, the attack was unsuccessful and Gorringe's force suffered over 21,000 casualties.

On 29 April Gen Townshend and his force in Kut surrendered, the officers and men of the 2nd/7th Gurkha Rifles being among those who went into captivity in Turkish prisoner-of-war camps, where they endured great hardship for the rest of the war. The surrender of Kut had major political ramifications for Britain and thereafter responsibility for the campaign in Mesopotamia was taken over by the War Office in London, which despatched Lt Gen Sir Stanley Maude to assume command.

A dynamic and energetic officer, Maude's influence was soon felt and by early 1917 operations against the Turks were being mounted once again. One of the first was carried out by two companies of the 2nd/4th Gurkha Rifles, who routed Turkish troops from Dahra Bend, near the junction of the Tigris and Hai rivers, taking more than 350 prisoners. In late February the 1st/2nd KEO and 2nd/9th Gurkha Rifles took part in an attack by 37 Indian Infantry Brigade across the Tigris, some 6 miles upriver of Kut, as part of a plan to capture an entire Turkish force. Crossing the 4-mile wide

Tigris at Shumran Bend in boats rowed by men of a battalion of The Royal Hampshire Regiment and the Royal Engineers, leading elements of the two battalions came under heavy fire. Despite suffering serious casualties, however, they succeeded in establishing a beachhead which was subsequently reinforced by the remainder of both battalions. It was for his gallantry and leadership during this action that Maj G.C. Wheeler of the 2nd/9th won the Victoria Cross.

Two days of fierce fighting ensued before the Turks were forced into a full-scale retreat on 25 February. The way to Baghdad was open at last and on 11 March troops of The Buffs entered the city without opposition, followed by the 2nd/4th Gurkha Rifles and the rest of 37 Indian Infantry Brigade.

Despite the capture of Baghdad, the campaign in Mesopotamia continued and the British Imperial forces pursued their advance up the Tigris, their next objective being a large Turkish force under Gen Ismail Hakki Bey, based near Mosul in the north of the country. On 27 September 1917 a battle took place at Ramadi with 42 Indian Infantry Brigade, comprising the 1st/5th, 2nd/5th and 2nd/6th Gurkha Rifles, with the 1st Battalion The Dorset Regiment in support, attacking and defeating a Turkish force after some fierce fighting before the advance up the Tigris was resumed.

The last major action of the Mesopotamian campaign took place in October 1917 under the auspices of 1 Indian Corps which had assembled in the area of Tekrit, to the south of the main Turkish positions at Sharqat, 70 miles south of Mosul. Three Gurkha battalions, the 1st/7th, 1st/8th and 1st/10th Gurkha Rifles, took part in the battle which commenced on 24 October. The 1st/7th, on active service for the first time in the First World War, carried out a forced march of 36 miles to the north in support of British cavalry deployed to prevent a Turkish withdrawal. Meanwhile, the 1st/8th and 1st/10th Gurkha Rifles were advancing from the south over a series of ridges, often under heavy fire, clearing a number of Turkish outposts as they did so. On 29 October, realising he was trapped, Ismail Hakki Bey surrendered. The campaign in Mesopotamia, which had cost the British Imperial forces over 30,000 killed, was finally over.

* * *

The following year of 1918 found six Gurkha battalions, including the newly formed 11th Gurkha Rifles, of which four battalions were formed in May, taking part in a move designed to release British units for service on the Western Front. During September the British Imperial forces under Gen Sir Edmund Allenby manoeuvred themselves into positions for a final onslaught against the Turks. While giving the impression of advancing inland around the Turkish left flank, Allenby in fact intended to attack the Turks' right and had concentrated his forces accordingly. The battle began on 11 September at El Kefr where the 2nd/3rd QAO Gurkha Rifles encountered stiff opposition, coming under fire from a machine-gun which held up the battalion's advance, causing heavy casualties. At this point Rifleman Karnabahadur Thapa went forward with a Lewis gun and knocked out the enemy machine-gun, enabling his company to move forward. He was later awarded the Victoria Cross for this exploit.

On 19 September began the battle of Megiddo, which was to result in ultimate victory for the British in Palestine. Among the units present at this final action were the 2nd/7th Gurkha Rifles, reformed as a new battalion following the capture of their predecessors at Kut. At 4.30 a.m. on the 19th they carried out a night attack to take the last line of Turkish trenches. No sooner had they achieved their objective than they came under fire from Turkish machine-guns in a village some distance away. Such was the degree of confusion in the darkness that the battalion seemed to be on its own; there were no communications or orders from the brigade headquarters and it was impossible to discern what was happening on either flank. The 2nd/7th thus continued their advance until eventually they made contact with friendly units on their left.

Despite the apparent confusion, the 2nd/7th and other battalions in the attacking force had in fact succeeded in forcing the Turks back into the hills, allowing Allenby's cavalry to push north with great rapidity. His entire force followed suit, the Gurkhas and their British counterparts marching at such a pace that they outstripped their logistical support. Sweeping past Jezreel, they headed for Nazareth and the Sea of Galilee. On 31 October 1918 came the news that Turkey had surrendered. The campaign in Palestine was over.

Thus the First World War ended for the regiments of the Indian Army's Gurkha Brigade, whose men had distinguished themselves greatly during the conflict. Over 114,000 Gurkhas had served in them, suffering approximately 20,000 casualties. In demonstrating his fighting prowess to the world, the Gurkha soldier had established a reputation which would endure for years to come.

CHAPTER 3

THE SECOND WORLD WAR

While peace might have returned to a war-shattered Europe, the same could not be said for India's North West Frontier. Gurkha battalions found themselves once again on campaign in Waziristan, where large numbers of tribesmen were bent on causing trouble. This was against a backdrop of massive demobilisation by the Indian Army, which had grown from a pre-war strength of 155,423 to a total of 573,484 by the end of 1918. The twenty years or so between the First and Second World Wars saw battalions carrying out regular tours on the frontier which proved excellent training as young officers, NCOs and riflemen were pitted against the wily Pakhtun tribesmen, all of whom were superb marksmen. The 1st/2nd KEO Gurkha Rifles, commanded by Lt Col Francis 'Gertie' Tuker, devoted much time during the latter part of the 1930s to ambushing and patrolling at night, practices which, although apparently not entirely approved of by those in authority, proved to be highly effective and stood the battalion in good stead during the years to come.

In 1940, with Britain and its empire by then at war with Germany, the Gurkha Brigade once again underwent rapid expansion, eventually more than doubling its size. The raising of extra battalions involved the arrival of large numbers of raw young recruits from the hills of Nepal, who underwent seven months of training at the ten regimental training centres before joining their battalions as riflemen. Meanwhile, regiments saw a considerable number of their highly experienced regular officers being posted away to the headquarters of newly formed brigades. These were replaced by young Emergency Commissioned Officers (ECOs) from Britain, many of whom had never travelled outside Europe and thus had little knowledge of Nepal and even less of Gurkhas. Six months later, on completion of their training at an officer cadet school, they joined their respective battalions as newly commissioned second lieutenants and began the tasks of not only mastering the language of Gurkhali but also learning all about their soldiers, their customs and background. Much reliance and responsibility was placed on the shoulders of the Gurkha Viceroy Commissioned Officers (VCO), who proved to be an essential link between the British officers and the NCOs and riflemen. It says much for them that the expansion of the Gurkha Brigade, while not without its problems, proceeded relatively smoothly.

The spring of 1941 found 10th Indian Division, under Maj Gen W.J. 'Bill' Slim, in Iraq, where it confronted and defeated the forces of the pro-German government of

A Zakha Khed Afridi tribesman on the North West Frontier.

Members of the 5th Royal Gurkha Rifles on the North West Frontier in 1923.

A Gurkha scout gives the signal to advance during operations in North Africa.

Rashid Ali. The 2nd/7th Gurkha Rifles took part in this brief campaign, during which they saw action and suffered a few casualties. Shortly afterwards the battalion was joined by the 1st/2nd KEO and 2nd/10th Gurkha Rifles with whom in July it marched north into Persia, where the Shah had refused to expel Germans holding key posts in his administration. The Persian Army, however, had little appetite for battle and swiftly capitulated.

Six months later the 1st/2nd KEO and 2nd/7th Gurkha Rifles joined 4th Indian Division, under the former's old Commandant, Maj Gen Francis Tuker. Soon afterwards the 1st/2nd were despatched to Cyprus as part of 7 Indian Infantry Brigade while the 2nd/7th accompanied 11 Indian Infantry Brigade to North Africa and the Western Desert where, as part of 2nd South African Division, they found themselves at Tobruk, the scene of an eight-month-long siege which had ended in December 1940.

June 1941 found the 2nd/7th Gurkha Rifles, a battalion commanded by Lt Col A.W. Orgill and largely composed of regular soldiers with considerable pre-war service, taking part in the second battle of Tobruk. 11 Indian Infantry Brigade had arrived to find there was little in the way of prepared defences around the town's 35-mile-long perimeter, most of its minefields and barbed wire defences having been removed for use elsewhere. During early June Lt Gen Neil Ritchie's Eighth Army was heavily mauled by Rommel's Afrika Korps and driven back to the extent that by 13 June Tobruk formed part of the front line, becoming the foremost defended area.

On 21 June the Germans launched an attack on 11 Indian Infantry Brigade, concentrating on its Indian battalion, the 2nd Battalion 5th Mahratta Light Infantry, which received a merciless pounding from German artillery and Stuka dive-bombers before being assaulted by Afrika Korps infantry. Such was the lack of depth to the brigade's positions, caused by its being stretched over such a wide front, that it was impossible for any support to be given to the Mahrattas, who were soon overrun, as was the whole brigade shortly afterwards. Meanwhile, the 2nd/7th Gurkha Rifles and the brigade's third infantry unit, the 2nd Battalion The Queen's Own Cameron Highlanders, fought on despite the fact that the Germans had penetrated through to Tobruk itself, splitting 2nd South African Division's area in two. During the night of 20/21 June the 2nd/7th fought off a number of attacks and during the following morning B Company repelled an assault by two Italian battalions which later mounted a second attack supported by a German unit. It was not until midday that the company, its ammunition exhausted, finally surrendered. D Company had surrendered earlier, its ammunition all expended, but C Company and Battalion Headquarters fought on grimly until Lt Col Orgill, realising that the situation was hopeless, ordered his men to lay down their arms. Some succeeded in breaking out and escaping, making their way across the desert to rejoin the Eighth Army, but the remainder of the battalion marched away into captivity along with their comrades of The Cameron Highlanders, who continued fighting until 22 June.

Another Gurkha battalion whose officers and men also found themselves prisoners of war was the 2nd/4th PWO Gurkha Rifles (the title 'Prince of Wales's Own' had been granted in 1924). Part of 5th Indian Division's 10 Indian Infantry Brigade, it had been deployed into the desert at a location known as Point 180, 10 miles east of the defensive area called the 'Knightsbridge Box'. Like the 2nd/7th, the 2nd/4th found themselves isolated and overrun by German armour, against which the battalion's 2-pounder anti-tank guns were useless. After 48 hours of hard fighting, by which time the rest of 5th Indian Division had been destroyed, the battalion was overrun on 6 June. Two other units, the 2nd/3rd QAO and 2nd/8th Gurkha Rifles, also fell prey to the Afrika Korps in the Western Desert. The latter first saw action on 28 June and suffered heavy casualties, the remnants of the battalion eventually making their way across the desert to El Alamein which was reached three days later.

Meanwhile, following the fall of Tobruk, the 1st/2nd KEO Gurkha Rifles had been transferred from Cyprus to the Egyptian capital Cairo where they rejoined 7 Indian Infantry Brigade and the rest of 4th Indian Division. Shortly after its arrival, however, the battalion suffered a devastating blow when nearly all the members of Headquarter

Gurkha soldiers pass a line of Bren carriers in Tunisia during their service with the Eighth Army.

Gurkha soldiers serving with the Eighth Army in Tunisia sharpen their kukris.

Company, watching a Royal Engineers' demonstration of mining, were killed when a sapper unintentionally inserted a detonator into a live mine and initiated it. In all, 68 officers and men were killed in the blast and 85 severely injured, the majority being members of the battalion's signals, mortar and motor transport (MT) platoons. Shortly afterwards the battalion left Cairo and deployed into the desert where it received reinforcements to replace those lost so tragically.

A month later, on 23 October, the battle of El Alamein took place with 4th Indian Division deployed on a flank. Its role was to mount a series of attacks as part of a deception plan by Eighth Army's new commander, Gen Bernard Montgomery, to prevent

Gurkha soldiers pictured while serving in North Africa with the Eighth Army. They are seen here playing a Nepalese card game which is a cross between bridge and whist.

A Gurkha motorcycle despatch rider in Tunisia.

Field Marshal Rommel from calling on reinforcements from his forces further inland when the British attack took place. The 1st/2nd KEO Gurkha Rifles, along with the 1st/9th, were formed into a number of columns which conducted a series of raids against German and Italian forces, capturing some 2,000 of the latter in the process. Following the breakthrough Montgomery's forces set off in pursuit of the retreating Afrika Korps but 4th Indian Division was given the task of remaining behind and clearing the battlefield. This was primarily due to the shortage of transport, which resulted in certain divisions and brigades being forced to remain in situ until they could be moved forward. Maj Gen Tuker took the opportunity of this respite to train his men further, honing them to a fine edge. It was not until four months later, in March 1943, that the division resumed its place among the foremost elements of the Eighth Army – by which time the latter had reached Tunisia, where it was preparing to confront Rommel's forces drawn up along the Mareth Line, a series of fortifications following a natural barrier of mountains and salt marshes leading inland to the Matmata Mountains.

At Tuker's request 4th Indian Division was given the task of attacking and seizing a vital feature called the Fatnassa Heights, the capture of which would open the way for a strong thrust behind the German and Italian line. It was strongly defended by the Afrika Korps but on the night of 5 April the 1st/2nd KEO and 1st/9th Gurkha Rifles succeeded in scaling the heights and locating the main enemy artillery. A large number of German gunners fell to the Gurkhas' kukris as the latter stormed the gun positions. By dawn on 6 April the feature had been taken by the 1st/2nd, and 7 Indian Infantry Brigade was able to push through. During this action a section led by Subedar Lalbahadur Thapa, the second-in-command of D Company of the 1st/2nd, stormed a number of enemy positions on the top of the most important part of the heights, killing a large number of enemy and putting the remainder to flight. Following the battle Lalbahadur was immediately awarded the Victoria Cross for his gallantry.

Gurkhas with kukris drawn storm an objective during operations in Tunisia.

Gurkhas in a shell-wrecked house in Jubatti, Tunisia.

Gurkhas advance with kukris drawn during a dawn attack in Tunisia.

The Germans reacted by launching a series of counter-attacks and it was not long before the 1st/9th Gurkha Rifles also distinguished themselves in a night attack on a feature called the Djebel Garci where the battalion was subjected to a strong German counter-attack lasting three days and nights. Much of the fighting was at close quarters where the Gurkhas' kukris once again took a heavy toll, eventually forcing the enemy to withdraw after suffering heavy casualties. The following days saw further enemy counter-attacks broken up by British artillery while German resistance became particularly stiff in the area of Enfidaville in the mountains. At this juncture Maj Gen Tuker proposed that the main British thrust should be switched to the narrow coastal plain north of Enfidaville.

On 12 May all German resistance in Tunisia was finally overcome and the campaign ended with the 1st/2nd KEO Gurkha Rifles capturing the 1,000-strong headquarters of Gen Hans von Arnim, the German Commander-in-Chief of Axis forces in North Africa.

Over the following months 4th Indian Division was withdrawn from the Eighth Army, being transferred initially to Egypt and then Palestine, Syria and, ultimately, Lebanon, where it retrained as a mountain division. At the same time, 5 and 7 Indian Infantry Brigades were joined by a newly formed 11 Indian Infantry Brigade, its predecessor having been captured in Tobruk along with the 2nd/7th Gurkha Rifles and the 2nd Battalion The Queen's Own Cameron Highlanders. Both these battalions had also been reformed as components of the brigade and at the end of 1943 returned with the rest of 4th Indian Division to the Eighth Army which by then was in southern Italy.

Landing at Taranto on 8 December 1943, the division was initially deployed on the Adriatic coast before being transferred, along with 2nd New Zealand Division commanded by Maj Gen Parkinson, to an area south of Cassino in central Italy. With three Gurkha units in the ranks of its three brigades, namely the 1st/2nd KEO, 2nd/7th and 1st/9th Gurkha Rifles, the division formed part of II New Zealand Corps, commanded by Lt Gen Sir Bernard Freyberg VC, which in turn was a component of the Fifth US Army under Gen Mark Clark.

Already in Italy was 8th Indian Division, which had arrived in September 1943 as part of the Eighth Army, its order of battle including the 1st/5th Royal Gurkha Rifles (the title 'Royal' had been granted in 1921). An advance northwards had brought it to a point south of the River Sangro where the battalion took part in an assault river crossing with the task of attacking the village of Mozzagrogna, which was heavily defended by the Germans. Bitter fighting took place, with the battalion succeeding in seizing parts of the village. Eventually, however, it was ordered to withdraw in order that a heavy artillery barrage could be brought down on the enemy. With much of the fighting taking place at close quarters, this was no easy task and the shelling caused more casualties among the Gurkha ranks than those of the enemy. Following the barrage, the village was seized after a fierce action by the 1st Battalion 12th Frontier Force Regiment supported by armour. The Germans launched a series of strong counter-attacks but these were repulsed and by 1 December the Sangro and its crossing points were firmly in Allied hands.

Men of the 7th Gurkha Rifles take the opportunity to clean their weapons and sharpen their kukris at Tavaleto in Italy during a lull in the fighting.

February 1944 found II New Zealand Corps preparing for an assault on the main German defensive positions. These hinged on the mountainous area to the north-east of Cassino, and were linked to a series of strongpoints on Monte Cassino itself, which was surmounted by a large monastery established in AD 529. The German defences, manned by crack parachute units of the 1st Fallschirmjägerdivision, comprised a complex of well-sited positions protected by minefields and supported in depth by artillery and mortars. Moreover, from their positions on Monte Cassino and further to the north-east on Monte Cairo, the enemy could observe the entire area in front of them. The task facing Lt Gen Freyberg and his corps was thus a formidable one.

The Allies possessed air superiority in Italy and this, combined with assurances from the commander of his air assets, was a major factor in the decision by Gen Sir Harold Alexander, the Allied commander-in-chief, to agree to a frontal assault by II New Zealand Corps. Unfortunately, Maj Gen Tuker, who had earlier proposed an outflanking attack against less well-defended locations in the German defences, was no longer in command of 4th Indian Division after falling victim to ethmoiditis, a serious complaint from which he had suffered previously. He was thus unable to argue against a plan that relied for success on heavy fire support rather than surprise.

American troops of 34th US Infantry Division had already established a foothold on an area of high ground to the north-east of the monastery when, in early February, the 1st/2nd KEO Gurkha Rifles moved up to relieve them. On their arrival the latter found evidence of hard fighting: over 150 enemy lay dead in just one sector forward of the American positions, while one of 34th Division's nine regiments, each of which comprised three battalions, had been reduced to a total strength of less than 200 men.

On 15 February the assault on Monte Cassino commenced with a series of heavy bombing raids on the monastery. Three days later, at 4.00 a.m. on 18 February, the ground assault began. The 1st/2nd, tasked with capturing the monastery itself, started the advance on their objective which lay some 800 yards away, while a battalion of The Royal Sussex began its attack on a nearby strongpoint on a feature called Point 593. As B and C Companies breasted the crest in front of them, they came under withering fire from enemy machine-guns that caused heavy casualties. Seeking cover in the nearby scrub, the Gurkhas encountered cunningly concealed anti-personnel minefields and within minutes both companies had suffered 50 per cent casualties. The Commandant, Lt Col James Showers, was hit and fell, as did a number of other officers. Dawn on the following day found the survivors in positions close to their start line, having suffered casualties numbering almost 150 killed, wounded or missing.

The Royal Sussex battalion also failed in its attempt to seize Point 593. Despite heavy enemy fire, its three leading companies succeeded in reaching the crest of the feature but withdrew after seeing three green flares. These had been fired by the Germans but, by an unfortunate coincidence, this was the battalion's prearranged signal for withdrawal. Meanwhile, below the mountain, 2nd New Zealand Division was also seeing some hard fighting during its efforts to take the town of Cassino. Once again, however, fierce resistance on the part of the enemy doomed these to failure.

The second attack on Monte Cassino was postponed for almost three weeks owing to bad weather. During this period 4th Indian Division units patrolled actively at night and a number of skirmishes took place, with the Germans continually bringing down artillery and mortar fire on the division's forward positions.

By the middle of March the weather had improved sufficiently and on the 15th a massive raid was carried out on Cassino and the monastery by 500 bombers. At midday 600 guns opened fire and 6 New Zealand and 5 Indian Infantry Brigades advanced under a protective curtain of shellfire. The latter was to push through the town and advance up the mountain towards the monastery. Unfortunately the advance of both brigades was hampered by the destruction wrought by the bombing, the collapsed buildings and rubble providing excellent cover for the town's defenders while preventing Allied tanks from moving up in support of the infantry.

One of 5 Indian Infantry Brigade's battalions was the 1st/9th Gurkha Rifles, whose objective was an outcrop just below the monastery; marked on maps as Point 935, it was better known as Hangman's Hill. Under cover of darkness, C and D Companies were sent out in advance of the battalion's main body with the task of seizing the objective. C Company, commanded by Capt Michael Drinkall, moved along a track and then headed across to a forming-up point, where the men dumped their packs before moving to their start line. From there the company advanced silently up the mountainside with drawn kukris, heading for a small enemy outpost in a cave, which it reached just before dawn. The Gurkhas attacked shortly afterwards but unfortunately some of the enemy escaped and raised the alarm. The response was fire from a single mortar, which wounded Capt Drinkall and his second-in-command. Shortly afterwards, however, the weapon and its crew were put out of action by a Gurkha NCO, Naik (Cpl) Amarbahadur Khattri, who went forward on his own to silence it.

Dawn broke to find C Company clinging tenuously to its positions on Hangman's Hill under heavy enemy fire. Its problems were made all the worse by the fact that its radio providing rear link communications with the battalion headquarters had become inoperable. Capt Drinkall was on the point of deciding to withdraw after nightfall when the set suddenly came to life and he was able to make contact with the Commandant, Lt Col George Nangle, who ordered him to continue holding out while the rest of the battalion made its way up to Hangman's Hill. This proved easier said than done, however, and it was not until dawn on 18 March that the leading element of the battalion appeared. Fortunately it did so just as German paratroops launched an attack that threatened to overrun C Company, and the Germans were beaten off.

For the following nine days the 1st/9th grimly held on to Hangman's Hill which was only a short distance from the outer reaches of the monastery. Meanwhile, the Germans attempted unsuccessfully to cut the battalion's line of communications and supply which passed through Castle Hill, held by a battalion of The Essex Regiment reinforced by A Company 2nd/7th Gurkha Rifles. By 25 March, however, it had become apparent that II New Zealand Corps' second attack had failed and, following nightfall, the 1st/9th, together with detachments of The Essex Regiment and the Rajputana Rifles, began to withdraw from Hangman's Hill. The battalion had paid a heavy price: German reports later stated that 185 Gurkha dead were found on the feature.

The end of the month saw the 1st/2nd KEO and 2nd/7th Gurkha Rifles relieved, by which time 2nd New Zealand and 4th Indian Divisions had been in action for nearly six weeks. Shortly afterwards the latter was transferred to Orsogno on the Adriatic front and thus missed the final assault on Cassino, which took place on 11 May. Its place was taken by 8th Indian Division, whose 17 Indian Infantry Brigade was tasked with carrying out an assault river crossing across the Liri. The 1st/5th Royal Gurkha Rifles were initially in reserve, their task being to move through the brigade's beachhead on the west bank and seize the village of San Angelo, a major strongpoint in the German defensive complex called the Gustav Line. Its capture would give the Allied forces access to Route 6, the main road to Rome.

The crossing took place on 12 May but the brigade's leading unit, the 1st Battalion Royal Fusiliers, became pinned down on the far side and twelve of its sixteen assault

The Rt Hon Leopold Amery, Secretary of State for India and Burma, visits the position of the 1st/5th Royal Gurkha Rifles who served with 8th Indian Division in 1944.

boats were destroyed. Using the remaining four, the 1st/5th Royal Gurkha Rifles began ferrying their companies across the river but it was not until four hours later that the entire battalion had been landed on the far bank. By this time an initial assault by one of its companies on San Angelo had been repulsed.

The following day was spent under heavy fire and it was not until the evening that Canadian tanks reached the west bank and moved up in support of the battalion, which thereafter began its second attack on San Angelo on the morning of 14 May. The supporting armour, however, became bogged down in the marshy terrain but, preceded by a heavy artillery barrage, the 1st/5th succeeded in gaining a foothold in the village. Heavy fighting ensued and it was not until the afternoon of the 14th that the battalion captured San Angelo, by which time it had paid the heavy price of 41 officers and men killed and 129 wounded.

By this time the third and final Allied assault had been launched on Monte Cassino. Having suffered very heavy casualties, the Germans were unable to withstand such an overwhelming onslaught and eventually they withdrew. On 18 May troops of II Polish Corps, commanded by Gen Wladyslaw Anders, stormed the bomb-shattered monastery and shortly afterwards the Polish flag could be seen flying over the ruins. The road to Rome was open.

Elsewhere other Gurkha units were also taking part in the campaign to push the Germans northwards through Italy. Among the formations advancing slowly up the Adriatic coast in the face of strong enemy resistance was 43 Gurkha Lorried Infantry Brigade, comprising the 2nd/6th, 2nd/8th and 2nd/10th Gurkha Rifles. Shortly after the fall of Cassino, however, resistance collapsed as the German forces in the region abandoned their positions and withdrew north. In central Italy, meanwhile, two battalions, the 2nd/3rd QAO and 2nd/4th PWO Gurkha Rifles, forming part of 10th Indian Division, saw heavy fighting in the Tiber Valley, along which the Germans were withdrawing to the Gothic Line, their next defensive complex.

As the Allied forces inexorably pushed forward in pursuit of the withdrawing German forces, 4th Indian Division was in the forefront of the fighting. During July and into early August the 1st/2nd KEO and 2nd/7th Gurkha Rifles were heavily involved in several actions. The 1st/2nd was given the task of attacking the Pian di Maggio, a crescent-shaped feature near Arezzo. The Germans, however, put up a stiff resistance and the Commandant, Lt Col Gordon Richardson, was forced to commit his reserve of his fourth rifle company before the battalion could take its objective. Similarly, the 2nd/7th had to capture a feature called the Poggio del Grillo, its attack being mounted after a night march of 3 miles over difficult terrain. The battalion achieved complete surprise and the enemy pulled back without putting up a fight, although they launched a series of counter-attacks during the following three days before withdrawing completely.

The end of August found 4th Indian Division in the foothills of the Apennines in north-east Italy, holding the left-hand sector on the Allies' western flank. Following resumption of the advance northwards by 5, 7 and 11 Indian Infantry Brigades, the 1st/9th Gurkha Rifles were involved in heavy fighting in the area of Monte Calvo. On the night of 2/3 September the 1st/2nd KEO Gurkha Rifles carried out a successful night attack on the village of Auditore. This was followed by an assault in the early hours of the following morning on the Poggio San Giovanni, a steep hill behind it. Fierce opposition was encountered but the battalion succeeded in taking its objective, only to find itself lacking the British tanks tasked with joining it on the feature. The situation became serious as German self-propelled guns appeared, the Gurkhas finding themselves hard-pressed until the belated arrival of their supporting armour. On the following night the 2nd/7th Gurkha Rifles mounted an attack on the hilltop village of Tavoleto, capturing it in the early hours of 4 September after heavy fighting.

4th Indian Division continued its advance, heading for San Marino, a small, landlocked Italian republic in north-eastern Italy. The Germans had established a number of strongpoints on the route leading to it and in mid-September the 1st/9th Gurkha Rifles were tasked with capturing two of them, Points 343 and 366, situated on a feature dominating the division's line of advance. Stiff opposition was encountered, with further problems being caused by supporting armour becoming bogged down in the marshy terrain. Eventually, after prolonged heavy fighting, both strongpoints were taken and the division was able to continue its advance on San Marino.

Meanwhile, mid-September found 43 Gurkha Lorried Infantry Brigade leading an attack on the night of the 12th on a feature called Passano Ridge. In the van were the 2nd/10th Gurkha Rifles advancing over difficult, broken terrain towards the objective. Fierce fighting took place at close quarters before the battalion succeeded in driving off the Germans, who retaliated by bringing down heavy concen-

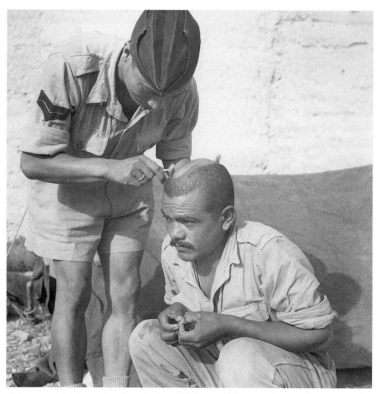

Gurkhas kept their hair very short during the Second World War and often shaved their heads retaining a tuft of hair the size of a calf's hoof, known as the *tupi*, to distinguish them as Hindus.

trations of mortar and artillery fire, causing severe casualties among the Gurkhas.

The advance was resumed with the 2nd/6th Gurkha Rifles leading the way, the brigade subsequently carrying out a crossing of the River Marino with the task of securing several features along the Mulazzano Ridge on the northern bank. Following a heavy bombardment by Allied artillery, this was achieved without much difficulty. Thereafter there was a pause during which the brigade was transferred to 56th London Division and given the task of crossing the River Marecchia and establishing a bridgehead on the far bank.

The crossing took place before dawn on 23 September. There was no supporting fire from armour or artillery, as the intelligence staff at Headquarters 1st Armoured Division were sceptical about reports indicating clearly that the Germans were well prepared to put up stiff opposition to a crossing. All too soon these reports proved to be accurate: the leading battalions, the 2nd/8th Gurkha Rifles on the right and the 2nd/10th on the left, came under heavy machine-gun fire as they crossed the river. Fortunately, much of it went high, enabling the Gurkhas to reach their objectives. Shortly afterwards, however, D Company of the 2nd/10th was subjected to an enemy counter-attack supported by tanks and was overrun despite the best efforts of

C Company to come to its aid. During the evening the 2nd/6th Gurkha Rifles moved through to relieve the 2nd/8th, subsequently mounting a night attack and driving the enemy off the crest of the feature. Shortly afterwards the brigade was joined by some British tanks which had managed to cross the river. By midday on 24 September the battle was over.

On 6 October the brigade was transferred to 10th Indian Division, deployed in the mountains to the south of Bologna. Leaving behind their lorries, the men took to their feet, with support weapons and equipment being carried by mules. Crossing the River Fiumicino with the 2nd/6th Gurkha Rifles in the lead, they captured the feature of Monte Codruzzo before dawn on 11 October, taking the enemy force holding it completely by surprise. Thereafter the brigade made its way along the ridge to Monte Chicco, on which was situated an enemy strongpoint known as the White House. Once again it was the 2nd/6th who led the attack, using their kukris in the prolonged close-quarter fighting which took place before the Gurkhas overcame all resistance and took their objective. Their casualties comprised 20 killed and 60 wounded, the latter including their Commandant, Lt Col G.F.X. Bulfield, who had been shot in the knee.

The brigade took part in one further important action before the onset of winter, the crossing of the River Ronco, beyond which lay the town of Forli. The river itself was a major obstacle, being some 12 feet in depth and in spate, and thus crossing it was a hazardous process. The problem was solved by the use of an aqueduct, across which a company of the 2nd/8th Gurkha Rifles crossed initially on 28 October to establish a bridgehead. On the following day they were joined by the 2nd/6th, now commanded by Lt Col Wyn Amoore, and the 2nd/10th, who pushed forwards and enlarged the bridgehead to a depth of over 3,000 yards.

The brigade saw further action throughout the winter of 1944, in December operating along the Montone and Lamone rivers, and subsequently taking part in an attack on Faenza under command of 2nd New Zealand Division.

The spring of 1945 found the Allied forces in Italy launching a major offensive. The Senio and Santerno rivers were crossed on 9 April with II Polish Corps in the lead. On 10 April 43 Gurkha Lorried Infantry Brigade, still under command of 2nd New Zealand Division, began its advance but saw little action during the following two or three days. On 16 April its leading element, the 2nd/10th Gurkha Rifles, spearheaded an attack across the River Sillaro, which, while successful, saw the battalion suffer heavy casualties as it seized its objectives on the far bank of the river. A battle group of A Squadron 14th/20th The King's Royal Hussars and two companies of the 2nd/6th Gurkha Rifles, the latter mounted in Kangaroo armoured troop carriers, then moved through and set off in pursuit of the withdrawing enemy heading for the town of Medicina, to the east of Bologna, which was held by German paratroops of 4th Fallschirmjägerdivision. The speed and momentum of the combined assault by the Gurkhas and Hussars took the enemy by surprise and by nightfall the town was in Allied hands.

The next major obstacle facing 2nd New Zealand Division was the River Gaiana which, while fordable by infantry, could not be crossed by armour owing to its banks, which were up to 20 feet in height. It was defended by German paratroops, who were well dug in and could be relied upon to offer stiff resistance. At 9 o'clock on the night of 16 April, following a heavy artillery bombardment, 43 Gurkha Lorried Infantry Brigade began its assault with the 2nd/6th Gurkha Rifles leading the way. The enemy responded with heavy and accurate fire, which inflicted severe casualties among A and D Companies, who were leading the way. Eventually the survivors were ordered to retire. A second assault was carried out on the night of 17 April by the 2nd/8th and 2nd/10th Gurkha Rifles. This proved successful and at last the entire brigade crossed the river. This was the last major action in which 43 Gurkha Lorried Infantry Brigade took part. On 2 May 1945 the German forces in northern Italy surrendered unconditionally and the campaign came to an end.

In the meantime 4th Indian Division had left Italy and had been transferred to Greece, its three brigades arriving at the end of November at Salonika, Athens and Patras along with other British forces occupying the country in the wake of the German withdrawal north through the Balkans. The British initially received a warm welcome but it was not long before they encountered opposition from Communist guerrillas of the People's Liberation Army (ELAS), who had been supported and supplied with arms by the Allies during the war.

In Patras 11 Indian Infantry Brigade faced a force of guerrillas of approximately divisional strength, while 7 Indian Infantry Brigade at Salonika was confronted by a further 8,000, both forces being supported by artillery. The end came late in November when a force of several thousand guerrillas advanced on Athens with the intention of seizing the capital. They were prevented from doing so by a combined force of 5 Indian Infantry Brigade, 2 Independent Parachute Brigade Group, 23 Armoured Brigade, the Greek Mountain Brigade and elements of the Greek National Guard. The fighting in the city was fierce, and the 1st/9th Gurkha Rifles suffered 10 killed and 60 wounded, but on 18 December further British reinforcements arrived in the form of 4th Infantry Division. Eventually the ELAS forces were driven out of Athens and on 14 January an operation by C Company 2nd/7th Gurkha Rifles cleared them from Patras after a short but fierce action which saw 32 guerrillas killed, 38 wounded and a number taken prisoner. During the following weeks units of 4th Indian Division were deployed to rural areas where they disarmed members of ELAS. At the end of December 1945 the division left Greece and departed by sea for India.

CHAPTER 4

THE WAR IN BURMA

While the Gurkha battalions of 4th and 10th Indian Divisions and 43 Gurkha Lorried Infantry Brigade fought their respective ways across the deserts of North Africa and up the length of Italy, the rest of the Indian Army's Gurkha Brigade had been fighting a very different war on the other side of the world.

On 7 December 1941 Japanese aircraft struck at the US naval base at Pearl Harbor on the island of Hawaii. The American losses were heavy: 8 battleships damaged and 5 sunk along with 3 light cruisers, 3 destroyers, 3 smaller vessels and 188 aircraft. A total of 2,403 people were killed during the attack, and 1,178 wounded. On the following day, 8 December, troops of the Japanese Twenty-Fifth Army landed in northern Malaya, while to the south Japanese aircraft carried out bombing raids on Singapore.

At that time the 2nd/1st KGO, 2nd/2nd KEO and 2nd/9th Gurkha Rifles were stationed in Malaya as part of 11th Indian Division. The 2nd/2nd had been deployed to the north of Alor Setar, on the west coast of Malaya, approximately 50 miles south of the border with Siam (now Thailand). The British, however, vacillated over whether to defend the border or adopt a defensive line to the south. In the event neither proved possible and thus it was not long before columns of British, Indian and Australian troops were retreating south with the enemy hard on their heels. Attempts were made to fight delaying actions and on 11 December the 2nd/2nd had their first brush with the enemy, following which the battalion continued marching south for the next four days and three nights to rejoin the rest of the division.

On 7 January 11th Indian Division fought a major action on the Slim River against the Japanese but within a matter of hours its area had been penetrated by the enemy, with both brigade headquarters being overrun by a force of 50 enemy tanks. The 2nd/2nd and 2nd/9th meanwhile found themselves cut off on the northern bank of the river. The 2nd/2nd was split into two halves, each comprising two companies. B and D Companies succeeded in crossing to the south via a partly destroyed railway bridge while A and C Companies, together with members of the 2nd/9th Gurkha Rifles, had to resort to improvised means. On reaching the south bank, however, the latter force encountered enemy troops who had cut off their line of withdrawal. Splitting up into a number of small groups, the remnants of both companies headed off into the jungle, through the terrain of razor-backed foliage which covered the ridges and hills, in a bid

Gurkhas in Burma prepare to mount a final assault on an objective.

to head south to the fortress of Singapore. Only a few succeeded in escaping, while others remained at large in the jungle before eventually being captured.

The remainder of both battalions succeeded in rejoining 11th Indian Division which, after five weeks of continual fighting, took up defensive positions 25 miles north of the Straits of Johore. By this time the decision to abandon Malaya had been taken by the Supreme Allied Commander South West Pacific, Gen Sir Archibald Wavell, and on 31 January 1942, as the last Allied units withdrew to Singapore, the causeway connecting it to the Malayan mainland was blown up.

Singapore soon found itself under siege. 11th Indian Division was tasked with defending the northern sector of the island with Australian troops on its left occupying the north-west. It was not long, however, before the Japanese launched a series of attacks, the first taking place on the night of 8/9 February when enemy troops crossed the straits and launched an assault against the Australians. Unable to resist this onslaught, the latter withdrew, exposing 11th Indian Division's left flank and leaving it no choice but to follow suit. As it did so, however, it encountered enemy troops to the rear, a force of 5,000 having infiltrated on to the island under cover of darkness.

The division withdrew to a new defensive perimeter where the remaining forces on the island prepared to make a last stand. The remnants of the 2nd/1st KGO, 2nd/2nd KEO and 2nd/9th Gurkha Rifles in particular were prepared to fight to the last man and thus it was with disbelief and dismay, following a ceasefire which came into force at 4 p.m. on 15 February, that they received the order to lay down their weapons and surrender.

A total of 85,000 British, Gurkha, Indian and Australian troops were marched away into captivity on that infamous day. The Japanese immediately separated the Gurkhas and Indians from their British officers prior to attempting to persuade them to join the Indian National Army (INA), a force of turncoats under the command of Subhas Chandra Bhose. Among those who suffered greatly during three years of captivity in the brutal Japanese PoW camps in Singapore was Subedar Major Harising Bohra of the 2nd/2nd KEO Gurkha Rifles. He and his fellow VCOs were subjected to appalling treatment, prompting him to write a letter to the Japanese in which he stated that as prisoners of war he and his men were entitled to fair and honourable treatment. This so enraged his captors that they subjected him to a series of severe beatings, which caused internal injuries and ultimately resulted in his death in May 1944. His conduct was an example to the men of the 2nd/2nd and 2nd/9th, the vast majority of whom remained steadfastly loyal. Only 26 members of the 2nd/2nd, led by Rifleman Dhanbahadur Rana, joined the INA but, when later posted to Burma, they promptly deserted. Taking with them a map with the Japanese positions marked on it, they made their way to the British lines.

Japan's invasion of Burma began on 16 December 1941 when the 143rd Regiment of 55th Division crossed the Burma–Siam border and captured Victoria Point. This was followed by air raids on Rangoon on 23 and 25 December and thereafter there was a lull until 15 January 1942, when a battalion of the 112th Regiment also crossed the border, capturing the town of Tavoy and its airfield on 19 January. On 21 January the Fifteenth Army crossed the border with two divisions, the 33rd and 55th, heading south for the capital, Rangoon, the location of the headquarters of the British Twenty-Fourth Army, commanded by Lt Gen H.J. Hutton who also held the appointment of General Officer Commanding (GOC) Burma. Its port was crucial to the British as all resupply and reinforcements had to come by sea, there being no roads linking India and Burma.

The Twenty-Fourth Army principally consisted of I Burma Corps comprising 1st Burma Division covering the northern half of the country and 17th Indian Division, commanded by Maj Gen John Smyth VC, deployed in the south. The latter consisted of 48 Indian Infantry Brigade, comprising the 1st/3rd QAO and 1st/4th PWO Gurkha Rifles and the 2nd/5th Royal Gurkha Rifles; and 16 Indian Infantry Brigade, which included the 1st/7th in its order of battle. In addition to the Twenty-Fourth Army,

Lt P.P. Dunkley MC and Bar (left), Maj M.D. Mulroney and men of 3rd/10th Gurkha Rifles examine a Japanese gelignite bomb following the capture of Scraggy on the Burma border, 25 July 1944.

there were two Chinese armies (each equivalent in size to a British or Indian division) in eastern-central Burma under the command of Generalissimo Chiang Kai Shek.

Hutton's orders from Gen Wavell, who was also Commander-in-Chief India, were to stem the Japanese advance and hold Rangoon. He was ill-equipped to do so, however, as 17th Indian Division was an untried and incomplete formation while 1st Burma Division was of poor quality. Within 17th Indian Division, 16 Indian Infantry Brigade was initially deployed along the Siamese frontier, its forward elements covering the crossing points most likely to be used by the enemy. D Company 1st/7th Gurkha Rifles was the first to make contact with the Japanese, coming under fire from mortars and machine-guns. At the same time the other companies were subjected to attacks by dive-bombers, preventing them from providing support for D Company, which was soon surrounded. It was not long before the rest of the battalion found that the Japanese had infiltrated round behind most of its positions, forcing it to withdraw swiftly to avoid being cut off. A week later the battalion reached Kywegan where subsequently it was joined by D Company which had succeeded in breaking out and heading for the River Salween. Having commandeered a barge, the company sailed downriver to rejoin the battalion.

In danger of being outflanked by the Japanese, whose speed of advance was such that there was no opportunity to launch any form of counter-attack, 17th Indian Division fought a series of rearguard actions, withdrawing through southern Burma from riverline to riverline until it reached the River Sittang, a 1,200 yard-wide waterway forming a major obstacle, where Maj Gen John Smyth intended to make his stand. The principal crossing point was the Sittang Bridge, situated just to the north of the river's estuary to the north-east of Rangoon, where the division established a bridge demolition guard to hold it until such time as the last of its units had crossed to the west, at which point the bridge would be blown.

Well aware of the significance of the bridge, the Japanese were hard on the division's heels. In mid-February Smyth learned that a second enemy force was moving west, heading directly for the bridge with the intention of blowing it and thus cutting the British line of withdrawal. The enemy succeeded in interposing a number of roadblocks between the bridge and those British and Indian formations and units, among them 16 and 48 Indian Infantry Brigades, desperately trying to reach it before being cut off. The only Gurkha unit among those troops who succeeded were the 1st/4th PWO Gurkha Rifles. The 1st/3rd QAO and the 2nd/5th Royal Gurkha Rifles, along with most of 16 and 48 Indian Infantry Brigades, attempted to fight their way through with artillery support but were pinned down by heavy enemy fire and thus failed to do so.

By this time there was increasing concern in London and Delhi over the swiftly deteriorating situation in Burma and the decision was taken to replace Lt Gen Hutton as Commander Twenty-Fourth Army and GOC Burma with Lt Gen Sir Harold Alexander, who was despatched by air from Britain on 27 February.

Meanwhile, by the afternoon of 23 February the demolition guard force had suffered heavy casualties, and it had become apparent that the bridge had to be destroyed or it would fall into Japanese hands and thus leave the road to Rangoon open. Faced with an agonising decision which would leave much of his division trapped to the east of the river, Maj Gen Smyth nevertheless gave the order for the bridge to be blown.

Fashioning crude rafts from wood or bamboo for the wounded, small groups of men attempted to swim across the 1,200 yard-wide Sittang. Approximately 2,000 men succeeded in reaching the far bank but many others perished, either drowning or being swept out to sea by the strong current. Others were captured by the Japanese. By the time the division reorganised, the missing in its Gurkha battalions alone were numbered in their hundreds, with the two battalions of the 7th Gurkha Rifles having lost an estimated 350 all ranks. Some of these had been taken prisoner but even after the war, when all the prisoners had been recovered, the regiment was still unable to account for 300 officers and men, the majority of whom were believed to have drowned while trying to cross the Sittang. The four sorely depleted battalions were amalgamated temporarily, the 1st/3rd and 2nd/5th joining forces while the 1st/7th and 3rd/7th did likewise. These two temporary units came under the command of a

American medical volunteer Jeffrey Potter tends a Gurkha hit by shrapnel during action in the Sittang Bend area where Japanese resistance was strong.

reformed 48 Indian Infantry Brigade, which was briefly the sole component of 17th Indian Division.

By 24 February the division numbered only 3,400 troops, some 2,000 of whom did not even have rifles, and had lost all its heavy equipment, much of which had fallen into the hands of the enemy. It was impossible to hold the west bank of the Sittang with such a weak force and so Smyth withdrew some 20 to 30 miles from the river and regrouped around the towns of Waw and Pegu. Fortunately the Japanese were forced to wait for their bridging equipment to arrive before they could cross the Sittang, giving Smyth a week's respite and the opportunity for him to be reinforced by

A lone Gurkha soldier passes along an empty street in Pegu, 50 miles north of Rangoon. The value of the road and rail town was considerable and the Japanese fought bitterly to retain it.

63 Indian Infantry Brigade, one of its three battalions being the 1st/10th Gurkha Rifles, and 7 Armoured Brigade, an all-British formation.

The new GOC Burma, Lt Gen Alexander, arrived in Rangoon on 5 March. He found the Burmese capital in a state of chaos, the Governor of Burma, Sir Reginald Dorman-Smith, having ordered its evacuation some days beforehand. The city was being subjected to air attacks by the Japanese, with looting and arson committed by inmates released from the city's jails and lunatic asylums adding to the general sense of pandemonium. Alexander spent only an hour in the city before heading 40 miles north-east to Twenty-Fourth Army headquarters, where he assumed command from Lt Gen Hutton, who became chief-of-staff.

By this time the Japanese had crossed the Sittang and two divisions were advancing in columns, one heading south-west via Pegu to Rangoon, while the other advanced westwards to cut the roads leading north from the capital before turning towards the city itself. Alexander was under orders from Wavell to defend Rangoon and thus cancelled Hutton's previous orders for 17th Indian Division to withdraw from Pegu and concentrate north of the capital. He decided instead to form a defensive line by linking up with 1st Burma Division, the nearest elements of which were 40 miles to the north. Alexander planned to close the gap by launching a series of simultaneous attacks from the north and south by both divisions. He ignored the advice of Hutton and other members of his staff, who pointed out that 17th Indian Division was in no state to confront two well-trained and well-equipped Japanese divisions.

On 6 March 63 Indian Infantry Brigade lost its commander when he and a small group comprising the commanding officers of his three battalions and members of his staff set off on a reconnaissance. Unknown to them, a Japanese force had succeeded in making its way undetected round Pegu, which was held by 48 Indian Infantry Brigade, some 50 miles to the north-east of Rangoon. The group was travelling in a number of personnel carriers and these were ambushed by the enemy. The second vehicle, whose passengers included the brigadier and his three commanding officers, was badly hit and all aboard were either killed or wounded. Despite his injuries, the driver succeeded in reversing his vehicle out of the area and driving it back to the brigade headquarters

Elsewhere 17th Indian Division's attacks made no progress and 1st Burma Division failed to advance south. It rapidly became apparent to Alexander that his plan had failed and he thus abandoned any idea of saving Rangoon. On the night of 6 March he gave orders for the city to be abandoned and all remaining installations to be destroyed. On 7 March he and two-thirds of his forces withdrew from the capital and headed north for Upper Burma in a 20-mile long convoy of vehicles, their withdrawal being covered by a rearguard.

Meanwhile, the northernmost of the two Japanese divisions had reached the road 20 miles north of the capital and had established a roadblock. That night Alexander ordered a brigade attack to clear it at dawn on the following day but just before the assault was about to commence it was found that the enemy had abandoned their positions. It transpired that the roadblock had been established to provide temporary flanking protection for the enemy division while it crossed to the west of the road before swinging south towards Rangoon, its commander hell-bent on reaching the capital before his rival commanding the division to the south.

Alexander subsequently established a new defensive line between Prome and Toungoo with I Burma Corps, from mid-March onwards commanded by Lt Gen Sir William Slim, holding the floor of the Irrawaddy Valley. Generalissimo Chiang Kai Shek's Chinese forces, recently increased by a third army (division), meanwhile held the Sittang Valley and the Shan States, an area along the Siamese border. During April, however, Alexander was forced to withdraw further north to protect the vital oilfields at Yenangyaung. To the north lay Mandalay and the large depots filled with arms, equipment and food which had been transferred there earlier from Rangoon and thus during this period Alexander was able to use these resources to sustain and re-equip his hard-pressed forces as there was no support forthcoming from India. Due to Japanese air superiority and a shortage of aircraft, all RAF aircraft in Burma having been destroyed by the Japanese in two raids, resupply by air was impossible while the absence of a road meant nothing could be despatched overland. A 60-mile-long route was under construction from Imphal in Assam to Tamu, just over the border into Burma, but it had not yet been completed.

In mid-April the Japanese launched a major offensive. In the Sittang Valley Chiang Kai Shek's forces were quickly overrun by the enemy, who moved swiftly through the Shan States to Lashio, where they succeeded in cutting the Burma Road, the main route between China and Burma. Shortly afterwards they captured Yenangyaung and its oilfields. I Burma Corps and the Fifth Chinese Army held firm but it soon became apparent to Alexander that he had no choice but to withdraw his forces to India without delay. He himself remained with his troops while sending a large part of his headquarters and staff to India by air.

A major obstacle to the Japanese advance was the Irrawaddy, a huge river with only one bridge spanning it at Ava. This was prepared for demolition and the withdrawal commenced. The rearguard was provided by 48 Indian Infantry Brigade, who manned positions to the east of the town of Kyaukse through which the rest of I Burma Corps, along with the Chinese Fifth Army, passed. On the night of 27 April troops of the Japanese élite 18th 'Chrysanthemum' Division approached and were within only 100 yards of the Gurkhas' positions before the latter opened fire. Having suffered heavy losses, the enemy withdrew under harassing fire from I Burma Corps artillery. Two hours later they reappeared, but once again were beaten off. On the following morning D Company 1st/7th Gurkha Rifles mounted a counter-attack and forced the enemy even further back, inflicting more casualties as they did so. The rest of the day saw further attacks and counter-attacks taking place until the late afternoon, when the brigade headquarters was informed that the last of I Burma Corps, together with two of Chiang Kai Shek's divisions, had withdrawn across the bridge at Ava. Moving by battalions, 48 Indian Infantry Brigade pulled back and headed for the bridge, which was blown at midnight on 30 April.

The withdrawal to India was a race not only against the Japanese but also against the weather. The monsoon rains, due in mid-May, would turn the road to the frontier and Assam into an impassable quagmire, giving Alexander's force only two weeks to reach India. Without further ado, they headed north-west from the Irrawaddy to the River Chindwin, a distance of 100 miles. Meanwhile, the Japanese were hard on their heels. There was no bridge over the Chindwin and thus Alexander was heading for a crossing point at Monywa. This was seized by an enemy force advancing from the south, and he was forced to head further north to Shwegyin, from where he and his men could be ferried to Kalewa on the west bank of the Chindwin.

The Japanese approached Shwegyin as the ferrying operation was under way, with troops and vehicles embarked aboard river steamers which transported them upriver to Kalewa. They encountered the rearguard, once again provided by 48 Indian Infantry Brigade, and on 10 May launched an attack on the brigade's Indian unit, a battalion of the 9th Jat Regiment, which was beaten off with the help of three companies of the 1st/7th Gurkha Rifles. Despite this, the Japanese brought down harassing fire on the ferry point as I Burma Corps and the two Chinese divisions were crossing to Kalewa, forcing them to leave behind most of their vehicles and all of 7 Armoured Brigade's remaining tanks.

Having crossed the Chindwin, Alexander's force faced a further trek of 100 miles to Tamu and the Assam border. The remaining 90 vehicles were used to carry the wounded and sick while all other personnel, numbering some 36,000, moved on foot, accompanied by hundreds of thousands of refugees. Many died through illness, including cholera and smallpox, while others were struck down by cerebral malaria which also proved fatal in many cases. The rains arrived on 12 May but fortunately the road remained just usable for vehicles and four days later Alexander and the leading elements of the Twenty-Fourth Army arrived in Assam, the rearguard following them on 20 May.

17th Indian Division now moved to Imphal, itself in a serious state of disrepair as a result of Japanese bombing. Exhausted and sorely depleted in number, the division was in desperate need of rest and recuperation as well as reinforcement. This, together with the incessant rain, resulted in no major operations being mounted by the British until early 1943.

During the rest of 1942 one Gurkha unit found itself operating behind Japanese lines. A newly raised battalion commanded by Lt Col L.A. Alexander, the 3rd/2nd KEO Gurkha Rifles was assigned as one of three infantry battalions to 77 Infantry Brigade, commanded by Brigadier Orde Wingate and dubbed the 'Chindits'. The others were the 13th Battalion The King's Regiment, commanded by Lt Col S.A. Cooke, and the 2nd Battalion The Burma Rifles, under Lt Col L.G. Wheeler, a unit recruited from Karen tribesmen.

The brigade comprised three elements. 1 Group, commanded by Lt Col Alexander, consisted of four columns. The 3rd/2nd, which included 300 men of the 10th Gurkha Rifles in its ranks, was divided between the columns, its platoons and sections mixed in with their British counterparts of the 13th King's. Its soldiers, mostly very young and inexperienced, found themselves serving under officers who not only were unknown to them, but also were not familiar with Gurkhas and did not speak Gurkhali. Used to their own tight-knit communities of the battalion and its companies, they understandably felt lost when placed among outsiders. The second element was 2 Group, commanded by Lt Col Cooke and comprising a further three columns, while the third consisted of the Burma Rifles battalion and 142nd Commando Company.

Wingate, a highly unorthodox soldier, had little knowledge of, or interest in, Gurkhas and failed to understand that the young Nepalese hillmen, some only sixteen years of age, required a different style of leadership from the older, experienced British soldiers in his brigade. His first operation, codenamed Longcloth, took place in mid-February 1943. He divided his brigade into two elements: Lt Col Alexander with 1 and 2 Columns was tasked with carrying out a diversionary move by crossing the Chindwin at Auktaung, while Wingate and the remainder of the brigade crossed at Tonhe. The entire force penetrated deep into Japanese-held territory but only 3 Column, led by Maj Michael Calvert, achieved anything of significance. Part of this column comprised C Company 3rd/2nd Gurkha Rifles, which frequently found itself in contact with the enemy as Calvert proceeded to carry out a number of demolition tasks as well as causing general mayhem throughout his area of operations. In so doing, however, he stirred up a hornets' nest and eventually was forced to split his column of 360 men into nine groups of 40 to exfiltrate back to India via different routes. In the process they suffered heavy casualties and it was a significantly reduced force of only 200 that finally returned safely to Assam. The 3rd/2nd KEO Gurkha Rifles lost 446 all ranks, of whom 150 later returned by various means.

The other columns had also suffered heavy casualties and by June only two-thirds of 77 Infantry Brigade had succeeded in making their way back. Wingate had, in the words of one critic, 'lost a thousand men in a series of operations which ranged from conclusive victory to complete fiasco'. Operation Longcloth is probably best summed up by Maj (later Brig) Bernard Fergusson of the Black Watch, who commanded 5 Column:

> What did we accomplish? Not much that was tangible. What there was became distorted in the glare of publicity soon after our return. We blew up bits of a railway, which did not take long to repair; we gathered some useful intelligence; we distracted the Japanese from some minor operations, and possibly from some bigger ones; we killed a few hundreds of an enemy which number eighty millions; we proved that it was feasible to maintain a force by supply dropping alone.

Despite the paucity of success achieved in his first expedition, Wingate succeeded in gaining support at high level for his concept of long-range, deep penetration operations. He was promoted to the rank of major general and the Chindits were expanded to form 3rd Indian Infantry Division, which became better known as 'Special Force'.

Wingate's new force comprised six formations, each of which was allocated a codename: 3 West African (Thunder), 14 (Javelin), 16 (Enterprise), 77 (Emphasis) and 111 (Profound) Infantry Brigades and the 5307th Composite Unit (Provisional) (Galahad), a US Army raiding regiment of three battalions, later to become better known as 'Merrill's Marauders'. In addition, it possessed a two-battalion formation known as 'Morris Force', named after its commander, Brigadier J.R. Morris, and comprising the 3rd/4th PWO and 4th/9th Gurkha Rifles. Two other Gurkha units, the 3rd/9th and 3rd/6th Gurkha Rifles, were components of 77 and 111 Infantry Brigades respectively. Other elements of Special Force included 'Dah Force', a unit of Kachin tribesmen, and 'Bladet' (Blain's Detachment), a unit of gliderborne commando sappers. Dedicated artillery support was provided by 'R', 'S' and 'U' Troops of 160 Field Regiment RA and 'W', 'X', 'Y' and 'Z' Troops of 69 Light Anti-Aircraft Regiment RA.

The basic Chindit unit was the independent column, each battalion being organised into two such sub-units. Each column comprised a rifle company of four platoons; a support platoon equipped with two 3-inch mortars and two Vickers .303 medium machine-guns; a reconnaissance platoon, including a section of the Burma Rifles; and a commando platoon, the latter trained in demolitions and sabotage.

Special Force also possessed its own organic air support in the form of a United States Army Air Force (USAAF) unit which was formed during the latter part of 1943 specifically to provide air support for Chindit operations. Its roles were threefold: to transport the Chindit columns into their areas of operations through glider and airlanding operations; to provide air resupply, casualty evacuation and extraction by air; and to provide close air support. Initially called Project 9, the unit underwent a number of changes of name before being designated the 1st Air Commando Group USAAF. It was equipped with C-47 Dakota transports, 100 CG-4A Waco gliders (each capable of accommodating fifteen fully equipped troops), 25 TG-5 training gliders and a dozen UC-64 light bushplanes. For casualty evacuation from jungle landing strips, it was also equipped with 100 L-1 and L-5 Sentinel Vigilant light aircraft. For its close air support role, it possessed 30 P-51A Mustangs and twelve B-25H Mitchell medium bombers.

Wingate's second expedition, Operation Thursday, was scheduled for early March 1944. He had conceived the idea of establishing a series of fortified bases in the jungle, each possessing an airstrip and being defended by its own garrison. The aim of the operation was to cut the two principal Japanese lines of supply: the railway between Myitkina and Mandalay to the south, and the road linking Myitkina and Bhamo.

The plan for the first phase of Thursday was for 16 Infantry Brigade, commanded by Brig Bernard Fergusson, to march from Ledo south-east into Burma and head for Indaw on the railway, where it was to capture and secure two Japanese airfields. While en route, it was to assist US and Chinese forces, advancing on its left under Gen 'Vinegar Joe' Stilwell, by detaching two columns to take and occupy Lonkin, which was then held by a detachment of Japanese guarding the left flank of the 18th Chrysanthemum Division. After securing Indaw, the brigade was to push on to the south to a location codenamed Aberdeen, where it was to establish a stronghold which would thereafter be garrisoned by the 6th Battalion The Nigerian Regiment.

Meanwhile 111 Infantry Brigade, under Brig W.D.A. 'Joe' Lentaigne, would be landed by glider east of the railway at a location codenamed Piccadilly. Thereafter it would head for the area south of Indaw and, by cutting the railway with explosives, would block any Japanese forces approaching from the south to counter 16 Infantry Brigade's operations. In the meantime 77 Infantry Brigade, led by Calvert, would be landed east of the railway at a location codenamed Broadway, from where it would march to the railway line and establish a strongly fortified blocking position. The brigade was also to develop Broadway as a stronghold, garrisoning it with two of Calvert's columns and the 3rd/9th Gurkha Rifles, the latter having been allocated to Special Force as an extra unit for the task.

Morris Force, comprising the 4th/9th Gurkha Rifles, would be landed at another location, codenamed Chowringhee, to the east of the Irrawaddy River, and would head for the mountains which lay to the east of the road between Myitkina and Bhamo. There it would establish a base from which it was to mount raiding operations. Dah Force, commanded by Lt Col D.C. Herring, would be landed in the jungle to the east of the Irrawaddy at Templecombe and would raise bands of guerrillas from the Kachin tribes in the area, thereafter operating in support of Morris Force.

The second phase of Operation Thursday would see 3 West African and 14 Infantry Brigades being flown into Aberdeen.

By now 16 Infantry Brigade had already entered Burma, having crossed the River Chindwin four days earlier, when the operation began, on the morning of 5 March. At the last minute, however, there was a hitch. Both 77 and 111 Infantry Brigades were due to take off from Hailakandi and Lalaghat in India but, thirty minutes before H-hour, air photographic reconnaissance revealed that the landing area at Piccadilly had been blocked by trees felled, as it transpired, during routine forestry operations. The decision was thus taken to fly two of 111 Infantry Brigade's battalions into Broadway while the remainder of the brigade would be landed at Chowringhee.

At 6.15 p.m. the first C-47 Dakota tugs, towing the gliders carrying 77 Infantry Brigade, took off for Broadway. A number of the gliders were overloaded and nine suffered broken tow ropes, being forced to land east of the Chindwin in the areas of three Japanese headquarters, inadvertently creating a diversion. Eight others, suffering various problems, landed west of the river. Some of the leading gliders landing at Broadway encountered tree stumps or ground that had been ploughed, and were wrecked as a result. Others, coming in to land too fast as a result of their heavy loads, cannoned into them on landing, causing further casualties. Of the 54 gliders tasked with landing at Broadway, 37 succeeded in reaching it. In all, 30 men died and 33 were injured during the landings, and most of the gliders were destroyed.

As patrols were despatched into the surrounding jungle to check for any enemy presence, Brig Calvert signalled the codeword Soyalink back to Headquarters Special Force, instructing it to halt any further flights until the landing strip had been cleared of wreckage and improved sufficiently for further landings to take place. By late afternoon a 4,700ft-long airstrip had been cleared and that night a total of 62 C-47 sorties were flown into Broadway. By first light on 8 March 77 Infantry Brigade had concentrated and at noon began heading for its objective. By 11 March a total of 9,000 men, along with quantities of weapons, equipment and some 1,200 mules and 175 ponies, had been landed 200 miles behind Japanese lines.

The 3rd/9th Gurkha Rifles remained at Broadway to defend it, along with two columns of the 1st Battalion The King's Regiment, which were responsible for patrolling outside the stronghold perimeter and acting as a mobile reserve in any counter-attacks. The other Gurkha battalion in Calvert's brigade, the 3rd/6th Gurkha Rifles, formed part of a powerful column comprising the 1st Battalion The South Staffordshire Regiment, an assault company and brigade headquarters. This headed for Mawlu, near where it would establish a blocking position codenamed White City close to Henu, where the foothills of the Gangaw mountain range met the railway. Meanwhile two further columns, one located at Mawhun, where it blew up the railway bridge over the Ledan River, and the other at Pinwe, provided protection on Calvert's northern and southern flanks respectively.

The initial fighting centred on 77 Infantry Brigade, with the first major action being the capture of a feature called Pagoda Hill; this dominated the site of White City, which was on seven small hills. It was captured on 17 March by the 1st Battalion The South Staffordshire Regiment, supported by the 3rd/6th Gurkha Rifles, after some very hard fighting, involving a considerable amount of hand-to-hand combat in which bayonets and kukris played a large part in killing a significant number of enemy.

White City was developed into a stronghold that became the target for a series of powerful counter-attacks as the Japanese sought to dislodge Calvert and his men. Bitter fighting ensued and the Chindits suffered heavy casualties. The brigade was now ordered to move over 150 miles to the north to capture the town of Mogaung in support of Gen Stilwell's Chinese forces advancing on Myitkina. The march proved to be an exhausting and harrowing one, not least because the monsoon rains had come, and by the time the brigade arrived at Mogaung all its units were reduced drastically in strength, each numbering no more than 230 officers and men, of whom many were suffering from malaria, dysentery or trench foot.

Mogaung was a difficult objective owing to its location between two rivers. Running along the town's western perimeter was the Namyin, while to the north was the Mogaung. The only feasible approach was from the south-east along a narrow route, called the Pin Hmi Road, sited on a causeway with flooded marshes on either side; a deep river, bridged only where the road crossed it, prevented any flanking moves. The brigade's start line was a ridge some 2 miles to the south-east of the town. The terrain in between was open and flat, interspersed with villages fortified by the Japanese with well-sited bunkers, their garrison being estimated at approximately 3,500, comprising the 128th Regiment of 53rd Division reinforced by a further battalion and support troops.

The battle for Mogaung began during the first week of June and lasted for sixteen days. During the first three days the brigade was involved in some hard fighting as it captured a number of objectives outside the town; in each instance these were subjected to initial air attacks by P-51A Mustang fighter-bombers of the 1st Air Commando Group USAAF, followed by a barrage of mortar and machine-gun fire behind which the infantry moved up to attack. On 8 June Pin Hmi village was captured by the 1st Battalion The Lancashire Fusiliers, who were ordered to take the bridge on the following day. The latter was a difficult objective to attack, however, as the approaches to it on either side of the road consisted of low-lying ground; moreover the enemy were well dug-in around the bridge itself. Twenty-four hours of fierce fighting saw the Fusiliers fail to take their objective despite incurring heavy casualties.

At this juncture Calvert adopted a change of tactics. By attempting to capture Mogaung from the south, he succeeded in cutting off the enemy around Pin Hmi, forcing them to withdraw. The 3rd/6th Gurkha Rifles were tasked with capturing Mahaung and then advancing into Mogaung from the south-east. The 1st Battalion The South Staffordshire Regiment was then to take the Pin Hmi bridge from the rear.

C Company of the 3rd/6th attacked Mahaung on 9 June and routed the enemy, who quickly counter-attacked the battalion's other companies. Meanwhile, by late afternoon the South Staffordshires had captured the southern half of Naungkaitaw and succeeded in reaching the road but could advance no further. A and B Companies of the 3rd/6th were despatched to reinforce them, while the remainder of the battalion withdrew to provide protection for the brigade headquarters.

At first light on the following morning the South Staffordshires blocked the road while the two Gurkha companies advanced on the Pin Hmi bridge from the Japanese rear, moving down either side of the road. A Company, on the right, encountered stiff resistance from enemy throwing grenades, which held it up and caused some 30 casualties. B Company's leading platoon meanwhile was held up by heavy fire some 20 yards from the bridge and suffered heavy casualties. The platoon commander, Capt Michael Allmand, advanced single-handed and engaged the Japanese at close quarters with grenades and his kukri, killing three of them. Inspired by his example, the surviving members of his platoon followed him and eventually succeeded in clearing the rest of the enemy positions.

This action enabled the Lancashire Fusiliers to begin their advance on Mogaung, moving up the road to a location known as the Court House, which they captured – together with an enemy battery of three guns positioned close to it. The South Staffordshires and thereafter the 3rd/6th Gurkha Rifles took the lead as the brigade pressed on until it reached the suburb of Natgiyon which formed the eastern bastion of the enemy's defensive positions in Mogaung itself. On 13 June the 3rd/6th was ordered to take Natgiyon; it proved to be a difficult task, with the Gurkhas having to fight through thick scrub infested by enemy snipers and machine-guns, which inflicted heavy casualties. It was during this action that Capt Allmand, who had assumed command of B Company after his superior officers had become casualties, distinguished himself again by advancing single-handed under heavy fire through long grass and swampy terrain, knocking out a number of enemy machine-gun positions before leading his company on to the ridge that was its objective. After two days of bitter fighting the battalion succeeded in establishing itself on the eastern edge of Natgiyon, with its right flank resting on the bank of the Mogaung River and its left linked with the South Staffordshires, who occupied the south-eastern corner of Natgiyon, the Lancashire Fusiliers being on their left.

On the night of 18/19 June reinforcements arrived in the form of the Chinese 114th Regiment, which crossed the Mogaung some 800 yards behind the 3rd/6th. The Chinese brought with them four 75mm guns to engage the Japanese artillery, which had been shelling Calvert's brigade incessantly from positions to the west. The South Staffordshires and 3rd/6th Gurkha Rifles were thereafter tasked with taking Natgiyon while the Chinese attacked from the south.

The attack was launched on 21 June with A Company of the 3rd/6th, supported by mortars, putting in a probing attack to reconnoitre the enemy positions covering the railway line and bridge. It became apparent that the enemy possessed a large number of automatic weapons and were strongly established in a number of buildings, among them a strongpoint known as the Red House. That night the Lancashire Fusiliers, supported by a heavy mortar barrage, captured Naungkaitaw in the face of fierce enemy resistance and thus were able to advance 77 Infantry Brigade's left flank almost to the railway line.

In the early hours of 23 June a final assault was launched on the railway line and the bridge to the north of the town. C Company of the 3rd/6th Gurkha Rifles, on the right of the battalion, headed for the bridge while B Company, in the centre, tackled the Red House with grenades, PIATs (Projector Infantry Anti-Tank) and flamethrowers. Once again Capt Allmand played a prominent role by advancing over the muddy terrain, pitted with shellholes, before attacking an enemy machine-gun position single-handed. No sooner had he knocked it out than he was hit and fell, mortally wounded. He died that night while awaiting evacuation by air to India. For this and his previous exploits he was subsequently awarded a posthumous Victoria Cross.

Meanwhile one of B Company's platoons had been pinned down by heavy fire from the Red House and its leading section was wiped out except for the section commander and two riflemen. These three charged the building but two of them, the section commander and one of the riflemen, fell, seriously wounded. The remaining man, Rifleman Tulbahadur Pun, seized the section's Bren light machine-gun and, under heavy fire, charged across the remaining 30 yards of ground to the Red House, killing three enemy, routing five more and capturing two machine-guns. He then provided covering fire for the remainder of his platoon as it came forward. For his gallantry in this action Tulbahadur was awarded the Victoria Cross.

Following further heavy fighting Mogaung fell to 77 Infantry Brigade on 24 June. After sixteen days of bitter fighting three understrength British and Gurkha infantry battalions had overcome an enemy force of over 3,500 men. Such were their casualties, however, that by the time the battle was over the brigade's strength had been whittled down from over 2,355 men to just 806.

Following the fall of Mogaung the remnants of the Japanese 18th and 53rd Divisions withdrew to the south-west to positions in the areas of the towns of Taungni and Sahmaw from which they could control the roads leading south. Special Force was given the task of capturing both towns and two enemy strongpoints nicknamed Point 2171 and Hill 60.

111 Infantry Brigade, comprising three columns of the 3rd/4th PWO and 3rd/9th Gurkha Rifles, was tasked with seizing Point 2171, a feature held in strength by the enemy and overlooking the Mogaung River. By this time the brigade was commanded by Maj John Masters, previously the Brigade Major, Brig 'Joe' Lentaigne having been promoted to major general and appointed commander of Special Force following the death of Maj Gen Wingate in an air crash on 24 March.

The approach march to Point 2171 took three days, following which the brigade spent the next four days driving in the enemy's outposts and clearing the designated area of its start line for its advance on its objective. On 9 July the 3rd/9th Gurkha Rifles launched their attack, for which an air strike had been requested. This, however, failed to materialise and thus the battalion was forced to storm Point 2171 without air support, incurring heavy casualties in the process. During the attack, which was carried out by two companies simultaneously from the front and rear of the objective, 30 men were lost, among them the commander of the frontal assault company and one of his Gurkha officers. The Commandant, Lt Col Alec Harper, and a group of men were pinned down by a machine gun until Maj F.G. 'Jim' Blaker, calling on his men to follow, charged its position. Hit by a hail of fire, he was killed outright but the Gurkhas stormed forward, the two companies meeting on the crest of Point 2171. Maj Blaker was subsequently awarded a posthumous Victoria Cross, the third Chindit officer to be awarded the decoration.

The 3rd/9th Gurkha Rifles held Point 2171 for several days, despite being subjected to a number of counter-attacks, but eventually the enemy succeeded in working their way round to his rear and Maj (later Brig) John Masters was forced to withdraw the battalion.

* * *

Meanwhile Morris Force, the other Gurkha element within Special Force, comprising the 4th/9th Gurkha Rifles, commanded by Lt Col J.R. 'Jumbo' Morris, had been carrying out the task of blocking the Bhamo–Myitkina road in support of the advance of Gen Stilwell's Chinese forces towards it.

Flown into Chowringhee on the night of 6/7 March 1944, the 4th/9th, divided into two columns numbered 49 and 94 respectively, landed without incident and initially deployed to protect the perimeter of the landing strip, while Headquarters 111 Infantry Brigade and the 3rd/4th PWO Gurkha Rifles, organised into 30 and 40

Columns, landed and prepared for the move to the west. They were followed by Wingate, who, experiencing a premonition that the landing strip would shortly be under threat, ordered it to be abandoned and the remainder of 111 Infantry Brigade, the 1st Battalion The Cameronians (Scottish Rifles) and the 2nd Battalion The King's Own Royal Regiment, to be flown into Piccadilly instead; in the event, due to another change of plan, they were flown into Broadway. Shortly afterwards he was proved right as no sooner had 1st Air Commando USAAF recovered all the undamaged gliders by the process of 'snatching' them off the ground than Japanese bombers made an appearance and cratered the landing strip.

By that time 111 Infantry Brigade was a few miles away, preparing to cross the Irrawaddy before moving further west. The river was approximately 900 yards wide at the selected crossing point, so its crossing was a major undertaking involving the use of assault boats flown in by gliders, which landed on a makeshift landing strip established on the east bank. Initially, on the night of 11 March, an advance guard from 30 Column was ferried across to secure a bridgehead but problems were encountered with the boats' outboard engines, which resulted in only the brigade headquarters and the major part of the column being on the west bank by dawn on 12 March. Further difficulties were experienced with the brigade's mules, which refused to swim across the river. Such was Brig Lentaigne's anxiety over the increasing risk of interception that he decided to abandon all his heavy weapons and equipment, apart from two mortars and two radio sets, and combine his headquarters and 30 Column into a single force which would press on westwards to join up with the remainder of the brigade. 40 Column, still on the east bank, was ordered to follow Morris Force, which was by then heading east towards the Bhamo–Myitkina road.

The two columns of Morris Force, with 40 Column moving up behind, crossed the Shweli River and headed east along the road leading to Bhamo, blowing bridges as they went, before circling round to the north. Avoiding Sinlumkaba, which was held in strength by the enemy, the entire force moved along the Burmese/Chinese border before crossing the Taiping River, a tributary of the Irrawaddy. Thereafter it headed downstream to a point where the road crossed the river via a suspension bridge, which they blew up, together with a vehicle ferry nearby.

Six more bridges suffered the same fate. One was at Myothit, a town on the banks of the Taiping River, where 94 Column, commanded by Maj Peter Cane, struck one night. A suspension bridge over the river was destroyed, along with a ferry nearby, and telephone lines were cut for a distance of 5 miles from the town. A rice mill supplying food for the enemy was blown up and 25 tons of rice burned. Meanwhile on the northern bank an ambush accounted for a truck carrying enemy soldiers, nine of whom were killed.

By mid-April the enemy lines of communications and supply along the road had been severely hampered, forcing the Japanese to divert up to 1,000 troops and a considerable amount of engineering equipment and plant to repair the road and the blown bridges. On 3 May 40 Column of the 3rd/4th PWO Gurkha Rifles succeeded in joining up with Morris Force and by the middle of the month the three Gurkha columns had destroyed eight large bridges, several small ones and two ferries. In addition, they had succeeded in blowing up a large section of the road where it ran along a cliff face, sending it plummeting down into the gorge below.

On 25 May Morris Force was ordered to head north, where it was to come under the command of an American task force led by Brig Gen Frank Merrill who, until laid low by a heart attack, commanded the 5307th Composite Unit (Provisional). Morris Force, however, was by then split into two elements: Morris and his headquarters were with the 3rd/4th PWO Gurkha Rifles' 40 Column in the mountains 4 miles from the Chinese border, while 49 and 94 Columns were engaged in blocking the crossing points on the Nam Tabet River. Once Morris Force had reassembled, it took some five days of forced marching through the mountains for it to reach the Myitkina area. On its arrival it was tasked with seizing and securing two villages, Waingmaw and Maingna, on the east bank of the Irrawaddy opposite Myitkina, which dominated the ferry points from where the Japanese despatched reinforcements and supplies across the river.

Morris learned that Waingmaw was only lightly defended and thus launched his attack on the village without delay. In fact the Japanese heavily outnumbered Morris Force, which carried out three assaults, penetrating the Japanese defences and killing 130 enemy. On each occasion the Japanese counter-attacked and eventually a combination of insufficient strength and lack of ammunition forced Morris to withdraw his men. Shortly afterwards he met the American task force commander, Brig Gen Hayden Boatner, who had replaced Merrill after the latter had suffered another heart attack. Boatner granted Morris's request for air support for the attack on Maingna but this proved to be inaccurate, with the P-51A Mustang fighter-bombers dropping their bombs on Morris Force's start line, fortunately without causing casualties, and the B-25 Mitchell light bombers dropping half of theirs in the Irrawaddy; the remainder landed on the target area but failed to explode. Just as Morris Force was about to begin its assault, the attack was aborted by the task force headquarters, which had learned that the bombs were of a new delayed-action type. During the following twelve hours explosions could be heard from the direction of Maingna as the bombs went off.

By this time the physical and mental condition of Morris Force had deteriorated considerably and on 17 July it was withdrawn, being flown out of Myitkina Airfield to India where, following a period of rest and recuperation, the 4th/9th Gurkha Rifles were reinforced with new drafts of riflemen and began retraining. Operation Thursday was, however, the Chindits' swansong and shortly afterwards Special Force was disbanded and its units dispersed among other formations.

* * *

Meanwhile other Gurkha battalions had taken part in major actions in the Arakan, at Imphal and in the area of Kohima.

These Gurkha soldiers, pictured in the Burma jungle within sight and sound of Japanese units, inspect a souvenir they have taken from their enemy during fighting patrols.

In the spring of 1943 the British made an unsuccessful attempt to eject the Japanese from the Arakan, the coastal region which extends the full length of western Burma. Ideal for defensive operations, the coast comprised a large number of islands formed by tidal rivers, while the terrain inland was hilly and covered in dense jungle through which there were few tracks. Like everywhere in Burma, it was subject to very heavy rains during the monsoon season.

Throughout most of 1943 17 Indian Division's two brigades, including the 1st/7th and 1st/10th Gurkha Rifles, had been observing the Tiddim road, the main approach along which the Japanese would advance on Imphal. Any operations during this period were of a minor nature and both battalions played their respective parts. Likewise, in 23rd Indian Division, the 3rd/10th was involved in operations in the 150-mile-wide sector at the southern end of the Imphal plain.

In December 1943 the British began a second offensive in the Arakan to drive out the Japanese. Owing to a lack of landing craft in South East Asia, it had to be carried out overland rather than being launched via a series of landings along the Arakan coast. Taking part was XV Indian Corps, commanded by Lt Gen Sir Philip Christison, which comprised 5th and 7th Indian Divisions, commanded by Major-Generals Harold Briggs and Frank Messervy respectively. Both formations included Gurkha battalions in their orders of battle.

The offensive began well, encountering only light resistance from the Japanese. In early January 1944, however, in the area of Razabil, the picture changed when the enemy hit back and inflicted heavy casualties. The British advance halted as troops were redeployed and roads constructed to enable vital logistical support to be brought forward. Renewal of the advance was scheduled for 7 February but this was pre-empted by the Japanese with a force under Lt Gen Tadashi Hanaya which counter-attacked, achieving complete surprise and severing links between 5th and 7th Indian Divisions.

The Japanese succeeded in skirting around 7th Indian Division's left flank and overran the divisional headquarters. Maj Gen Frank Messervy and the majority of his staff succeeded in avoiding capture and reached XV Indian Corps' administrative area, dubbed the 'Admin Box', which was manned by the Corps's support troops and others who had become separated from their units in the fighting. Among them were two companies of the 4th/8th Gurkha Rifles, the 25th Dragoons and elements of 9 Indian Infantry Brigade which formed part of 5th Indian Division. The Admin Box was situated in a bowl surrounded by hills which dominated it, and from where the Japanese bombarded it with artillery, mortars and machine-guns for eighteen days.

The enemy also launched attacks and succeeded in reaching the Box's hospital, where they bayoneted the wounded lying on stretchers and shot six doctors, only withdrawing at dawn on the following day in the face of a counter-attack. They did so using wounded medical personnel as human shields; these men were subsequently murdered in cold blood. Such was the much-vaunted Bushido code of honour.

Meanwhile, throughout 7th Indian Division's area its three brigades were stemming the advance of the Japanese. The latter, equipped with only limited supplies, had relied on the British withdrawing for the success of their operation, as it was impossible for them to bring forward sufficient supplies along the jungle tracks they had used for launching their attack. Lt Gen Hanaya had counted on capturing supply dumps, along with weapons and vehicles, to sustain his operations. In the event, however, he was disappointed, as the British, having learned the lessons of the 1942 campaign, had sited their brigades in defensive boxes. Resupplied by air, each was able to hold out against the fierce onslaught of the Japanese while 5th Indian Division advanced from the west and 26th Indian Division approached from the north.

Dawn on 24 February saw the arrival of 5th Indian Division at XV Indian Corps's Admin Box, where it found over 500 wounded men requiring evacuation to India. Among the relieving troops were the 1st/8th Gurkha Rifles, who had lost 3 officers and 23 other ranks during the fighting around the Admin Box. Meanwhile the 4th/1st KGO Gurkha Rifles had also seen heavy fighting on a feature nicknamed 'Abel', repelling a number of heavy attacks while being shelled constantly by 150mm guns at a range of only 3,000 yards. On 22 February the Japanese launched another powerful attack and a two-hour-long battle ensued, during which the 4th/1st suffered heavy casualties but held firm. Thereafter the attacks on 'Abel' continued until the beginning of March when the 4th/1st was relieved; by that time it had lost six British officers, two VCOs and 225 other ranks killed or wounded. The end of May 1944 saw the arrival of the monsoon season and the end of the second Arakan campaign, which was the turning point of the war in Burma.

Meanwhile there was still fierce fighting further north in Assam, in the areas of two British defensive bastions around the villages of Imphal and Kohima, key objectives of the Japanese Fifteenth Army under Gen Renya Mutaguchi. The latter had planned to capture both these villages before advancing a further 30 miles to the north and cutting the Bengal–Assam railway, the main line of communications and supply for Gen Stilwell and his Chinese forces. Thereafter he intended to head west towards the border with East Bengal and onwards into India, bypassing both the British Fourteenth Army, commanded by Gen Sir William Slim, and Stilwell's forces. Although outnumbered and outgunned, Mutaguchi was relying on the superior mobility of his forces to infiltrate through the British lines and surround their formations, which had in the past withdrawn when threatened with being outflanked and cut off. On this occasion, however, Gen Slim was well aware of the Japanese intentions and had laid plans for swift reinforcement by air, rail and road. Moreover, as in the Arakan, brigades that were cut off would stand firm in their defensive boxes which would be resupplied by air.

Using the 15th, 31st and 33rd Divisions, numbering about a hundred thousand men in total, Mutaguchi launched his attack on the British IV Corps on 6 March. His 31st Division, commanded by Maj Gen Kotoku Sato, advanced through the Somra Hills, emerging on the Imphal–Kohima road and cutting the remaining link between IV Corps and the rest of Fourteenth Army. Thereafter it advanced over the Kohima ridge and isolated Kohima itself, where the garrison, commanded by Col Hugh Richards, comprised the 4th Battalion The Royal West Kent Regiment under Lt Col John Laverty, the 3rd Battalion Assam Regiment (which included a number of Nepalese hillmen in its ranks) and a half-trained battalion of Nepalese state troops. The entire force numbered approximately 1,200 men, including some administrative personnel, convalescents and a small number of civilians; facing it was a fully manned Japanese division of 12,000 troops.

Totally cut off, the garrison at Kohima was successfully resupplied from the air and held out for sixteen days and nights, being subjected to a constant and murderous barrage of artillery, mortar and machine-gun fire. Under remorseless pressure from the Japanese, it was slowly forced to contract its defensive perimeter until eventually it occupied only a single hilltop. At that juncture, however, troops of 2nd Infantry Division, forming the leading element of the British XXXIII Corps under Lt Gen Sir Montagu Stopford, had advanced from Dimapur and succeeded in breaking through and relieving the beleaguered garrison.

A Gurkha Bren gunner returns from a fighting patrol after contact with the Japanese near Laya Station in 1945.

The Japanese, however, launched an all-out attack to capture Kohima and on the night of 22 April concentrated their assault on a feature called 'Garrison Hill', which was held by the 1st Battalion The Royal Berkshire Regiment and the 2nd Battalion The Durham Light Infantry, the latter bearing the brunt of the attack. Preceded by a heavy barrage of artillery, mortar and machine-gun fire, waves of enemy infantry attacked uphill but both battalions held firm, the Durhams launching a counter-attack at dawn on the following day. During the night they lost 15 officers and over 100 men but the losses suffered by the Japanese were greater, amounting to the equivalent of four companies.

The fighting at Kohima lasted a further seven weeks, during which the gap between the British and Japanese positions was no more than the width of the tennis court of the District Commissioner's bungalow. Eventually, however, the British succeeded in winching a Grant tank of the 149th Royal Tank Regiment up the steep hillside and into a position from which it was able to bring fire to bear against the enemy bunkers. During these weeks of fighting several units of 7th Indian Division became involved, among them the 4th/1st KGO Gurkha Rifles, who captured 'Basha Hill' and were then subjected to a series of fierce counter-attacks by the Japanese before continuing their advance. During the following three days the battalion encountered stiff resistance before being relieved by the 4th/5th Royal Gurkha Rifles.

Eventually, however, on the night of 6 June, the Japanese 31st Division withdrew from Kohima, the battle having lasted a total of 64 days. Short of medical supplies and ammunition, and reduced to little more than a disorganised rabble, the Japanese retreated across the Chindwin and back into Burma.

Meanwhile there had been equally fierce fighting around Imphal. Prior to the Japanese advance, 17th Indian Division, whose order of battle included several Gurkha battalions, had been deployed to the east of Imphal. On reporting the movement west of several Japanese columns, the division, commanded by Maj Gen D.T. 'Punch' Cowan, was ordered to withdraw to Tiddim, because of the risk of being cut off by enemy forces cutting the road near the Tuitum Ridge, where three Gurkha battalions, the 1st/3rd QAO, 1st/4th PWO and 1st/10th Gurkha Rifles, engaged the advance elements of Mutaguchi's force, destroying half of them. Thereafter the 1st/10th provided the rearguard covering the first stage of the withdrawal of the division, repelling a number of attacks by the Japanese until relieved by the 1st/3rd QAO Gurkha Rifles.

As 17th Indian Division withdrew westwards, other Gurkha battalions played a major part in covering the withdrawal, among them the 2nd/5th Royal Gurkha Rifles who suffered almost 250 casualties during the fighting along the Tiddim Road. After three weeks, during which it suffered losses of some 1,200 men, the division reached Imphal during the first week in April.

* * *

Meanwhile 20th Indian Division had been guarding another possible enemy approach route from the south-east. The road from Tamu to Imphal ran over the mountains via a pass through the 6,000ft-high Shenam Ridge which separated the Kabaw Valley from the Manipur Plain. From late May to 24 June bitter fighting took place for control of the Shenam Ridge, on which the foremost defended area was a peak nicknamed 'Scraggy', which was defended by 37 Gurkha Infantry Brigade, comprising the 3rd/3rd QAO, 3rd/5th and 3rd/10th Gurkha Rifles. On 24 June, following a counter-attack led by the 3rd/10th, the Japanese withdrew and the battle for the Shenam Ridge was over.

In the meantime, though, the Japanese had succeeded in advancing to Imphal across the Manipur Plain from the south. In the area of the village of Bishenpur, some 16 miles to the south-west of Imphal, where the Tiddim Road joined a track from the village of Silchar to the west, another significant battle took place during which a sergeant of the 1st Battalion The West Yorkshire Regiment and three Gurkha riflemen, two of the 3rd/5th and one of the 1st/7th, won the Victoria Cross.

The latter was Rifleman Ganju Lama of B Company 1st/7th Gurkha Rifles, part of 48 Indian Infantry Brigade. On 12 June the brigade's positions just north of the village of Ningthookong were subjected to an intense artillery barrage that preceded an attack by enemy infantry supported by tanks. The latter succeeded in penetrating the brigade's outer perimeter and were threatening to overrun its positions. B and D Companies of the 1st/7th launched an immediate counter-attack and initially made considerable progress before being halted by fire from the enemy tanks. Rifleman Ganju Lama, a PIAT operator in one of B Company's platoons, crawled forwards and engaged the enemy armour from a flank. Despite having been wounded already in his left wrist, right hand and one leg, he opened fire from a range of only 30 yards, destroying the leading tank with his first round and another with his second. As the crews abandoned their blazing vehicles, Ganju Lama attacked them with grenades, extracting the pins with his teeth because of his broken hand. It was only after he had killed them all that he permitted himself to be evacuated to the Regimental Aid Post to have his wounds dressed.

Four weeks earlier Ganju had won the Military Medal for a similar feat of arms. On 17 May the 1st/7th had been pushing forwards to milestone 33 on the Tiddim Road. The battalion had been tasked with clearing an enemy force from a complex of bunkers and roadblocks impeding the advance of 17th Indian Division to relieve Imphal. B Company was in the lead when it was held up by fire from a number of light tanks. Despite heavy fire from the enemy tanks, Ganju Lama crawled to a flanking position from where he fired two rounds, knocking out a tank with his second shot. Providing covering fire for his platoon as it withdrew, he engaged the remaining tanks, knocking out another before crawling to safety.

32 Indian Infantry Brigade, which comprised the 3rd/8th and 4th/2nd KEO Gurkha Rifles, also played a major role in the fighting in this area, as did the 1st/4th PWO Gurkha Rifles, who had been detached from 17th Indian Division to assist in

Queen Elizabeth and HRH The Duke of Edinburgh pose with five Gurkhas who all hold the Victoria Cross. Left to right: Rambahadur Limbu, Talbahadur Pun, Ganju Lama, Bhanbhagta Gurung and Agansing Rai. They are pictured here at the British Embassy in Kathmandu.

blocking the Japanese advance. The battalion was involved in a number of actions in the area of a feature named Scrub Ridge, during which several of its British officers, including the Commandant, Lt Col Wilfred Oldham, were killed in fighting at close quarters.

By this time Gen Mutaguchi realised that his exhausted forces, sorely depleted by heavy losses amounting to some 30,000 after almost four months of fighting, had no hope of achieving their objectives. On 2 July he issued the order for his troops to withdraw and thus, suffering from malnutrition and sickness from which hundreds died daily, the remnants of the Japanese Fifteenth Army headed back into Burma.

It was now the turn of the British to follow up in pursuit. In November 1944 the leading brigades of Gen Slim's Fourteenth Army crossed the Chindwin and headed for the Irrawaddy. Slim's plan was to advance across the North Burma Plain in a two-pronged thrust, the left making for Mandalay while the right aimed for Meiktila, 70 miles to the south.

The Japanese withdrew across the Irrawaddy on the night of 14 January 1945, taking up positions to launch counter-attacks on the British bridgeheads as they were established on the east bank. Fierce fighting ensued and it was not until 26 February that 19th Indian Division, which included the 4th/4th PWO, 1st/6th and 4th/6th Gurkha Rifles in its order of battle, succeeded in breaking out of its bridgehead, initially encountering stiff opposition and making slow progress as it advanced across the plain towards Mandalay.

17th Indian Division had also crossed the Irrawaddy and was heading for Meiktila. At the same time, in a move designed to draw off the enemy forces defending Mandalay, 20th Indian Division landed opposite Myinlu. This formation contained five Gurkha battalions, namely the 1st/1st and 3rd/1st KGO, 3rd/8th and 4th/2nd KEO and 4th/10th Gurkha Rifles. The latter captured the village of

The 4th/6th Gurkha Rifles crossing the Irrawaddy in January 1945.

Members of the 4th/10th Gurkha Rifles advance through Prone during victory celebrations near Galle Face in Colombo in 1945 after the defeat of the Japanese.

Talingon on 16 February but soon found themselves involved in a prolonged battle which lasted ten days during which the battalion was subjected to numerous counter-attacks by the Japanese 16th Regiment. These were beaten off with the aid of artillery fire, which at one point was accidentally called down on one of the companies' positions. When the battle ended on 26 February, the 4th/10th had suffered 50 killed and 127 wounded while Japanese losses numbered 953, of whom 500 had been killed.

Meanwhile in 19th Indian Division, the 4th/4th PWO, 1st/6th and 4th/6th Gurkha Rifles were heavily involved in the fighting to capture the village of Kyaukmyaung, a key objective which had to be taken before the attack on Mandalay could be launched. The village eventually fell and by 7 March the leading elements of the division had reached Mandalay.

By now 17th Indian Division had advanced across the plain to Meiktila, and 48 and 63 Gurkha Infantry Brigades took the town on 7 March. No sooner had the division occupied it, however, than it found itself under siege from strong enemy forces which succeeded in cutting the division's line of supply and threatened its hold on the town's

Soldiers of the 1st/3rd Gurkha Rifles unload a Dakota at an airstrip near Meiktila in the heart of Burma. The brilliantly conceived Meiktila operation cut deeply into the Japanese communications system.

airfields. It was not until the end of March that the division succeeded in breaking the enemy stranglehold.

In Mandalay, meanwhile, 19th Indian Division was fighting its way into the city where one feature, Mandalay Hill, was proving a tough nut to crack. Almost a mile long and some 700 feet high, it was honeycombed with tunnels and passages occupied by the enemy. By 10 March the 4th/4th PWO Gurkha Rifles and the 2nd Battalion The Royal Berkshire Regiment had cleared much of the hill but were still encountering fierce resistance from small groups of enemy rearguards. These were engaged by the 4th/4th, whose Gurkhas went into the tunnels after the enemy, accounting for a large number with their kukris.

Another feature, Fort Dufferin, also posed a major problem. With 30ft-high walls extending over a length of 2,500 yards and surrounded by a moat 40 yards wide, it was a formidable obstacle that proved highly resistant to artillery fire and bombing, which inflicted only slight damage. Its Japanese defenders beat off several attempts by infantry to scale the walls, the 1st/6th Gurkha Rifles being among those who attempted to do so. 19th Indian Division prepared to mount a full-scale assault on 24 March but, on the night of 19/20 March, the Japanese suddenly withdrew.

Thereafter Gen Slim launched his forces towards Rangoon, tasking them with capturing the Burmese capital and its vital port by the middle of May, before the onset of the monsoon season and the heavy rains that would turn the Burmese plains into quagmires impassable to wheeled or even tracked vehicles.

An amphibious operation, codenamed Dracula, had been planned for the capture of Rangoon but it was decided at the end of March that the plans should be

The road to Mandalay. Gurkhas pictured on their way to the historic Burmese town.

modified. The earliest date by which the weather conditions would be suitable for the operation was 2 May, leaving a month to prepare. Dracula involved a landing by 26th Indian Division, with naval and air support, on both banks of the Rangoon River south of the city and halfway between Elephant Point and the Bassein Creek. The river itself had been mined by the Japanese, as well as by Allied aircraft, so minesweepers would have to precede the landing craft and other vessels carrying the division. Moreover, the Japanese had sited coastal defences on the west bank of the river and these would have to be neutralised before the minesweepers could enter the river mouth. This was to be carried out by a composite force from 44th Indian Airborne Division; a detailed account of the airborne phase of Dracula is given in Chapter 8, which tells the story of the Gurkha parachute battalions in the Indian Army's wartime airborne forces.

Dracula commenced in the early hours of 1 May, the airborne force dropping from its Dakota transports at 5.45 a.m., and throughout that day it secured its objectives and cleared enemy forces from bunkers and defensive positions, calling in air support to silence fire from some small craft on the river. On the following morning the vessels carrying 26th Indian Division appeared and headed upriver. Thereafter 36 and 71

Gurkhas march through Rangoon as the Burma campaign comes to a close. They had fought through jungle, lived in foxholes and endured conditions of extreme hardship during the conflict.

Indian Infantry Brigades landed on the east and west banks and advanced on the city, which was occupied without resistance on 6 May.

By this time the war was approaching its end, although large numbers of enemy in Central Burma attempted to fight their way out of the net which closed around them. In mid-July a major attempt at a break-out took place, but this was crushed by 17th and 19th Indian Divisions who inflicted massive losses on the Japanese. On 25 July the Japanese forces in the country surrendered and the war in Burma was over. On 14 August, following the dropping of the atomic bombs on Hiroshima and Nagasaki, Japan surrendered unconditionally.

Now began a curious and little-known phase of the war in which the former enemy turned ally in a number of South East Asian regional operations to control nationalist insurgents. During the following months Gurkha units played a major role in maintaining security in the former Japanese-occupied territories. 20th Indian Division, which included five Gurkha battalions in its order of battle, was despatched to Indochina, where it landed in Saigon to find a state of war between the French colonial authorities, who were attempting to re-establish their rule over the region, and the communist Viet Minh under Ho Chi Minh, who were determined to prevent them from doing so. The division deployed in support of the French, pending the arrival of French forces in the country, but such was the size of the task that its commander, Maj Gen Douglas Gracey, was forced to employ captured Japanese troops to assist in maintaining order.

Commanded by Maj Gen D.C. Hawthorn, and including four Gurkha battalions in its order of battle, 23rd Indian Division meanwhile had been sent to the Indonesian island of Java, where in-surrection had broken out following the Japanese surrender. On 19 October the 3rd/10th Gurkha Rifles, commanded by Lt Col Dick Edwards, landed at Semarang, where they encountered fighting in progress between Indonesian nationalists and a battalion of Japanese troops attempting to keep law and order in the area. The 3rd/10th

A Japanese general surrenders to Lt Col O.N. Smith of the 1st/10th Gurkha Rifles in Burma, 1945.

HRH The Duke of Edinburgh inspects Gurkhas in Saigon, escorted by the future King of Siam.

A Gurkha stands guard over a group of Indonesian civilians who had been caught looting.

Gurkhas on parade in India. Soldiers of an Indian unit can be seen in the background.

Gurkhas pictured aboard landing craft taking part in the Allied landings on Bali in 1946.

were followed by a composite brigade of 23rd Indian Division, under the division's Commander Royal Artillery (CRA), Brig Richard Bethell. During the following months the division's Gurkha battalions found themselves deployed on peacekeeping operations in various parts of Indonesia.

By 1946 the situation in South East Asia had stabilised sufficiently to allow Indian Army formations to be withdrawn from the region. On their return to India some of the Gurkha battalions raised for wartime service were disbanded. In all, around 120,000 Gurkhas had served in 52 battalions during the war against Germany, Italy and Japan, suffering 20,000 casualties. Some of the regular battalions, notably those of the 6th, 7th and 10th Gurkha Rifles, remained in Burma while the remainder, including both those of the 2nd KEO Gurkha Rifles, returned to India.

CHAPTER 5

PARTITION AND
THE MALAYAN EMERGENCY

The end of the Second World War brought with it political turmoil in India, with nationalists led by Mahatma Gandhi demanding independence from Britain. Meanwhile war broke out between Muslims and Hindus throughout the sub-continent and huge numbers of people died, the total later estimated as being higher than those killed in all the battles fought by the British during the Second World War. Gurkha battalions were among the Indian Army units deployed on internal security operations to maintain law and order.

With the announcement of the forthcoming creation of the state of Pakistan came the news that the regiments of the Indian Army would be divided between the two countries. In addition, it had been decided that four regiments of Gurkhas, the 2nd KEO and the 6th, 7th and 10th Gurkha Rifles, would be transferred to the British Army while the remainder would be retained by the Indian Army. The Viceroy Commissioned Officers (VCOs) and other ranks of the four regiments were given the choice of staying with them and transferring to the British Army, or remaining in India and being transferred to another regiment. Alternatively, they could opt for discharge and return to Nepal with a small gratuity. It was a period of great difficulty and sadness for all concerned, in particular for the Gurkhas in those regiments being retained by India whose British officers departed, either returning to Britain or transferring to other regiments. They were handed over to Indian officers who were unknown to them. Fortunately, however, the Indians carefully selected officers of very high calibre and integrity to serve with Gurkhas, a number of them having served with Punjabi, Baluch or Frontier Force regiments that had been handed over to Pakistan.

Within some of the eight battalions being transferred to the British Army, a surprisingly high percentage of VCOs and other ranks chose to remain in India and transfer to other regiments. In the case of the 2nd/7th Gurkha Rifles at Ahmedabad, all but 40 of the 729-strong battalion did so, while the 2nd/6th, based in Delhi, lost 692 out of 781. The two battalions of the 2nd KEO Gurkha Rifles, based at Poona and Dinapore respectively, did rather better, with the 1st Battalion losing 377 out of 717 VCOs and men and the 2nd 242 out of 834.

Indian Army Gurkhas on parade in New Delhi.

On 1 January 1948, following the granting of independence to India and the birth of Pakistan in August 1947, the 2nd, 6th, 7th and 10th Gurkha Rifles were officially transferred to the British Army and Headquarters British Gurkhas was established in Delhi to organise the transfer of their eight battalions from India. This began during February and continued until the end of March.

The principal home of the British Army's Brigade of Gurkhas, as it was called, was to be Malaya, with two battalions based in Hong Kong and Singapore. A new formation, 17th Gurkha Division, was already in the process of being formed, comprising 26, 48 and 63 Gurkha Infantry Brigades based at Johore Bahru, Seremban and Kuala Lipis respectively. Each of these would comprise two Gurkha and one British infantry battalions. In addition, the decision had been taken to form Gurkha specialist support troops in the form of squadrons of the Gurkha Engineers, Gurkha Signals, Gurkha Army Service Corps and a divisional military police company. The story of the Gurkha Corps units is recounted in Chapter 9.

The major problem was the shortage of trained manpower, in particular of senior King's Gurkha Officers (KGO) as the VCOs were redesignated. Moreover a shortage of British officers had resulted in a number of KGOs being recommissioned as Gurkha Commissioned Officers (GCOs), who were of the same status as their British counterparts. Those Gurkhas who had opted to remain in India had been replaced with untrained recruits from Nepal and one unit, the 2nd/2nd KEO Gurkha Rifles, had three training companies comprising 400 men under its command. Furthermore a high

At the time of the partition of India at the end of the Second World War there were ten Gurkha regiments in the Indian Army. As a result of negotiations between the Nepalese, British and Indian Governments (known as the 'Tri-Partite Agreement') four of these regiments, each of two battalions, were transferred to the British Army, the remainder staying with the new Indian Army.

proportion of the men of all eight battalions were absent in Nepal on their long leave periods to which they were entitled every three years.

On 16 June 1948 insurrection broke out in Malaya when three young Chinese men shot dead Mr Arthur Walker, the British manager of the Elphil Estate, a rubber plantation situated some 20 miles east of Sungei Siput, a tin-mining town north of Ipoh, the capital of the state of Perak. Thirty minutes later and 10 miles away, twelve armed Chinese shot dead the manager of the Sungei Siput Estate, Mr J. Alison, and his assistant, Ian Christian. The latter had served as an officer in the 8th Gurkha Rifles during the war and on the day prior to the attacks had visited the 2nd/2nd KEO Gurkha Rifles, confiding to friends among the battalion's British officers that he was convinced that trouble was brewing. Indeed, such was his concern that he borrowed a 9mm Luger pistol from one of the company commanders, Capt Johnny Lawes.

By the following day reports of other attacks were flooding into the federal capital of Kuala Lumpur. These heralded the start of a twelve-year-long war, dubbed the Malayan Emergency, in which the newly formed Brigade of Gurkhas would play a major role.

The men who had carried out the murders were members of the Malayan People's Anti-British Army (MPABA), an organisation that had sprung from a guerrilla movement formed in Malaya during the Second World War to fight the Japanese forces which had occupied the country after December 1941. Resistance to the Japanese had come mainly from the Malayan Communist Party (MCP), headed by an individual named Ong Boon Hua (better known by his alias of Chin Peng), who formed the Malayan People's Anti-Japanese Army (MPAJA). Numbering some 7,000 guerrillas and organised in eight regiments, the MPAJA was supported by a highly secret civilian organisation, the Malayan People's Anti-Japanese Union (MPAJU) which supplied the guerrillas with food, medical supplies, recruits and funds, as well as gathering intelligence and distributing propaganda.

In 1943 contact with the MPAJA was established by Force 136, the Asian and Far Eastern arm of the Special Operations Executive (SOE) based in Colombo on the island of Ceylon (Sri Lanka). Thereafter Force 136 supplied weapons, equipment and training, the latter being provided by British officers landed by submarine or parachuted into the jungle, and by 1945 the guerrillas were a well-armed and highly trained force. Towards the end of the year, following the surrender of Japan and the return of British forces to Malaya, the MPAJA was demobilised and disbanded, handing over its arms to the Malayan authorities.

The return of British rule to Malaya was followed by a proposal to make the country into a single Malayan Union, incorporating all its nine states but excluding Singapore. This drew strong objections from the Malay population, who were opposed to any reduction in the autonomy of the individual states, each of which was ruled by its own sultan, and to the granting of citizenship and political rights to non-Malays living in the country. The outcome was the formation in 1946 of the United Malays National Organisation (UMNO), followed by a series of strikes, demonstrations and boycotts which forced the British to climb down and begin negotiations with UMNO. These in turn led in 1948 to the establishment of the Federation of Malaya which united the states, secured the positions of the sultans and guaranteed the rights of Malays.

These developments caused considerable alarm throughout the Chinese population and in the MCP, which decided to pursue its twin aims of expulsion of the British and achieving communist domination of Malaya through armed insurrection. It mobilised its military wing, renaming it the Malayan People's Anti-British Army (MPABA), and formed eight regiments ranging in strength from 200 to 700, deployed in a number of jungle camps, some of which had been constructed during the war. Two regiments were based in Johore and two in Pahang, the remainder being located in Selangor, Negri Sembilan, Kedah and Perak, the latter being the largest with a strength of 700 guerrillas. In addition to the regiments that remained within their respective states, there were a number of independent sub-units which had a roving brief and were free to operate throughout their allocated areas of operations.

The MPABA was well equipped with weapons acquired from SOE during the war and hidden in well-concealed caches. On the disbandment of the MPAJA in 1945, each guerrilla had received a gratuity of Malay $350 in return for his weapons. The organisation, however, had concealed large quantities of arms dropped by Force 136 while reporting them as not received owing to airdrops having gone astray. Moreover it had removed weapons from Japanese armouries following the surrender.

The MCP's strategy was divided into three stages, completion of which, in Chin Peng's estimation, would take ten years. The first would consist of attacks on rubber plantations and tin mines, as well as on members of the police and government officials in towns and villages. Its aim was to force the federal government to evacuate the countryside, which was to be secured by the MPABA as 'liberated areas'. The second stage would comprise the establishment of bases where additional recruits, attracted by the successes in the first stage, were to be trained and the guerrillas' strength increased in preparation for the third phase. This would see MPABA forces breaking out of the 'liberated areas' and attacking towns and other major targets, such as railway installations, before seeking to engage British forces.

The MCP had expected to receive support from China for the third phase but it was to be disappointed. China was already heavily committed to crushing the nationalist forces of Chiang Kai Shek and thus could not afford to provide any material support. Chin Peng could, however, rely on considerable support from another source, the MPAJU, which had since been renamed the Min Yuen (People's Movement), whose members existed at all levels among Malaya's Chinese population. They ranged from wealthy merchants and members of the professional classes to taxi drivers, domestic servants and barbers.

The attacks on 16 June caught the federal government totally by surprise and the reaction of the authorities was slow, particularly in view of the fact that the Malayan Security Service had issued a number of warnings beforehand. During the previous year there had been over 300 strikes organised by the MCP on rubber plantations and in tin mines, and in January the police had been forced to open fire on a group of rioters, killing seven of them. Tension had been growing ever since but despite the increasing expressions of concern, the government, and in particular the High Commissioner, Sir Edward Gent, took no action, refusing requests for protection and dismissing reports of impending trouble as alarmist. Even following the first attacks, Gent would only agree to declare a state of emergency in certain areas of Perak and Johore. On 23 June, however, following an outcry from the press and public, this was extended throughout Malaya and emergency measures including curfews and special powers of search, arrest and detention were introduced immediately.

Military forces in Malaya at this time comprised the fledgling 17th Gurkha Division, with its six understrength battalions, and three battalions of The Malay Regiment which were also undermanned. Also available were the two additional Gurkha battalions in Hong Kong and Singapore.

The police numbered some 10,200 all ranks, its divisions covering Malaya's nine states and the settlements of Penang and Malacca, with stations in each district and town. It was, however, understrength and suffering from poor morale, lacking the numbers, weapons and equipment to counter the Communist Terrorists or CT (as the MPABA were dubbed) effectively. As the latter continued to attack rubber estates, tin mines and isolated police stations, as well as ambushing traffic on remote roads, it became clear that additional manpower was needed swiftly to provide sufficient protection. This resulted in the formation of the Special Constabulary, recruited almost entirely from Malays, whose armed constables took over static guard duties and provided bodyguards for estate managers and tin mine owners. A few weeks after its mobilisation, it was reinforced by several hundred British NCOs demobilised from the Palestine Police following Britain's withdrawal from Palestine in June 1948. Within six months the Special Constabulary would number some 30,000 men.

In those early days responsibility for military operations against the CT fell almost solely on the six Gurkha battalions, whose half-trained young riflemen found themselves being deployed on operations in an environment totally foreign to them. They had to assimilate the skills of jungle warfare and at the same time operate against an enemy habitually at ease living and operating in the jungle. The fact that they learned to do so within a very short time is testament to the dedication and professionalism with which they applied themselves to their new role.

One of the initial successes against the CT occurred on 12 July, less than a month after the initial CT attacks. In the district of Ipoh in central Perak, Capt Nick Neill, commanding B Company of the 2nd/2nd KEO Gurkha Rifles, received information concerning a large group of some fifty CT who had been spotted in their camp. On the following day, before first light, Neill and elements of B Company were led by the informant through a rubber estate to a track leading to the CT camp. As dawn broke the Gurkhas moved swiftly and silently towards their objective but as they did so a group of ten CT appeared from a lean-to shelter and attempted to flee into the jungle. Neill, however, reacted swiftly and opened fire with his Sten gun, firing three bursts and hitting seven of the terrorists.

Finding the terrorists was likened to searching for a needle in a haystack. It required weeks of patrolling; success, as in Neill's contact, depended largely on reliable, up-to-date intelligence combined with a large amount of luck. In the early days of the Emergency, though, intelligence was difficult to come by as the CT conducted a campaign of terror among the local population, who were understandably reluctant to provide information to the security forces.

Among the operations that took place during the early months of the Emergency were those carried out by Ferret Force, an ad hoc composite unit formed from British, Gurkha and Malay troops led by former officers of the wartime Force 136. Commanded by Lt Col John Davis, who had served as a police officer in Malaya before the Second World War and with Force 136 during the conflict, it comprised a headquarters and six groups, each of the latter consisting of four sections. Guided by trackers in the form of Iban tribesmen brought in from the state of Sarawak on the island of Borneo, Ferret Force deployed its sections into the jungle to search for the CT. It achieved considerable success, locating terrorist camps and arms caches as well as accounting for a number of them. Between July and October 3 Group in Port Dickson, three of whose sections comprised men of the 2nd/2nd KEO Gurkha Rifles, killed ten terrorists in Pahang and Kelantan. Unfortunately, however, Ferret Force fell prey to bickering and disagreements between the police and the army over matters of policy, administration and methods of operation, and was disbanded in December after an existence of only a few months.

In the meantime a number of British units had arrived in Malaya from Britain to reinforce the sorely pressed Gurkha battalions. Among these were 2 Guards Brigade, the 1st Battalion The Royal Inniskilling Fusiliers, the 1st Battalion The Seaforth Highlanders and the 1st Battalion The Devonshire Regiment. All troops underwent training at the Far East Training Centre's Jungle Warfare Wing at Johore Bahru, formed in October 1948 by Lt Col Walter Walker of the 6th Gurkha Rifles. In due course this became an establishment in its own right as the Jungle Warfare School (JWS).

October 1948 saw the 1st/2nd KEO Gurkha Rifles, commanded by Lt Col Gordon Richardson, deployed to Malaya from Singapore where it had been tasked with internal security duties. The battalion moved to Johore where, relieving the 1st/10th, it joined the Seaforth Highlanders, Inniskilling Fusiliers and Devons. That same month, however, saw the 2nd/2nd KEO Gurkha Rifles suffer a grievous blow at the hands of the CT when on the evening of 5 October a strong force of terrorists established an ambush in the area of Sungei Siput, on the road to Lintang. At 6 p.m. a civilian truck carrying twenty Gurkhas of C Company, most of whom were newly joined recruits, drove into the ambush area and came under heavy fire from automatic weapons and rifles. The driver was killed in the first burst of fire and the truck careered out of control before hitting a culvert and overturning. Contrary to all orders and standard operating procedures, the vehicle was fitted with a canvas canopy and its tailboard was raised and fastened. The Gurkhas inside were trapped and unable to escape the murderous hail of fire directed into the vehicle; within a few seconds all had either been killed or seriously wounded. Having ceased fire, the CT came out of their ambush positions and collected two Bren guns, ten rifles, three Sten guns and a 2-inch mortar, along with a quantity of Mills No. 36 grenades and 2-inch mortar bombs, before withdrawing. They left behind ten dead and nine wounded Gurkhas lying in the wreckage of the truck.

The ambush resulted in the 2nd/2nd, under Lt Col E.G. 'Lakri' Woods, mounting Operation Kukri, whose aim was to locate and destroy the CT and their bases. The first phase was designed to nullify the source of logistical support for the terrorists: the removal of some 500 Chinese squatters who had settled on forestry reserve land in the area of Jalong during the Second World War and had remained there since. This was achieved without difficulty, the squatters being moved from Jalong to Sungei Siput, where they were joined by a further 5,000 who moved voluntarily from the nearby Sungei Kerbau valley.

The remaining squatter areas were kept under tight control, with large quantities of rice, very obviously out of all proportion to what was required by the squatters and their families, being confiscated and destroyed. These measures cut off the CT from their sources of food and other supplies and, supported by a squadron of the 4th Hussars and 3 Group of Ferret Force, the 2nd/2nd succeeded in accounting for twenty CT while a further forty were arrested during police raids in Sungei Siput and squatter camps in the area. Under such pressure the remaining terrorists in the area were forced to move to other areas.

On 7 November a patrol of Ferret Force's 4 Group discovered a large CT training camp in the hills to the west of Chemor, situated approximately 12 miles to the north of Ipoh. As the patrol approached the camp, it came under heavy fire from a force of about a hundred terrorists. One of its members was hit and the patrol withdrew.

B Company 2nd/2nd was tasked with attacking the camp and on 8 November carried out an approach march, reaching the area during the early afternoon. Covered by his second-in-command, Capt (KGO) Parsuram Gurung, Capt Neill went forward to carry out a close reconnaissance of the camp which was seemingly deserted. He found ten large huts used as barracks, a lecture hall, a rifle range and administrative areas. Moving to the far side of the camp, Neill beckoned to his two platoons, but no sooner had 4 Platoon begun to move forward than it came under heavy fire from high ground on the far side of the camp and two Gurkhas, Cpl Deobahadur Thapa and Rifleman Sarki Gurung, were killed.

At that moment the company sergeant major (CSM), WOII Shere Thapa, spotted a number of terrorists across a stream and charged, with Capt Neill and rifleman Kharbahadur Gurung following close behind. Shere Thapa killed one terrorist with his Sten gun while Neill and Kharbahadur accounted for two others. Meanwhile the rest of B Company became engaged in a fierce battle with the main CT force, which broke contact and withdrew shortly afterwards. A search of the surrounding area revealed a further four dead CT, bringing the total killed in the action to six.

In December 1948 an operation codenamed Sickle was launched in Johore by The Seaforth Highlanders and C Company 1st/2nd KEO Gurkha Rifles, commanded by Capt Scott Leathart, who was attached to them for the operation. The operation began on 10 December and four days later, acting on information obtained during the interrogation of a terrorist captured by the police on the 12th, C Company set off for a large CT camp designed to accommodate a hundred terrorists. Led by the prisoner and following a track which began some 2½ miles south of an area called Batu Anam, Leathart and his men headed east through a rubber estate before entering the jungle.

Such was the thickness of the jungle that it was only possible to move along the narrow, well-worn track. After about half a mile the leading element of the company came to a small unoccupied hut, thereafter encountering a further four huts, each with a deserted sentry position covering the track. Shortly afterwards it came to a track junction where a second track led off to the right. At this point the terrorist guide claimed he did not know which path to follow and thus Leathart divided his force in two, half continuing along the track the company had been following while the other moved off on the track to the right. Some five minutes later the latter group came under fire from a sentry who then disappeared into the jungle. Following up at the double for about 400 yards, the Gurkhas came to a camp that had just been abandoned. Large and well-built, it comprised nine wooden buildings used as barracks, a kitchen and dining hall, a lecture hall and an armourer's workshop. A search of the camp revealed two packs and cooked food for some fifty men.

Having destroyed the camp, C Company withdrew along the track in darkness, at one point coming under inaccurate and ineffective fire from two automatic weapons in the jungle. This was silenced by return fire from the company, which thereafter continued on its way.

At the beginning of 1949 Chin Peng convened a conference of MCP leaders which was also attended by senior officers of the People's Liberation Army (PLA) of China, some travelling via Thailand while others came by sea via the island of Hainan. Conducted in the jungle of Pahang, the purpose of the conference was to review the situation. During the first six months of the war the CT had killed 482 troops, police and civilians and wounded 404 while suffering losses of 406 killed and 268 captured. More importantly, however, the CT had been unable to declare any areas 'liberated' and the British were adopting increasingly tougher measures to counter the terrorists.

One of the first decisions taken at the conference was to change the name of the MPABA to the Malayan Races Liberation Army (MRLA), largely because of the declaration by Britain that Malaya would be granted independence in the near future. In Chin Peng's view the MPABA's name would be meaningless if there were no British to fight.

A major problem facing Chin Peng and his fellow leaders was that of poor communications, with messages sometimes taking weeks to arrive. The decision was thus taken to reactivate the jungle postal network established by the MPAJA, details of which had never been revealed to the Force 136 officers working with the guerrillas. The network criss-crossed the entire length and breadth of the country, with couriers travelling relatively short distances along jungle tracks, delivering and collecting messages to and from a series of carefully camouflaged 'letterboxes', each man knowing only the locations of those on his particular route. Schedules were carefully planned so that couriers never met one another when making deliveries or collections.

The conference also decided on a change of course politically, in response to mounting criticism that the terrorist campaign had been totally destructive and offered little or nothing in return. Chin Peng published an open letter in which he invited members of all races in Malaya to assist the MCP in its aims, claiming that a democratic future could only be assured by expelling the imperialists and establishing a 'People's Democratic Republic'. Victory, he claimed, would result in everyone over eighteen having the right to vote in a state 'controlled by united revolutions of all races' and in which all workers would be granted equality with the 'armies of state-controlled industries'. The statement was accompanied by promises of national and social insurance, free education, land grants and free supplies of seeds and agricultural implements. This shift in direction by the MCP was followed by a change of tactics in the field. Large-scale attacks became fewer, with terrorist-inspired incidents falling from a rate of 50 per week to an average of 26, while CT units switched to operating in small groups.

At the end of May 1949 a group of CT was located around Sungei Siput and pursued northwards by the 2nd/2nd KEO Gurkha Rifles into the area of operations of the 1st/6th Gurkha Rifles, who joined the chase. The two battalions thereafter pushed the terrorists further north into the Cameron Highlands, whose steep, jungle-covered mountains separated the states of Perak and Kelantan. Intelligence pointed to the presence of a large concentration of terrorists of the MRLA's 5th Regiment, which had established a base deep in the jungle, where it intended using the monsoon period for rest and training.

In early October Operation Smoke was launched with the 2nd/2nd KEO Gurkha Rifles, less D Company, deploying 6 miles to the north of the Cameron Highlands. D Company, commanded by Maj Pat Kent, meanwhile marched in via Lasah to the north of Sungei Siput, thereafter searching the Piah and Betis valleys before withdrawing and making its exit at Gua Musang, some 80 miles to the east. On the following morning, A, B and C Companies were transported to the Blue Valley, from which A Company, under Maj Tony Harrison, moved off towards the head of the Yum River and then made its way to the junction with the Plus before searching a valley. B and C Companies, under Capt Nick Neill and Capt Bill Truss, were meanwhile making their way with considerable difficulty through dense jungle. Progress was slow, at best 2,000 yards per day, with the heavy monsoon rains allowing only a three-hour 'window' in which resupply drops could be carried out by RAF aircraft.

After two weeks B and C Companies split up, with Capt Neill and his men heading west into the top of the Korbu Valley while C Company marched east to the head of the Mu. Thereafter both companies followed the line of the rivers, searching for traces of CT. On this occasion it was C Company that struck lucky when it came across a track used by the terrorists. While making their way along it, however, the Gurkhas encountered a group of CT carrying supplies to the 5th Regiment's main camp located nearby. A brief action ensued during which one terrorist was killed, the remainder escaping into the jungle. Shortly afterwards a senior CT commander approached the rearmost element of the company which was some 500 yards from the scene of the action. Oblivious to the presence of security forces in the area, he was apparently under the impression that the Gurkhas were members of his own unit. He was swiftly disabused of any such notion by a burst from a Bren gun, which unfortunately missed, allowing him to escape into the jungle.

Following this contact C Company followed up with caution and eventually reached the 5th Regiment camp, which was found to be abandoned. Subsequent searches of the surrounding area were hampered by heavy rain which obliterated tracks and, although C Company deployed a number of ambushes and patrols, no trace of the enemy was found.

The operation ended on 7 November. Despite the fact that only one terrorist had been killed, Smoke was deemed a success as the 5th Regiment had been forced to abandon its camps and its lines of supply had been disrupted by other units deployed into areas where the terrorists grew food.

In January 1950 a major action was fought by the 1st/2nd KEO Gurkha Rifles in the state of Johore. The commander of B Company, Maj Peter Richardson, was informed that a large group of CT was operating in the area north of Labis and was ordered to eliminate as many of its members as possible. Richardson deployed into the area with 3 and 4 Platoons, the majority of his force being young, untried riflemen, and in the early hours of 22 January moved into an area of overgrown rubber plantation. At first light he and his men headed off in the direction of Labis but shortly afterwards 3 Platoon came under fire. Richardson, accompanied by two riflemen, was moving with 4 Platoon, commanded by his CSM, WOII Bhimbahadur Pun, following up a short distance behind.

Richardson soon found himself in the ambush killing ground and, together with two young Gurkhas, charged the CT, killing two terrorists with his Sten gun and then shooting a third, who had just killed one of the two Gurkhas with a *parang* (long jungle knife). Meanwhile the CSM, WOII Bhimbahadur Pun, had swiftly manoeuvred 4 Platoon behind the terrorists' position, forcing them to try to escape across some padi fields. Here they came under fire from both platoons who, despite the difficult visibility caused by the early morning mist, succeeded in killing a large number of terrorists.

A search of the area revealed twenty-two bodies, two Sten guns, a Thompson submachine-gun, eight rifles and quantities of .303 and 9mm ammunition. Months later it was learned that the total number of CT casualties was thirty-five killed and wounded, the dead including a notorious terrorist named Yap Piow, the commander of CT in the Labis area, and his second-in-command. This was the highest number of terrorists killed in a single operation and remained so throughout the rest of the Emergency. Maj Peter Richardson was later awarded the DSO and CSM Bhimbahadur Pun the DCM for this action.

Meanwhile British forces in Malaya had been reorganised. Under the command of Headquarters Malaya, based in the federal capital of Kuala Lumpur, the country was divided into the districts of North and South Malaya with their respective headquarters at Kamunting in Perak and Seremban in Negri Sembilan respectively. Troops in North Malaya comprised: 3 Commando Brigade at Ipoh in Perak; 1 Malay Brigade at Kota Bahru in northern Kelantan; and the 1st Battalion The King's Own Yorkshire Light Infantry stationed on the island of Penang. In South Malaya were: 18 Infantry Brigade, based in Kuala Lumpur; 26 Gurkha Infantry Brigade at Johore Bahru; and 63 Gurkha Infantry Brigade at Seremban. By this time 48 Gurkha Infantry Brigade was based at Kuala Lipis in Pahang, under the direct command of Headquarters Malaya. Additional troops, in the form of 28 Infantry Brigade and a further two infantry battalions, together with artillery, armour and engineer units, were also available.

In early May 1951 the CT demonstrated that they were still a force to be reckoned with. On the nights of 30 April/1 May and 1/2 May, in the area of Segamat in northern Johore, the twenty-strong Pioneer Platoon of the 1st/2nd KEO Gurkha Rifles, commanded by Sgt Manbahadur Pun, was deployed to the area north of a squatter resettlement camp at Buloh Kasap where it laid ambushes on tracks leading from the north. No terrorists appeared, but on the morning of 2 May, after the ambushes had been lifted and the platoon was concentrated at the resettlement camp prior to carrying out a number of patrol tasks, a Chinese man reported that a group of labourers on the rubber estate to the east of the camp had been robbed of their identity cards by seven terrorists.

Accompanied by two policemen as guides, the platoon left the camp and moved through the rubber estate, travelling astride the road leading through it. Ahead of it, however, was a very large force of 300 CT who, it was later learned, had been in position for 48 hours. Sited in depth with interlocking arcs of fire, their positions covered a front of between 400 and 500 yards. Advancing in open formation, Sgt Manbahadur and his platoon, preceded by scouts, had moved well into the ambush killing area when they were subjected to a murderous volume of fire from the front and both flanks. Four Gurkhas and both policemen died immediately, while a number of others were wounded.

The platoon, including the wounded, reacted swiftly and returned fire. A swamp to the east prevented withdrawal in that direction, while the rubber estate, with its total absence of undergrowth, provided no cover for any outflanking movement. The only course open to Sgt Manbahadur was to force a breach through the CT and extricate his platoon. This he proceeded to do by leading a charge against the nearest terrorist positions, thereafter providing covering fire for the surviving members of his platoon as they carried out their wounded, and organising a rearguard action to cover their withdrawal.

Back at the resettlement camp, Sgt Manbahadur assembled a force of eleven policemen and, with two members of his platoon, returned to the ambush area to retrieve the bodies of the Gurkhas and two policemen who had died during the action. By this time the terrorists had withdrawn, taking with them a Bren gun, three Sten guns, an Owen submachine-gun and three rifles. As was later learned, they had suffered eleven killed and wounded. Manbahadur Pun was later awarded the DCM for his gallantry in this and other actions.

It was not long, however, before the 1st/2nd exacted revenge for the ambush. On 22 May information was received that a group of some thirty terrorists, members of the MRLA's 8th Independent Platoon, had been observed in the area of the Chuan Hin San rubber estate. On 27 May four ten-man groups of CT were spotted in an area to the east of the Ayer Panas road. On the following morning B Company moved in transport to the area and, having debussed and crossed the road, deployed with its left flank on the east bank of a large swamp called the Anak Ayer Merah and its right on the western side of the road.

On the left was 4 Platoon, which lost contact with the remainder of the company shortly after it began its advance. The platoon commander, Capt (KGO) Lachhiman

Gurung, sent a section forward across the swamp but it came under heavy fire at close range as it emerged. The Gurkhas immediately charged, forcing the terrorists to withdraw, before taking up a position to cover a second section and the platoon headquarters as they crossed the swamp, the third section remaining on the east bank. 5 Platoon meanwhile was moving up towards the sound of the firing when it spotted three CT withdrawing westwards on the far side of the swamp. As the platoon advanced through a padi field adjoining the swamp, it came under heavy fire and one Gurkha was killed. At this stage Lachhiman realised that the terrorists were attempting to escape to the west and so manoeuvred the two sections with him round to where they were able to join forces with 5 Platoon, one Gurkha being killed during the process.

As 4 and 5 Platoons returned the terrorists' fire, the latter stood their ground rather than withdrawing, as was normally the case, only beginning to pull back as the two platoons began skirmishing forward. As the Gurkhas paused to fix bayonets, the CT broke and ran, heading towards the east. While crossing the swamp, however, they were exposed to the Gurkhas' fire and a number were killed. Following the action twelve bodies (eight male and four female) were recovered, along with a Thompson submachine-gun, two Sten guns and three rifles. It was later learned that the CT had suffered a further eight killed, bringing the total of their dead to twenty, and fifteen wounded. Furthermore Special Branch reported that the group had comprised a number of senior terrorists and an escort en route to a meeting in the Labis area. The apparent reluctance of the CT to withdraw following the initial contact with B Company had been the escort covering the escape of their leaders.

The latter part of 1951 saw the CT score a major blow against the British. During the first week of October a 50-strong force, comprising terrorists of 24 and 30 Companies of the 6th Regiment MRLA under command of a leading CT named Siu Mah, moved into the area of Fraser's Hill, a popular hill resort in Pahang. On 4 October, armed with three Bren guns, Sten guns and rifles, it established an ambush on the narrow winding road leading up to the resort. Covering a front of some 200 yards around a sharp bend, the terrorists were positioned on a bank approximately 20 feet above the road and were hidden behind screens fashioned from palm leaves and *atap*. During the following two days Siu Mah waited for a military convoy, which, a member of the Min Yuen had informed him, would shortly be passing along the road. The principal purpose of the ambush was to capture much-needed weapons and ammunition once the troops in the convoy had been killed.

By noon on the third day there had been no sign of the convoy, and Siu Mah had decided to withdraw his force when, at 1 p.m., two vehicles appeared on the bend. The first was a Land Rover carrying six policemen, while the second was a black Rolls-Royce in which the High Commissioner of Malaya, Sir Henry Gurney, was travelling with his wife and private secretary. Seconds later both vehicles were raked by heavy fire which killed five of the policemen, the sixth escaping injury and returning the terrorists' fire. A few seconds later Sir Henry Gurney stepped from the Rolls-Royce and proceeded to walk calmly towards the terrorists, who cut him down in a hail of bullets. At this juncture Siu Mah gave the order to withdraw and he and his men disappeared into the jungle. Lady Gurney and Sir Henry's private secretary, Mr D.J. Staples, survived unscathed and it was later concluded that Sir Henry had deliberately exposed himself in order to draw the terrorists' fire away from his wife.

Word of the ambush soon reached the security forces and A Squadron of the 12th Royal Lancers was despatched to investigate, its report being received at 3.30 p.m. Thereafter the response was swift and an operation, codenamed Pursuit, was launched to try to track down the terrorists. A force comprising the 2nd/2nd KEO Gurkha Rifles, 1st Battalion The Worcestershire Regiment, 12th Royal Lancers and 93 Field Battery RA, supported by RAF aircraft, was quickly deployed to follow up the CT, who had initially headed south-east before turning north-east.

The operation lasted approximately two months, being hampered by difficult terrain and appalling weather. Despite the difficulties, however, the 2nd/2nd succeeded in making first contact with elements of Siu Mah's force when an ambush laid by Headquarter Company shot dead two terrorists on 24 and 25 October respectively. On the 26th a 2nd/2nd patrol killed another, and on 6 November a C Company patrol accounted for a fourth after a brief action during which a CT succeeded in escaping. He was pursued by a patrol from D Company as he headed north. As dusk fell the patrol was moving along a stream searching for a location for a base for the night when its lead scout spotted a terrorist filling containers with water. The Gurkha opened fire, hitting the CT, but the latter picked himself up and ran off into an area of rubber nearby.

The patrol followed up at dawn the next morning and found a camp that had been occupied by seven men. Finding a fresh trail heading east, the Gurkhas set off in pursuit and continued doing so until 5.00 p.m. when fresh human faeces were discovered near the track. Moving forward with caution, the patrol eventually came upon a camp. The lead scout shot dead a CT sentry; as he did so a terrorist charged out of the undergrowth nearby and was killed immediately. The patrol then stormed the camp but by that time the other CT had fled, leaving behind them seven packs, a rifle and a shotgun. Following this action one of the dead CT was identified as the quartermaster of the MRLA's No. 24 Company, Lau Lee.

Operation Pursuit was terminated towards the end of November, by which time the 2nd/2nd KEO Gurkha Rifles had killed eight of the CT responsible for Sir Henry Gurney's death, suffering one Gurkha killed and one wounded in the process.

During 1951 casualties had escalated on both sides, with 504 members of the security forces and 1,079 CT killed, and 322 terrorists captured or having surrendered. The figures for the previous year had been 294 police and troops killed while the CT had suffered 942 losses. Civilian deaths had decreased, with 533 killed during 1951 compared to 646 in 1950.

February 1952 saw the arrival of Gen Sir Gerald Templer as High Commissioner. He also assumed the appointment of Director of Operations, replacing Lt Gen Sir Harold Briggs who had retired at the end of 1951 after a year in the post. The latter had been notable for instituting a number of measures, in particular a new strategy known as the Briggs Plan. Its four aims were: the domination of populated areas, thereby increasing the feeling of security among the population and resulting in a steady and increasing flow of information to the security forces; the break-up of the MCP organisation within the populated areas; the isolation of the CT from their sources of food and information within the populated areas; and the destruction of the terrorists by forcing them to attack the security forces on the latter's own ground. Under the plan half a million squatters were resettled into fortified villages, an idea originally conceived by Sir Henry Gurney. Administered by 'camp officers', these provided accommodation for the squatters (each family being allocated its own single-storey house with electricity), shops, a clinic, a school and a police post. Surrounded by a high perimeter fence, each village was protected by a detachment of armed police. In the area surrounding each village, outside the perimeter fence, each squatter family was allocated 2 acres of land for cultivation of crops. Each inhabitant of a village was issued with an identity card and access was strictly controlled.

Templer was a dynamic individual and his influence was soon felt at all levels throughout the security forces in Malaya. These had seen a considerable increase in their strength, numbering over 40,000 in total: 10,000 Gurkhas in 17th Gurkha Division comprising 26 and 99 Gurkha Infantry Brigades in Johore, 48 Gurkha Infantry Brigade in Pahang and 63 Gurkha Infantry Brigade in Negri Sembilan; 25,000 British troops (including RAF and Royal Navy personnel); five battalions of The Malay Regiment; two battalions of The King's African Rifles; and a battalion of The Fiji Infantry Regiment. In addition, there was the newly formed 22nd SAS Regiment (22 SAS) which had been formed in January from the Malayan Scouts (SAS) and a composite squadron of 21st SAS Regiment (Artists) (TA), and reinforced by a squadron of volunteers from Rhodesia. All these formations and units were supported by the RAF and the Royal Australian Air Force (RAAF), the latter providing bomber and transport squadrons.

The police in particular benefited from Templer's arrival. Their new Commissioner, Col Arthur Young, requested large amounts of much-needed weapons and equipment including 600 armoured personnel carriers, 120 armoured cars, 250 scout cars and large quantities of small arms. Templer not only gave his assent to the supply of these items but also seconded a number of army technical experts to Young's force. During the following year a total of £30 million was spent on re-equipping the police. At the same time considerable effort and resources were devoted to enhancing the Special Branch as Templer, a former Director of Military Intelligence at the War Office in London, was well aware that the foremost weapon against the CT was intelligence.

In February 1953 the 2nd/7th Gurkha Rifles carried out a highly successful operation following receipt of information about an area of cultivation spotted by the pilot of an Auster light aircraft while on a flight from Seremban in Negri Sembilan. By this time the CT had been forced to resort to growing their own food as a result of the success of the Briggs Plan in cutting them off from their sources of supply among the squatters. The area was approximately the size of a tennis court and had been camouflaged by the terrorists using cut saplings. The foliage on these, however, had died and thus the pilot had been able to observe the neat rows of cultivated vegetables underneath, along with the roof of a hut or basha (shelter).

Following his report the 1st Battalion The Gordon Highlanders was tasked with carrying out an attack on the area, with C Company 2nd/7th, commanded by Capt John Thornton, under command. While the Gordons approached the objective from the south, after dropping off a company tasked with laying ambushes to the east, C Company approached from the north and also established a number of ambushes.

Having headed southwards along a ridgeline, C Company established a base approximately a mile to the north of the cultivated area. By this time it was around 4 p.m. and Capt Thornton despatched seven three-man reconnaissance patrols to cover a fan-shaped area. One of these patrols, commanded by Acting Unpaid L/Cpl Rabilal Rai, spotted two terrorists washing in a stream. Suspecting their camp was nearby and leaving the two other members of his patrol to continue observing the two CT, Rabilal continued on his own and discovered approximately a dozen terrorists. He then proceeded to carry out a close reconnaissance around the camp's perimeter, with the aim of locating any sentry posts, before rejoining his two riflemen. Despatching one of his two men to report to Capt Thornton, Rabilal moved to an RV where he would meet the rest of C Company for an attack on the CT camp.

In the early hours of the following morning the company moved into stop positions before Thornton and nine of his Gurkhas charged the camp. Initially he thought the CT had escaped; in fact they had evacuated on hearing his approach but had encountered his stop groups, who killed eight of them.

In March 1953 one of the first operations in which Gurkhas were deployed by helicopter took place. Codenamed Gyroscope, its aim was the destruction of cultivated areas discovered by aerial photographic reconnaissance. The operation began on 27 March, when B Company of the 1st/2nd KEO Gurkha Rifles was taken by RAF Whirlwind helicopters into a landing zone (LZ) near a large cultivated area measuring some 400 by 200 yards. In the meantime a platoon from A Company and 1 Federal Jungle Company of the Royal Malay Police were placed in stop positions ready to cut off any CT attempting to escape.

B Company succeeded in approaching the cultivated area undetected and surprised one terrorist who was shot dead; others fled but encountered the stop groups, who succeeded in killing several. Another walked into an ambush later in the day but managed to escape. Thereafter the company proceeded to destroy the crops of sweet potatoes and tapioca using a chemical called Triaxone.

Further successes were scored against the CT during 1953, although in several cases success was only achieved after protracted operations. One such operation began in June, following an ambush by a group of twenty terrorists in the area of a rubber estate on the Pengarang. The 1st/10th Princess Mary's Own Gurkha Rifles (the additional title having been granted in 1950) were tasked with responding to this attack and deployed a platoon under Lt (QGO) Dhojbir Limbu to follow up. It took two days of painstaking searching before fresh tracks were found and the platoon was able to pursue its quarry. The CT, however, were well aware that the security forces would be hot on their trail and thus did their best to throw their pursuers off the scent, splitting into separate groups more than once during each day and meeting at prearranged RVs.

The chase became a lengthy affair, taking the pursuing Gurkhas through 25 miles of swamp, and soon they were in dire need of resupply. Lt Dhojbir, however, realised that halting to resupply would enable the terrorists to increase their lead and thus reduced his platoon's rations to one meal a day while continuing to pursue the CT non-stop throughout daylight hours.

By 8 July the platoon had exhausted its rations and Dhojbir knew that he had to make contact with the CT that day or give up the chase. At that juncture, however, the terrorists' tracks disappeared. Dhojbir divided his platoon into two groups in order to cover more ground while attempting to pick up the trail again and set off at the head of half his men. Fortunately, luck was with him and later that day he stumbled upon a camp on an island in the middle of a swamp. The terrorists were, however, on the alert and both sides spotted the other simultaneously. Despite being heavily outnumbered and under heavy fire from three light machine-guns, as well as a shower of grenades, Lt Dhojbir and his group put in an immediate assault on the camp. Two terrorists were killed as the Gurkhas charged, the remainder fleeing into the swamp, abandoning a number of weapons together with large quantities of food and ammunition. Subsequent identification of one of the dead CT revealed him to be a political commissar with a price of Malay $75,000 on his head.

* * *

A significant high point for The Brigade of Gurkhas had been the coronation of Her Majesty Queen Elizabeth II, which took place in London on 2 June 1953 – thereafter all KGOs were redesignated Queen's Gurkha Officers (QGOs). A contingent was sent from Malaya to take part in the parade, including a detachment of the 2nd KEO Gurkha Rifles, commanded by Maj Dudley Spain, which took with it the Queen's Truncheon that, as recounted in Chapter 1, had been presented to the regiment by Queen Victoria. Queen Elizabeth expressed a wish to see the Truncheon and so, on the morning of 4 June, Maj Spain and the Gurkha Major of the 2nd Battalion, Maj (QGO) Bahasa Rana, together with the Truncheon Jemadars, Lt (QGO) Kharakbahadur Ghale of the 1st Battalion and Lt (QGO) Kharakbahadur Thapa of the 2nd Battalion, presented themselves at Buckingham Palace. Following this occasion the Truncheon was fitted on the top of its upper staff with two silver collars engraved with the following inscription: 'The Queen's Truncheon was carried in the procession at Her Majesty's Coronation, 2nd June 1953. Inscribed by order of Her Majesty Queen Elizabeth II.'

The following year saw the departure in June of Gen Sir Gerald Templer from Malaya, being succeeded as High Commissioner by Sir Donald MacGillivray and as

Director of Operations by Lt Gen Sir Geoffrey Bourne, the latter also being GOC Malaya. During the two years of Templer's tenure the security situation had improved sufficiently to permit a gradual reduction in the strength of the police, the Special Constabulary and the Home Guard. Moreover the CT strength had declined by some 2,000 to an estimated total of 3,200, comprising 1,200 in Pahang, 1,000 in Perak, 500 in Negri Sembilan and a further 500 over the border in southern Thailand.

By 1955 the pattern of the campaign in Malaya had changed. By then the CT were operating in smaller numbers and had withdrawn their bases deeper into the jungle as the security forces, making increasing use of helicopters, probed ever deeper. Contacts were less frequent as the terrorists became more elusive, units spending increasingly lengthy periods fruitlessly searching the jungle.

At the beginning of 1956, however, a large band of some fifty CT was reported to be operating in the area of Fort Brooke, one of a number of jungle forts manned by companies of the Police Field Force (PFF), and to be terrorising the aboriginal tribes in the area. C Company of the 1st/6th Gurkha Rifles, commanded by Maj (GCO) Harkasing Rai, was tasked with investigating them.

An initial search found evidence that the CT had been in the area some four or five days before, heading west. On 2 January C Company, led by a team of Iban trackers, set off in pursuit and by 9 January, despite the efforts of the terrorists in employing every measure to shake off any pursuers, was only one day's march behind its quarry. At noon on the following day the leading scouts spotted a small hut ahead of them in the jungle. As the company deployed for an attack it came under fire from a CT sentry. Mounting an immediate assault, it charged, killing the sentry but coming under fire from the terrorists' camp some 200 yards away.

Major Harkasing and his men then proceeded to attack the camp, killing three more of the CT, who withdrew across a river close to the camp before bringing heavy fire to bear on the Gurkhas, preventing them from crossing the river in pursuit.

During the following days C Company lost contact with the terrorists and it was not until 11 March that their trail was picked up again. Before long the company was only two days' march behind the CT, who were well aware that they were being followed and were making every effort to elude their pursuers. They resorted to sleeping in caves rather than camping in the jungle, climbed sheer cliff faces and descended waterfalls, but all in vain; led by their trackers, the Gurkhas closed in remorselessly.

Eventually a patrol from the company spotted a group of fifteen terrorists in a small camp. Unfortunately last light was only a matter of minutes away, so Maj Harkasing decided to mount an attack at first light on the following morning. Before dawn C Company succeeded in crawling to within striking distance but was suddenly challenged by a CT sentry who opened fire, wounding two Gurkhas. The terrorists scattered, fleeing into the jungle in groups of two or three. Other companies of the 1st/6th Gurkha Rifles, however, had been deployed to the north, south and west and these encountered some of the fleeing CT groups. As a result of having suffered several casualties, the CT unit was disbanded and thereafter caused no further problems in the area of Fort Brooke.

Throughout the Malayan Emergency campaign a considerable amount of effort was directed at persuading the CT to surrender themselves to the security forces. An important measure introduced by Sir Henry Gurney just before his death was the announcement of rewards for information leading to the capture or killing of terrorists, the aim being to encourage CTs to turn themselves in and then subsequently 'sell out' their former comrades. Prominent CT leaders had prices placed on their heads, Chin Peng being worth Malay $80,000. In addition, rewards were offered to anyone who arranged the surrender of a known terrorist.

During late September 1956, in Negri Sembilan, a senior CT named Ah Fui, a member of the MCP's branch committee for the area of Kuala Pilah, made it known he was interested in surrendering and proposed a meeting in the jungle with Mr Gus Fletcher, the head of the Special Branch at Kuala Pilah. A Company of the 2nd/2nd KEO Gurkha Rifles, commanded by Maj Graham Vivian, was tasked with providing an escort for Fletcher and one of his officers. Three nights later, the Gurkhas having cordoned off the area, Fletcher met Ah Fui, who agreed to remain in the jungle and assist in the killing or capture of the MCP Branch Secretary, the official in charge of the CT in the area, and two others. In return Fletcher agreed that Ah Fui and his bodyguard, Tong Gah, would receive the officially laid down rewards.

A few nights later Vivian and Fletcher, accompanied by a section of A Company and one of Fletcher's officers, Inspector Tan, met Ah Fui and Tong Gah, who told them that the Branch Secretary, a woman, had arrived with another female terrorist and a CT courier, the latter bringing news of the arrival of a senior CT official within the next four or five days. A plan to capture the two women and the courier was hatched during this meeting and Fletcher gave Ah Fui a powerful sedative, with which he was to lace their coffee.

On the following evening Tong Gah arrived at the rendezvous and led Fletcher, Inspector Tan, Maj Vivian and his section of Gurkhas into the jungle to a spot near the terrorist camp where he left them. Three hours later Ah Fui appeared, somewhat anxious that the drug, added by him to the coffee drunk by both women, had succeeded merely in rendering the Branch Secretary dopey; after taking a sip and complaining about the taste the other woman had refused to drink any more. The courier meanwhile had drunk a mugful and appeared totally unaffected.

By this time darkness had fallen but Fletcher and Vivian decided to launch an immediate assault. Led by Ah Fui, they and the rest of their group made their way slowly and cautiously through the jungle to the camp, where Ah Fui, Inspector Tan and three Gurkhas took up position on one side while the remainder crept to the other. At a signal from Ah Fui, the entire group rushed the three terrorists, Tong Gah seizing the courier while Inspector Tan tackled the Branch Secretary, who was attempting to draw a pistol. Ah Fui meanwhile restrained the other female terrorist who, it transpired, was his girlfriend.

Four days later Fletcher and Vivian were back in the jungle to apprehend the senior CT official, who had by then been identified as one Sui Lam, the MCP's area treasurer; he had arrived with three bodyguards, one of them armed with a Bren gun. Accompanied by Inspector Tan and a section of Vivian's company, they were led by Ah Fui to a location some 100 yards from the camp, where Ah Fui left them. Several hours later Tong Gah appeared to report that although the terrorists had drunk the laced coffee the drug had not worked; the three bodyguards were, however, asleep and Sui Lam was lying on his bed, talking quietly to Ah Fui.

Once again it was decided to attack the camp without delay and, led by Tong Gah, Fletcher, Tan, Vivian and five Gurkhas crept through the pitch darkness, holding on to the belt of the man in front, until they reached the edge of the camp, where the remnants of a fire provided a dim light. The attack was carried out in a silent rush followed by a short burst of firing. Ah Fui had seized Sui Lam but unfortunately, in the darkness, Gus Fletcher fired upon him by mistake, enabling Sui Lam to escape into the jungle along with one of his bodyguards, the other two having been killed during the attack. Three days later, however, Sui Lam was shot dead while approaching a terrorist camp some 50 miles away; it transpired that he was killed by a patrol guided by the CT courier captured by Fletcher and Vivian's group on the first operation.

On 31 August 1957 the Federation of Malaya achieved independence under an Alliance government headed by Tunku Abdul Rahman. The arrangement favoured Malays politically, with the leaders of UMNO being appointed to most federal and state offices, and the position of Agong (King) to rotate in turn between the sultans. The Chinese in Malaya, however, were granted full rights of citizenship and were permitted to maintain their strong economic base within the country.

British and Commonwealth forces remained in Malaya under the terms of a newly drawn-up Agreement of Defence and Mutual Assistance, which was signed shortly after independence. This was a major blow to the CT, who by this time numbered approximately 1,830 men and women. Some 550 of these were active in central Perak while another 500 were in Johore. A further 550 were near the Thai border or across it in southern Thailand, while the remainder were spread throughout the rest of Malaya.

Following the launch in April of a major operation, codenamed Chieftain and targeted on 175 CT in southern Perak, further surrenders of CT took place during the latter part of 1957. One of these was of particular importance: an individual named Chow Fong, the political commissar in south Perak, gave himself up in October with his four bodyguards. He was of incalculable value to the security forces as he knew the identities of the CT commanders and of the district and branch members in his region. His defection was kept secret until July of the following year, when it was announced that 118 CT, including several high-ranking terrorists, had surrendered and that large quantities of weapons and ammunition had been captured by the security forces.

One of those who surrendered was Hor Lung, the CT commander for Johore and deputy head of the MCP under Chin Peng, who gave himself up at a rural police post on 5 April. Shortly afterwards, having been offered considerable financial inducement for himself and for any CT who turned themselves in, he agreed to go back into the jungle to persuade his men to surrender. During the following six months, while the security forces held back from conducting any operations in Johore, Hor Lung toured all his units and succeeded in persuading 160 CT, including 28 known hard-core commanders, to give themselves up. Only 81 refused to surrender and remained in the jungle. Having completed the task, Hor Lung was paid Malay $400,000 (£50,000 at 1958 exchange rate), which made him a wealthy man.

By January 1959 there were only an estimated 250 CT still active inside Malaya. One group of 35 remained in Pahang under the leadership of a senior terrorist named Ah Chun, until he was killed by a British officer out hunting big game in the jungle. In Perak another 170 CT were commanded by Siu Mah, notorious for having led the CT force which had murdered Sir Henry Gurney in October 1951. Eventually, however, he was betrayed by two of his men who gave themselves up and led a patrol of troops to a cave where he was waiting for them to return from collecting food. He was shot dead in the ensuing action, and Gurney's death was finally avenged. Meanwhile the security forces had been conducting a major operation targeted on the area in southern Perak where the CT were known to be operating. A total of 103 terrorists surrendered, among them two senior commanders, Chan Hong and Choy Foong, while several more were killed or captured. In Kelantan, meanwhile, the CT had split up into small groups of six or seven, being constantly harried by troops aided by aborigines, whose loyalty had been won over following a major 'hearts and minds' campaign.

By July 1959 the majority of the CT known to be still active in Malaya were believed to be in northern Perak and Kedah. There were, however, still large numbers of terrorists over the border. Agreement over joint operations was reached between the Malayan and Thai governments but it was never put into practice and the CT remained safe in their jungle bases in southern Thailand. Despite the threat still posed by them and those remaining in Malaya, the decision was taken to declare an end to the Emergency and this took place with a proclamation signed by the prime minister, Tunku Abdul Rahman, on 30 July 1960.

Although the Emergency was officially at an end, British forces in the form of 17th Gurkha Division and other troops remained in Malaya. There were, however, problems ahead for The Brigade of Gurkhas, not least of which was an announcement by the British government that the brigade's strength was to be reduced from 14,600 to 10,000.

During 1961 elements of the 1st/7th Duke of Edinburgh's Own Gurkha Rifles (the additional title having been granted in 1959) were deployed to assist the Federation Armed Forces in Malaya on operations against the CT, whose main base was by this time in Yala Province in southern Thailand. The number of terrorists believed to be still in Malaya had shrunk to 35, and all their names were known to the security forces, including that of their leader, Ah Soo Chye. They were believed to be in the region between the Thai border to the north and the Cameron Highlands to the south, in an area covering eastern Perak and western Kelantan through which ran the central mountainous divide. The entire area measured over 10,000 square miles of jungle-clad mountains.

The 1st/7th, commanded by Lt Col Richard Kenney, was deployed to Ipoh in central Perak on Operation Bamboo, which had begun three years earlier but had achieved little. Under command of 2 Federal Brigade, the battalion was tasked with helping to locating the CT and in October 1961 deployed two companies to the small town of Grik, 100 miles to the north of Ipoh. From there troops were deployed to aborigine jungle settlements from which they patrolled the surrounding areas. In December a patrol led by the commander of D Company, Maj John Cross, succeeded in discovering the route used by CT couriers travelling from southern Thailand to Perak and Kelantan.

During January 1962 the 1st/7th deployed A and C Companies to the north to patrol and lay ambushes along the Thai border, these being relieved by B and D Companies which were augmented by a squadron of 22 SAS, who had arrived from Britain ostensibly to carry out jungle training but were deployed on Bamboo none the less.

During February 1962 information was obtained by Maj Cross from an aborigine headman on the movements of Ah Soo Chye and his two lieutenants, along with details of the CTs' *modus operandi* and the assistance provided to them by aborigines. During a long patrol, which lasted from 19 March until 8 May, Cross, accompanied by nine Gurkhas and three aborigines, marched over the central mountain divide in search of Ah Soo Chye but failed to locate him. At the end of July Cross set off again and eventually established a patrol base where he and his Gurkhas remained while his aborigines searched for news of the CT. They were extracted by helicopter on 25 September but some four weeks later, on 26 October, he returned to the jungle in a third attempt to track down Ah Soo Chye and his group.

It was not until 12 January 1963 that Cross received details from two sources that the CT leader and three other terrorists had entered the area and were located only 4,000 yards away. He transmitted this information to the 1st/7th's battalion headquarters, naturally expecting it to mount an operation to follow up and capture Ah Soo Chye and his companions. Instead, however, he was informed that the battalion was being deployed to Brunei, the small British protectorate on the north-west coast of Borneo, where a rebellion had broken out five weeks earlier on 7 December 1962. Two days later Cross and his men were extracted by helicopter. The last Gurkha operation against the CT in Malaya was over.

CHAPTER 6

THE BRUNEI REBELLION

While peace had returned to Malaya, trouble was brewing across the South China Sea on the island of Borneo, fomented by Indonesia under its charismatic leader President Ahmed Sukarno, who had held power since December 1949 when Indonesia achieved independence from the Netherlands.

At the end of 1961 the Prime Minister of Malaya, Tunku Abdul Rahman, announced plans for the establishment of the Federation of Malaysia which would incorporate Malaya, Singapore, the Borneo states of Sarawak and North Borneo, and the oil- and natural gas-rich British protectorate of Brunei. His proposals had met with a receptive response from all except Brunei whose ruler, the Sultan Sir Omar Ali Saifuddin, declared that he wished Britain to continue exercising responsibility for Brunei's defence and external affairs.

Sukarno, however, had dreams of an alternative federation, called 'Maphilindo', which would incorporate Indonesia, the Philippines, Malaya, Singapore and the whole of Borneo. With a total population of 150 million and with massive natural resources, he envisaged it as a bloc capable of rivalling the United States, the Soviet Union and China in economic power. His plans, however, called for the removal of British forces from the region. This was unwelcome not only to the British but also to Tunku Abdul Rahman and the Prime Minister of Singapore, Lee Kwan Yew, both of whom feared the threat of communism from the north, where the United States was engaged in a major conflict in South Vietnam and, secretly, in Laos. The latter part of the 1950s had seen the advent of the 'Domino Theory' and the fear that the collapse of South Vietnam would be followed by the rest of South East Asia falling under communist domination. North Vietnam was already moving its forces covertly into Laos and Cambodia and it was feared that Thailand would be its next objective. Thus all military threat assessments and planning with regard to Malaya were concentrated on the north of the country and its northern neighbour.

Communism had also established a foothold in Indonesia, where in the late 1950s Sukarno had formed strong ties with the Indonesian Communist Party (PKI) in an effort to offset the power of the Indonesian Army following its crushing of an insurrection on the islands of Sulawesi and Sumatra in early 1958.

With a population that, in the early 1960s, numbered approximately 80 million, Indonesia comprises an archipelago of 3,670 islands covering around 3,200 miles from

Sumatra in the west to New Guinea in the east, and some 1,000 miles from north to south. In addition to Sumatra, the southern element of the island chain includes Java, Bali, Lombok, Sumbawa, Flores and Timor. To the north of these lies Borneo, the third largest island in the world, the greater part of which comprises Indonesian Kalimantan. Along its north-west coast stretch the states of Sarawak and North Borneo (collectively now known as East Malaysia), and the tiny sultanate of Brunei.

A British protectorate since 1888, Brunei covers an area of only 2,200 square miles but possesses huge resources of oil, natural gas and minerals. In the early 1960s its population numbered approximately 85,000, just over half of it Malay and a quarter Chinese, who lived predominantly in towns and *kampongs* (villages) along the low-lying coastal areas. The remainder consisted of indigenous tribes, including Iban and Punan, who inhabited the jungle-covered interior of the country, living mainly along the banks of the Brunei, Tutong and Belait rivers.

In 1929 oil was discovered in Brunei, resulting in the Sultan deriving a vast income as a result of a concession granted to the Shell Petroleum Company, making him possibly the wealthiest individual in the world. Little of this wealth was seen by the population, which suffered from a lack of health and education services, as well as from the inefficiency and corruption endemic among the ruling élite. This inevitably resulted in deep resentment, which eventually manifested itself in 1953 in a revolt that was suppressed without difficulty.

In 1962, under pressure from Britain, the Sultan made a half-hearted effort at introducing a façade of democracy by permitting elections for a legislative council. A limitation was placed on this, however, with the Sultan decreeing that only half the seats on the council would be contested, the remainder being filled by individuals nominated by him. The elections took place in September, with all the contested seats being won by the Partai Ra'ayat (People's Party) which proposed unification with Sarawak and North Borneo into a state sufficiently powerful to withstand domination by Malaya or Singapore, this being followed by federation with Malaysia. The Sultan, however, was opposed to any form of unification or federation, being reluctant to share his massive oil revenues.

The Partai Ra'ayat formed a military wing, the Tentera Nasional Kalimantan Utara (North Kalimantan Army), popularly known by its initials TNKU. This was led by A.M. Azahari, who had fought alongside the Indonesians against Dutch forces after their return in 1946 following the surrender of Japan and the arrival of Allied forces in Indonesia in the previous year. Through him, the TNKU enjoyed close links with the Sukarno regime in Indonesia, which provided training in guerrilla warfare for TNKU personnel, including their operational commander Yassan Affendi. By late 1962 it numbered approximately 4,000 men of whom only 2,250, however, were fully trained. Organised in fifteen companies of 150 men, they were poorly armed, possessing only a few military weapons, around 1,000 shotguns and large quantities of spears and *parangs*.

Initial signs of trouble appeared in April 1962, when a local newspaper reported that rebel groups were undergoing training in the jungle. This was ignored by the

Gurkhas of the 1st/2nd KEO Gurkha Rifles were the first to be deployed on the outbreak of the Brunei Rebellion in December 1962. The battalion was alerted at 11 p.m. on 7 December and the first company was air landed in Brunei, 900 miles away, at 9 a.m. the following day.

authorities. In early November, in neighbouring Sarawak, which was split into divisions for civil administration purposes, Richard Morris, the British Resident responsible for the Fifth Division, received information that trouble was brewing in Brunei. He informed the authorities in Sarawak's capital, Kuching, and an investigation was carried out by Special Branch, who found no evidence of any planned insurrection. On 23 November Morris received further information indicating that an uprising would take place in Brunei on 19 December. Once again, however, no firm evidence was available – but a warning was passed to the C-in-C Far East, Admiral Sir David Luce, who took the matter sufficiently seriously to order his Chief of Staff, Maj Gen Brian Wyldbore-Smith, to check contingency plans for counter-insurgency operations in Brunei.

On 6 December Richard Morris received a further report that the insurrection was to take place two days later. On the following day the British Resident in the Fourth

Division, John Fisher, was also informed that trouble was imminent and he alerted the authorities in Brunei. A detachment of the Sarawak Police Field Force (PFF) was deployed to the coastal town of Miri, approximately 20 miles west of the border with Brunei, while a detachment of the North Borneo PFF was flown from the capital of Jesselton to Brunei Town to reinforce the police there.

The insurrection began at 2 o'clock on the morning of 8 December with attacks taking place throughout Brunei. In the capital, Brunei Town, 300 rebels assaulted the Sultan's palace and the Prime Minister's residence. These were repulsed but the power station was captured by the rebels, who cut off all electricity. Meanwhile the TNKU was launching attacks on police stations in the towns of Tutong and Seria, and in the district of Temburong. At the same time it mounted others in the western region of North Borneo and in Sarawak's Fifth Division, where it succeeded in taking the main town of Limbang.

The first report of trouble reached HQ Far East Command in Singapore in the early hours of 8 December. Codenamed Ale, the contingency plan for deployment to Brunei called for a small tactical headquarters and two companies, supported by signals and engineer detachments, to be flown to Brunei Town, subsequent deployments being limited to the remainder of the battalion if so required. Shortly after receipt of the report, the Sultan requested British military assistance to put down the rebellion and Headquarters Far East Land Forces (FARELF) was instructed to put Ale into operation. The order was passed immediately to 17th Gurkha Division, commanded by Maj Gen Walter Walker and at 4 a.m. 99 Gurkha Infantry Brigade was ordered to place its stand-by unit, the 1st Battalion The Queen's Own Highlanders, on 48 hours' notice to deploy to Brunei. That battalion, however, was on exercise on the west coast of Malaysia, so the 1st/2nd KEO Gurkha Rifles, based at Slim Barracks in Singapore and commanded by Lt Col Gordon Shakespear, were placed on alert instead.

That afternoon a force comprising C and D Companies, together with a small command element under Maj Tony Lloyd Williams, took off from Singapore in three RAF Beverley transports, a Hastings and a Britannia. Fortunately the rebels had not seized control of the airfield, which was held by a force of police, and thus the three Beverleys carrying Lloyd Williams's tactical headquarters and C Company, the latter commanded by Maj Tony Lea, were able to land there unopposed. Meanwhile the Britannia and the Hastings carrying D Company, under Maj Bob Watterton, flew to the island of Labuan, the runway in Brunei being too short to accommodate them.

Lloyd Williams and his force landed at Brunei Town airfield during the evening of 8 December and advanced into the capital where they established themselves in the police station by 11 a.m. Thereafter, under cover of darkness, Maj Lea and two of his platoons headed west in vehicles commandeered from the local public works department towards the towns of Sengkurong, Tutong and ultimately Seria. They were to seize an airstrip at Anduki, to the east of Seria, and reinforce the police at the station at Panaga. En route they encountered rebels at a roadblock beyond Sengkurong, killing two of them before driving on to Tutong. As they entered Tutong, however, they came under fire from rebels in the town's police station. Returning the fire, Maj Lea and his men drove on but shortly afterwards came under heavy fire from rebels in positions in the upper storeys and on the roofs of buildings. The driver of the Land Rover in which Lea and his company headquarters were travelling was wounded and the vehicle went out of control, crashing into a ditch and overturning. Carrying the wounded Gurkha, along with a signaller who had also been hit, Lea and his company headquarters succeeded in taking cover in a market nearby, capturing a rebel in the process.

At dawn Lea's two platoons succeeded in making contact with him before beginning the process of clearing the rebels from the town. By the time they had completed the task, they had killed seven rebels, wounded twenty and captured approximately a hundred more. Their own casualties amounted to eight wounded.

During the night Maj Watterton arrived at Brunei Town with his company headquarters and two of his platoons, having been ferried by the RAF from Labuan to Brunei. Having landed, they advanced into the town, but on hearing the sound of firing they halted at one end of a government office building, not far from the police station, where Lloyd Williams had set up his headquarters. This firing was the result of an encounter between a patrol sent out by Lloyd Williams in response to a report of a sighting of a rebel in the area of the office building. Led by Lt David Stephens, the patrol had made its way down a road but came under fire from rebels positioned in the upper storeys of the office building and a post office nearby. Stephens was hit and seriously wounded, later dying of his wounds, as the rest of the patrol returned the rebels' fire. Meanwhile Gurkhas and police opened fire from the police station, from where half of the platoon immediately began running towards the north-east side of its perimeter to meet any attack from that direction. As they did so, however, they came under fire at a range of only 25 yards from a platoon-sized force of rebels, the Gurkha platoon commander and four of his men being wounded, one dying later of his wounds. The remainder nevertheless succeeded in reaching their positions and beating off the attack.

In the meantime Maj Watterton had been ordered by Lloyd Williams over the radio to attack the government office buildings from the rear. As one of his two platoons moved forward to do so, however, it came under fire from behind and was forced to change direction to meet this new threat. Shortly afterwards a group of men were observed some 200 yards away but it was impossible to identify them in the dark and D Company was forced to hold its fire.

At dawn on the following morning D Company attacked and cleared a number of buildings and the area around a hotel. Shortly afterwards its third platoon arrived from Labuan and searched the government offices, capturing four rebels. By 9 a.m. the whole of Brunei Town had been cleared and secured. Later that morning Lt Col Shakespear arrived with A Company, which was deployed immediately by air to secure an airfield and oilfield installations at Lutong, and further installations at Miri in Sarawak. That night several attempts by the rebels to infiltrate back into Brunei Town were foiled by the battalion.

In the early hours of 10 December the leading elements of the 1st Battalion The Queen's Own Highlanders, comprising the battalion's Tac HQ and A Company, the latter commanded by Maj Ian Cameron, flew from Singapore to the island of Labuan. There the Commanding Officer, Lt Col W.G. 'Charlie' McHardy, was briefed by Brig Jack Glennie, the Brigadier General Staff at HQ FARELF, who had been designated Force Commander. McHardy was given the task of dealing with rebels in the west of Brunei.

At 3.55 a.m. McHardy, his Tac HQ and A Company (less 2 Platoon which had been flown to Brunei Town on the previous evening) flew from Labuan in a Beverley transport to Brunei Town where they landed twenty minutes later, being met by 2 Platoon and members of Headquarter Company 1st/2nd KEO Gurkha Rifles. At 7 a.m. Brig Glennie arrived in a Twin Pioneer aircraft. Forty minutes later McHardy and Cameron, accompanied by the Commissioner of Police and two representatives of Brunei Shell Petroleum, carried out an aerial reconnaissance of Seria and Kuala Belait, the latter town being situated at the westernmost point of Brunei on the banks of the Sungei Belait. Following this, McHardy formulated his plans for two tactical airlanding operations at the western end of Seria and at the airstrip at Anduki.

At around noon a 90-strong force commanded by Capt Johnny Macdonald, comprising 40 men of A Company and a section of two 3-inch mortars, accompanied by Tac HQ and elements of Headquarter Company under the battalion's Adjutant, Capt Johnny Langlands, emplaned in a Beverley transport at Brunei Town airfield and shortly afterwards took off for Anduki. At the same time the remaining 60 men of A Company, under Maj Ian Cameron, emplaned in five Twin Pioneers of 209 Squadron RAF which headed for Seria. Also airborne was Lt Col McHardy in an Army Air Corps Beaver, being used as an airborne command post.

Some thirty minutes later the Beverley made a low-level approach from the sea and touched down less than a quarter of the way along the runway. No sooner had it halted than Capt Macdonald and his men deplaned at high speed and advanced on the airfield buildings. At a range of 250 yards 1 Platoon, commanded by 2nd Lt Donald Monro, came under fire from rebels, who also shot at the Beverley as it took off, hitting it but fortunately without causing any serious damage. The platoon put in an immediate attack on the airstrip buildings, clearing a group of rebels from the area of the control tower, before advancing on the Anduki police post at the entrance to the airfield where two rebels were killed and five captured. Shortly afterwards Lt Col McHardy, accompanied by the Commissioner of Police, landed in his Beaver.

Leaving Capt Langlands and Tac HQ to secure the airstrip and establish a roadblock on the road to Seria, Capt Macdonald and the rest of his force headed for Seria, advancing along the road towards the town to carry out their second task, the seizing of a bridge over the Sungei Bera approximately 1½ miles west of the airfield. As they did so they encountered nine rebels in two vehicles who were swiftly captured and disarmed. Shortly afterwards a Land Rover carrying a small group of armed rebels was observed heading at high speed towards 1 Platoon, which was nearing the bridge. On observing the troops, the vehicle's driver turned round and made off at speed, attempting to escape, but was brought to a halt by a well-aimed shot at one of its rear tyres. Three armed rebels jumped out and the platoon opened fire, hitting two of them, while the third escaped into the jungle. By 3.30 p.m. Macdonald's force had secured the bridge. Meanwhile members of Tac HQ had opened fire on a car that attempted to drive through their roadblock. The driver was killed.

In the meantime the rest of A Company had landed further west in its five Twin Pioneers. Although some of the aircraft became bogged down in the soft ground, the landing was completed successfully and at 3 p.m. Maj Cameron and his men reached the Panaga police station unseen by the rebels besieging it. Shortly afterwards, while establishing a roadblock, one of Cameron's two platoons came under fire from rebels in the local telecommunications centre. A section attack was mounted which resulted in two rebels throwing down their arms and surrendering. Throughout the rest of that afternoon fifteen rebels were captured, some being wounded in the process, along with a number of weapons and vehicles.

While this was going on B Company, commanded by Maj Neil Wimberley, had sailed at 8 p.m. on 9 December from Singapore to Labuan aboard a Royal Navy destroyer, HMS *Cavalier*. At first light on 10 December the company was flown from Labuan into Anduki from where it headed towards Seria. By midday, following some brushes with small groups of lightly armed rebels, it had reached the Shell Petroleum logistics area situated between the sea and the coastal road. Wimberley established his headquarters there along with the battalion's medium machine gun (MMG) platoon and a section of 3-inch mortars. The remainder of the company continued to head west, 6 Platoon leading the way with 5 Platoon in reserve. Shortly afterwards a rebel vehicle appeared and its driver was killed, several more rebels subsequently being captured. By 2 p.m. both platoons had linked up with A Company and the road between Anduki and Seria was clear.

At 9.30 a.m. on 11 December A Company was ordered to establish a roadblock in the area of the Royal Brunei Police mobile reserve unit barracks to the west of Seria, on the road to the town of Kuala Belait. Maj Cameron, with 2 Platoon and two sections of police, set off from the town in transport but en route encountered a vehicle which turned round and sped off. Debussing, the platoon, commanded by Lt Alastair McCall, followed up on foot. Reaching a roundabout, it continued westwards along the road to Kuala Belait but shortly afterwards a car appeared suddenly from the driveway of the Istana Kota Menggalela, the Sultan's country palace. The leading section opened fire on the vehicle, causing it to crash into a ditch, but almost immediately came under heavy fire from a force of rebels in the palace itself.

A fierce battle ensued, with the Highlanders skirmishing into the cover of jungle surrounding the grounds of the palace. Under covering fire from a section, Maj Cameron, Lt McCall and two soldiers succeeded in reaching the building and lobbing CS gas grenades through the ground-floor windows, McCall shooting dead an armed rebel at the same time. The rebels, however, stood their ground and thus the two

Gurkhas of 2 RGR on a jungle warfare exercise in Brunei.

officers, accompanied by a section, entered the palace and cleared the ground floor. As they moved upstairs the Highlanders encountered a rebel who surrendered. On entering the first room Cameron was confronted by five armed rebels who dropped their weapons as he fired a shot over their heads. The remainder of the palace was then cleared, a dead sniper being found in one of the rooms on the first floor. Eight rebels were captured during the action while five escaped, two being wounded as they did so. A search of the building uncovered a quantity of weapons, comprising a Bren gun, eight rifles and a Sten gun, together with a large amount of ammunition.

Having reorganised, 2 Platoon continued along the road towards the police mobile reserve unit barracks that lay approximately half a mile to the west of the palace. Two rebels were encountered during the advance, both being shot at and hit but escaping. Soon after the platoon reached the barracks a car approached and came under fire. The driver leaped out and, armed with a shotgun, began advancing on the platoon but was shot dead almost immediately. Having cleared the barracks, the platoon withdrew to the roundabout where it took up positions covering all three roads leading to it.

At midday B Company of the 1st/2nd KEO Gurkha Rifles, commanded by Maj Terry Bowring, was flown from Singapore into Anduki where it came under command of The Queen's Own Highlanders. Ordered by Lt Col McHardy to clear Kuala Belait, the company set off in Land Rovers at 1.15 p.m. in heavy rain, driving west through Seria, heading for the roundabout and the Highlanders' positions there. Pausing to consult the Managing Director of Brunei Shell Petroleum, P.M. Linton, who briefed Maj Bowring on the latest situation in Kuala Belait, the company drove on to the outskirts of the town where it debussed and began systematically clearing the town, encountering sporadic sniping as it did so.

Kuala Belait was held by a force of 800 rebels, whose main positions were in the town's government offices. Despite the size of the opposition, B Company succeeded in clearing the buildings by last light, being reinforced by The Queen's Own Highlanders' 5 Platoon, under 2nd Lt James Cassels, which occupied the police mobile reserve unit barracks.

At first light on the following morning, 12 December, having been joined by two Ferret scout cars of B Squadron The Queen's Royal Irish Hussars, B Company began to clear the rest of Kuala Belait. By 10 a.m. the police station had been secured and four European hostages released. During the two days of the operation, three rebels had been killed and seventeen captured, two of whom were wounded. Over the following five days a further twelve rebels were killed while attempting to cross the Sungei Belait under cover of darkness. Weapons and ammunition were recovered during searches of the town: 25 Lee Enfield No. 5 .303 jungle carbines, two shotguns, a .22 rifle, two pistols, two boxes of LMG magazines, some CS gas grenades, a quantity of .303 and 9mm ammunition and approximately 1,000 shotgun cartridges.

In the meantime Maj Wimberley and his company had mounted an operation to release a number of hostages being held in the police station at Seria by about fifty hard-core rebels, who had also established themselves in positions around some bungalows to the south of the station. At 8.30 a.m. on 12 December Wimberley conducted an aerial reconnaissance of the area. At 11.15 a.m. a force comprising 6 Platoon, the MMG Platoon and the mortar section set off and subsequently approached the police station from the west. Halting 200 yards short of the objective, 6 Platoon secured the area while the mortar section established two LMG positions on the roofs of a school and some flats nearby. The MMG Platoon, commanded by Lt Simon Taylor, then advanced on the police station, coming under fire at a range of 20 yards from rebels in a house some 50 yards from the station. Fire was returned and a small group of rebels was seen running between some houses, being engaged by the mortar section's LMGs.

At this juncture two RAF Hawker Hunter fighter-bombers arrived overhead and proceeded to 'beat up' the town while the MMG Platoon attacked the police station. One section moved into a position in a monsoon drain from which it covered the front of the station while another section and the platoon headquarters covered the crossroads outside. Meanwhile Lt Taylor and his third section succeeded in climbing over a 7ft-high wire fence at the rear and rushing the station building. Inside the Highlanders found the thirty hostages in the armoury and a further sixteen in one of the cells. In another room they found five rebels, two of whom had been wounded, a doctor and a female nurse.

Once the station had been cleared and occupied, 6 Platoon cleared the police barracks, encountering no rebels but finding a large quantity of rifles, shotguns and ammunition. It took another three hours before the buildings throughout the surrounding area had been cleared but by 3 p.m. B Company had accomplished all its allotted tasks.

Other British forces, meanwhile, were being deployed to Borneo, with overall command being exercised by Brig Glennie. 40 Commando RM was landed at Kuching, the state capital of Sarawak, from the commando carrier HMS *Albion*, while L Company of 42 Commando RM, under Capt Jeremy Moore, together with elements of Support Company, was despatched up the Sungei Limbang in two commandeered ramp cargo lighters (RCL) manned by Royal Navy personnel from the minesweepers HMS *Fiskerton* and *Chawton*, to the town of Limbang, in Sarawak's Fifth Division. Following a battle with the police, in which four policemen were killed and several wounded before being overrun, the town had been seized by a force of over 200 rebels. The latter had rounded up the eight Europeans living there, including the British Resident, Richard Morris, and his wife, and incarcerated them in the local jail, subsequently transferring them to the local hospital, which was converted into a detention centre. Comprising the hard-core element of the TNKU, this force was led by Salleh bin Sambas, a former constable in the Sarawak Police Force.

L Company reached Limbang at just after 6 a.m. on 12 December, coming under fire as the two RCLs approached a landing point some 30 yards upstream from the town's police station, which had been turned into a strongpoint by the rebels. In the leading

lighter two marines were killed and the coxswain wounded while in the second craft L Company's second-in-command and a sailor were wounded. Nevertheless Capt Moore and his force landed and, having rescued the hostages, proceeded to engage the rebels, eventually clearing them from the town – although sporadic sniping continued during the following 24 hours. L Company's casualties amounted to five dead and six wounded while rebel casualties numbered fifteen killed; subsequent reports indicated that a further twenty died of their wounds later.

In Sarawak's Fourth Division, meanwhile, on the morning of 12 December the 1st Battalion The Royal Green Jackets (1 RGJ), under Lt Col H.T. 'Todd' Sweeny, had landed, less A Company, at Miri from the cruiser HMS *Tiger*. Shortly afterwards B Company, commanded by Maj David Mostyn, was despatched in a landing craft belonging to the Shell Petroleum Company to a point further down the coast where two platoons were landed,

A rifleman of The Royal Gurkha Rifles shown here wearing the famous Gurkha hat.

thereafter marching overland to the town of Bekenu, on the Sungei Sibuti, which was being held by the TNKU. The third platoon was transferred to a launch in which it travelled up the Sibuti. By dawn on 13 December the two platoons had reached the town and at around 9.45 a.m. came under fire. During the ensuing action six rebels were killed and five taken prisoner, The Royal Green Jackets suffering no casualties. The remainder of the rebels escaped but two platoons pursued them upriver in the launch, capturing eight of them and releasing a hostage.

C Company, commanded by Maj Mark Pennell, meanwhile travelled a further 20 miles down the Sarawak coast to Niah, where it arrived at 6 p.m. on the 12th.

(*Opposite*): A QGO and soldiers of 2 RGR shown here in Brunei, wearing the tropical No. 6 Dress.

There it found an irregular force of local tribesmen, armed with shotguns, ready to defend the town against the TNKU. During the following days thousands of Iban, Kenyah and Kayan tribesmen in the Fourth Division answered the call of the British Resident, John Fisher, and appeared at Marudi, where they were issued with 12-gauge buckshot ammunition and deployed along the border with western Brunei to prevent the rebels infiltrating into Sarawak. Eventually they grew to a force of over 2,000, which was placed under the command of Tom Harrisson, the well-known curator of the Sarawak Museum, who, during the Second World War, had served with Force 136, the Asian and Far East arm of the Special Operations Executive, leading a large force of tribesmen against the Japanese forces occupying Borneo. Harrisson Force, as it was dubbed, blocked all the suspected rebel escape routes and during the following weeks captured about a hundred rebels along with quantities of arms and ammunition.

Within a week of the beginning of the rebellion, the British forces in Brunei and Sarawak had restored control. On the night of 13 December a large group of rebels attempted to infiltrate into the town of Tutong which, along with Brunei Town and Muara, was held by the 1st/2nd KEO Gurkha Rifles. The battalion mounted a successful ambush and accounted for twenty-six rebels, the remainder making good their escape. Meanwhile, in the areas of Limbang and Temburong, 42 Commando had established bases in kampongs along the Panduran, Temburong and Batu Apoi rivers, which were patrolled by troops in boats who enforced a ban on all movement by river.

On 20 December the Sultan suspended Brunei's constitution and declared a state of emergency, dissolving the Legislative Council and replacing it with a 14-member Emergency Council. Headed by himself, this comprised ten individuals nominated by him and four ex-officio members, among them the British High Commissioner. By this time forty rebels had been killed and approximately 1,900 arrested and detained. An estimated 1,500 TNKU supporters, who were considered unlikely to pose a serious threat, had been permitted to return to their homes. Among the security forces the total number of casualties were seven killed and twenty-eight wounded.

CHAPTER 7

THE BORNEO CONFRONTATION

Although the rebellion in Brunei had been suppressed, there was anxiety that insurrection might occur in neighbouring Sarawak and North Borneo and precautionary measures were taken to counter it. In western Sarawak the leaders of the Chinese Communist Organisation (CCO), a body which had not taken part in the rebellion but was considered to be a major threat, were detained and a pro-communist newspaper was closed down. In North Borneo police had received indications of possible unrest among the 30,000 Indonesians who formed part of its population and thus B Company of the 1st/2nd KEO Gurkha Rifles was flown from Brunei to Tawau on 17 December.

If President Sukarno had been harbouring hopes for a rapid British withdrawal following the end of the rebellion, these were swiftly dashed. On 19 December Maj Gen Walter Walker, the commander of 17th Gurkha Division, flew from Malaysia to Brunei to take up the appointments of Commander British Forces and Director of Operations in Borneo. He lost no time in implementing measures to round up all remaining elements of the TNKU by the end of August 1963, September having been set as the date for the creation of the Federation of Malaysia.

By the third week of January 1963 British forces in Borneo comprised 99 Gurkha Infantry Brigade, commanded by Brig A.G. 'Pat' Patterson and consisting of the 1st/2nd KEO Gurkha Rifles (subsequently relieved in early February by the 1st/7th), the 1st Battalion The Queen's Own Highlanders (less one company) and the 1st Battalion The Royal Green Jackets; 40 and 42 Commandos RM (the latter less one company) were allocated responsibility for Brunei and Eastern Sarawak. In Western Sarawak Lt Col John Strawson, the Commanding Officer of The Queen's Royal Irish Hussars (QRIH), was responsible for the security of the First, Second and Third Divisions, having under his command C Squadron QRIH, his own Regimental Tac HQ and elements of Headquarter Squadron, B Company 40 Commando, A Squadron 22 SAS and two Auster light aircraft. North Borneo, meanwhile, was garrisoned by a company of The Queen's Own Highlanders based at Tawau and a half-squadron of B Squadron QRIH of which elements were also in Brunei. In addition to these units were local security forces, including The Royal Brunei Malay Regiment, The Sarawak Rangers and elements of The Royal Malay Regiment, the police constabularies of each territory and Tom Harrisson's irregular force of tribesmen.

Following the failure of the rebellion, the TNKU split up into small groups. Walker nevertheless was convinced that Sukarno had far from given up and was well aware that the CCO also posed a major threat, having been expanding its influence and numbers so that by 1963 it comprised 1,000 hard-core activists with a further 3,500 available. Approximately 1,000 had received training from the Indonesian Army, carried out over the border in Kalimantan. Moreover the organisation could call on some 25,000 supporters. It was due to Walker's concern that 300 of its leading members had been arrested.

In April a new enemy appeared in the form of a force of irregulars known as Indonesian Border Terrorists (IBT). Comprising approximately 1,500 men supported by regular troops, they were organised in eight units deployed along the 1,000-mile-long border with Sarawak and North Borneo. Six of these were tasked with carrying out raids into Sarawak's First and Second Divisions, while the other two were targeted on the Fifth Division and North Borneo.

On 12 April a 30-strong force of IBT crossed from Kalimantan into the First Division and attacked a police post at Tebedu, situated 2 miles north of the border and some 20 miles east of Padawan. The Indonesians succeeded in taking the police detachment by surprise, having penetrated the perimeter fence by crawling through a culvert that led underneath it. A police corporal was killed and two constables wounded in the brief battle that followed, before the raiders turned their attention to the local bazaar, which they looted before withdrawing to the border.

The short distance from the village to the border meant that there was no time for the security forces to intercept the raiders before they reached it. Nevertheless two troops of C Squadron QRIH and a troop of B Company 40 Commando were despatched to Tebedu immediately, the latter occupying and fortifying the police station. Meanwhile Maj Gen Walker despatched his only reserve, B Company 1st Battalion The King's Own Yorkshire Light Infantry (KOYLI), from Brunei to Sarawak, along with six Whirlwind helicopters of the Fleet Air Arm's 846 Naval Air Squadron.

During the immediate aftermath of the raid the local people provided information about Indonesian units of approximately company strength located at three points along the border in the area. Although documents had been deliberately left behind by the raiders, to give the impression that Indonesian irregulars had carried out the attack, it later transpired that regular troops were responsible.

On 23 April, in the early hours, fifteen IBT attacked a police post at Gumbang in the First Division of Sarawak, only 200 yards inside the border with Kalimantan. The police detachment, however, had been reinforced with a half-section of C Company 40 Commando who returned the raiders' fire, killing two of them and wounding three. Once again the IBT left behind documents, on this occasion indicating that the raid had been carried out by the TNKU.

Another incursion took place on the night of 27 April when three IBT opened fire on the police post at Tebedu with an LMG and a shotgun. Once more, however, the police had been reinforced by marines of 40 Commando, who followed up after the raiders

L/Cpl Rambahadur Limbu VC leading a patrol of the 2nd/10th PMO Gurkha Rifles during operations in Borneo.

withdrew but lost the trail, despite the assistance of tracker dogs flown in by helicopter.

The following three weeks passed without incident but on 17 May the Indonesians struck again. On this occasion a force of thirteen IBT attacked a civilian target in the form of two boats owned by traders at Nangga San, a riverside village in the Second Division. Opening fire on the boats with automatic weapons and forcing their occupants to dive into the river, the raiders then looted both craft before absconding into the nearby jungle.

At that time the Second Division was the responsibility of the 2nd Battalion 10th PMO Gurkha Rifles, commanded by Lt Col Jim Fillingham, which had deployed a small tactical headquarters and two companies there, the remainder of the battalion being in the Third Division. Following the attack at Nangga San, the 2nd/10th was concentrated in the Second Division while the Third Division was handed over to the

1st/10th. Thereafter Lt Col Fillingham redeployed his battalion in such a manner that its companies covered virtually every track and known crossing place along the 120 miles of the border in the Second Division.

On 18 May in Brunei the 2nd/7th DEO Gurkha Rifles, commanded by Lt Col A.N. 'Knott' Seagrim, scored a success following its arrests a month earlier of two of the leaders of the TNKU, Sheikh Osman and Sheikh Salleh, the latter the brother of the organisation's leader, Azahari. These arrests had been followed on 17 May by that of a TNKU supporter who admitted under questioning by Special Branch that he had been taking food to a small group of rebels hiding in a large area of mangrove swamp, some 2,000 yards long by 800 yards wide, on the north bank of the Sungei Brunei near the village of Kampong Serdang.

The task of attacking the TNKU camp was given to B Company, under Maj David Cutfield. Based on an island in the estuary of the Sungei Brunei, the company had been tasked with denying use of the river to rebels and hunting down those groups reportedly hiding in the mangrove swamps. Shortly after first light on 18 May, accompanied by two Special Branch officers and the TNKU supporter acting as a guide, Cutfield and his company embarked in assault boats and headed into the mouth of the Sungei Brunei, making their way to the edge of the swamp. While 5 and 6 Platoons disembarked at the Kampong Serdang and north-eastern ends of the swamp respectively to establish cut-off groups, Cutfield and ten Gurkhas, along with the two Special Branch officers and the guide, entered the swamp in locally commandeered canoes. After a while they were forced to abandon them because of the shallow depth of the water and thereafter had to continue on foot, wading through deep mud. After one and a half hours, however, they had made little progress as the guide had lost his bearings. Making their way back to the river, Maj Cutfield and his group headed for Kampong Serdang, where more canoes were commandeered. Once again they entered the swamp, this time travelling up a small stream. After approximately an hour and a quarter they disembarked and went forward on foot for some 75 yards.

Spotting movement, Maj Cutfield opened fire, while one of the Special Branch officers called on the rebels to surrender. One rebel, Abdullah bin Jaffah, the TNKU's commander in that area, did so. But his companions had escaped, splitting up into two groups of four and five men who headed north and west respectively. Shortly afterwards the group heading north encountered Rifleman Nainabahadur Rai who was in a position by himself in a patch of overgrown rubber, some 100 yards from the next Gurkha in his cut-off group. The leading rebel, who was armed with a pistol, spotted Nainabahadur at a range of 30 yards and the entire group charged straight at him. At a range of just 15 yards he opened fire, killing the leading two men with a single bullet which passed through both bodies. The other two rebels took cover but Nainabahadur engaged and wounded both, taking them prisoner immediately afterwards. The two dead were both senior officials of the Partai Ra'ayat, while one of the two wounded was none other than the TNKU's overall commander, Yassan Affendi. Rifleman Rai was subsequently awarded the Military Medal for his part in this action.

Shortly afterwards the five rebels who had headed west were discovered and captured. One of them was Salleh bin Sambang, who had commanded the rebel force that opposed the landing of L Company 42 Commando at Limbang. On the following day another rebel surrendered himself to the security forces.

At the end of the first week of June a group of 54 young Chinese men was intercepted and arrested in the jungle while awaiting the arrival of a guide who was to lead them over the border. During this period it was estimated that some 650 Chinese, all members of the CCO, left Sarawak for Kalimantan. A large number reportedly underwent training in Sumatra, at a camp at Tanjong Sekupang, where they were initiated by Indonesian Army instructors into the skills of guerrilla warfare, subversion and sabotage. The latter included methods of blowing up bridges, railway lines, power stations, reservoirs and other similar types of target.

In addition to mainland Malaya, Singapore was also a principal target and the camp at Tanjong Sekupang was one of a number of bases established on Sumatra and the Rhio Islands from which attacks were launched. Agents were infiltrated into Singapore with orders to create terror and chaos through the use of bombings targeted on public utilities and areas where large numbers were gathered. In Malaya, meanwhile, other agents were tasked with encouraging Malay political parties to adopt repressive measures against the Chinese population.

Towards the end of June the 2nd/10th PMO Gurkha Rifles received information that a group of IBT had arrived at Mawang, a village in the border area opposite the Second Division. The battalion deployed cut-off groups by helicopter while setting off in pursuit of the raiders, who were intercepted, three being killed and two wounded. A few days later a 2nd/10th patrol ambushed further members of the group, killing one and capturing his Sten gun.

During August the Indonesians launched further attacks on the police post at the village of Gumbang, where a section of 42 Commando under Sgt Alastair Mackie and a section of Border Scouts were based. The first attack took place during the early hours of 17 August, with others following on the nights of the 21st and 22nd, all of which were beaten off without difficulty. On the 23rd, however, the Indonesians prepared to mount an attack with a strong force of 60 irregulars led by regular troops. On this occasion, however, Sgt Mackie and his section ambushed the raiders before they could reach the post and the latter withdrew after abandoning their mission.

Meanwhile a 60-strong force had crossed into the Third Division in mid-August and headed northwards along the Sungei Rajang in the direction of Song, which was its objective. News of this incursion was passed to the 2nd Battalion 6th QEO Gurkha Rifles, commanded by Lt Col E.T. 'Slim' Horsford, which on 16 August despatched a patrol from C Company under Lt Hugh Wallace to follow up. Having tracked the raiders downriver, Wallace and his men encountered them near a village and an engagement took place in which six raiders were killed. While carrying out a flanking move in this action, Wallace was wounded in the knee and was unable to walk. His Gurkha orderly remained with him, but he ordered the rest of his patrol to carry on.

At last light, however, he instructed his orderly to return to the C Company base to fetch help. The latter succeeded in reaching the base by first light on the following day and a patrol was despatched to rescue Wallace. By the time it reached his position, however, he was dead; during the night the Indonesians had located his position and, despite his putting up a stout resistance, had killed him.

The 2nd/6th reacted swiftly by deploying a platoon on the following day by helicopter to a cut-off position along the raiders' suspected route. Almost immediately the platoon made contact with the Indonesians, killing three of them. In the meantime the security forces were receiving information about the remainder of the force, 39 of whom were travelling downriver into the eastern area of the Third Division.

At this juncture the 1st/2nd KEO Gurkha Rifles, commanded by Lt Col Johnny Clements, took over responsibility for the Third Division, while the 2nd/6th moved to the Fifth Division. Towards the end of the month Clements received information that some of the raiders were moving up the Sungei Angkuah. Two platoons were already in the area and these set off in pursuit. Some 48 hours later, on 2 September, while moving up the riverbed, the leading platoon was spotted by the enemy, who opened fire at a range of about 400 yards. A fierce battle ensued, which resulted in one Indonesian being killed and a quantity of weapons and equipment being subsequently captured. Shortly afterwards a platoon of C Company, commanded by Lt (QGO) Lalitbahadur Gurung, encountered a group of the raiders, who opened fire and wounded a Gurkha. During the ensuing action, which took place at close quarters, five more enemy were killed.

On the following day it was D Company's turn when its second in command, Capt (QGO) Aitasing Gurung killed two of the raiders, one of them the commander of the force. On the next day an Indonesian was killed by an Iban tribesman and two weeks later another was captured. Capt Aitasing and Lt Lalitbahadur were both awarded the Military Cross for their performances in these actions.

The area that Walker had to defend was equivalent to the combined size of England and Scotland but the forces available to him were pathetically inadequate. His infantry comprised five battalions and Royal Marine commandos, one of which, the 1st Battalion The Royal Leicestershire Regiment, had been sent with two others from Hong Kong to assist in suppressing the rebellion in Brunei and had remained after the others had returned. Added to these was a squadron of the QRIH and an SAS squadron in Western Sarawak, where Headquarters 3 Commando Brigade, under Brig F.C. 'Billy' Barton RM, had assumed responsibility for security following the Tebedu raid in April, and a further half-squadron of the QRIH in North Borneo/Brunei. In addition to the lack of troops, a further handicap at this early stage of the conflict in Borneo was the limited amount of tactical air-mobility for the infantry and SAS, this being provided by approximately a dozen troop-carrying helicopters.

The limited size of his forces meant that Walker had to rely heavily on intelligence, which was supplied by an overstretched Special Branch and the SAS squadron – whose 16 four-man patrols were deployed along the 1,000-mile-long border, their operations being controlled by a forward regimental headquarters located initially in Brunei and thereafter with Walker's headquarters on the island of Labuan. There was a limit, however, to the area of ground that they could cover; thus, the British Resident in the Fourth Division, John Fisher, who was also Maj Gen Walker's brother-in-law, had conceived the idea of raising a force of indigenous tribesmen who would act as 'a thousand pairs of eyes and ears'.

Formed in early 1963, and initially numbering 300, the new force was called the Border Scouts. Trained by the SAS and the Gurkha Independent Parachute Company, the tribesmen were organised into sections commanded by Gurkhas. Initially the experiment was not a success owing to the recruitment of a large number of unsuitable candidates, who were then given the wrong type of training. Problems had arisen with the Scouts, but these were eventually resolved by Maj John Cross of the 7th DEO Gurkha Rifles, who was appointed Commandant of the force in late July 1963. Ridding it of unsuitable elements and implementing a retraining programme tailored for the intelligence-gathering role, he succeeded within seven months in rebuilding the Scouts, who ultimately numbered approximately 3,000.

On 16 September the Federation of Malaysia came into existence, comprising the eleven states of Malaya, the two Borneo states of Sarawak and North Borneo (the latter renamed Sabah), the island of Labuan, the federal territory of Wilayah Persekutuan, in which the capital Kuala Lumpur is located, and Singapore. Brunei continued to refuse to join the federation and subsequently Singapore left it after only two years of membership. Indonesia's reaction to the establishment of Malaysia was furious and violent, manifesting itself in the expulsion of the Malaysian ambassador and the sacking and burning of the British embassy. Ten days later the Indonesians launched a major incursion into Sarawak.

On the night of 26 September a raiding force between 150 and 200 strong, comprising IBT reinforced by a number of regular troops, crossed the border into the Third Division and headed down the Sungei Balui in longboats towards the isolated village of Long Jawi. The raiding force was commanded by a major named Muljono, an experienced guerrilla who had seen service against the Japanese in the Second World War and against the Dutch during the post-war period, and who had undergone training overseas, including a course at the British Army's own Jungle Warfare School at Kota Tinggi in Malaya.

Situated on the banks of the upper reaches of the Rajang River, Long Jawi lay some 30 miles from the border in Sarawak's Third Division. A large proportion of its population of approximately 500, predominantly Kenyan and Kayan tribespeople, originally hailed from Long Nawang, a large village just across the border in Kalimantan, and a considerable amount of trade was conducted between the two villages.

At Long Jawi there was a small Border Scout post manned by four Gurkhas (two junior NCOs and two riflemen, one of them a signaller), two PFF radio operators and twenty-one Border Scouts. The four Gurkhas were provided by the 1st/2nd KEO

Gurkha Rifles whose headquarters and A Company were located at Sibu, approximately 180 to 200 miles to the west. The battalion's other three rifle companies were well dispersed, with B Company at Sarike and Binatang, C Company at Kapit and D Company at Song. The battalion had 150 Border Scouts under command, their headquarters being at Belaga which lay some 70 miles to the north-west of Long Jawi. At Long Linau, between Belaga and Long Jawi, there was another Border Scout outpost. Communications between Belaga and its posts, frequently tenuous owing to the terrain and varying atmospheric conditions, were maintained by HF radio using carrier wave (morse) only.

The occupants of the village possessed little knowledge of the world outside the border area around them, and had no interest in the concept of Malaysia. Uncooperative in their attitude towards the small garrison, they had been reluctant to provide materials or labour for constructing defences. As a result the outpost's headquarters and signal centre was located in a school hut beside the longhouse instead of being sited to the east on a hill dominating the village.

On 25 September Capt John Burlison of the 1st/2nd arrived at Long Jawi with an escort and Cpl Tejbahadur Gurung, who was to relieve the NCO in command of the outpost, accompanied by two riflemen with an LMG to bolster the post's strength and firepower. Dismayed at finding the headquarters and signal centre in the school hut, Burlison persuaded the villagers to provide the necessary assistance to relocate them on the hill to the east and to prepare the necessary defensive positions there. By the time he left two days later, five trenches had been finished and a bunker for the signallers was almost completed. Problems were experienced, however, in re-erecting the radio antennae and thus the signallers and their sets could not move to the hill until new masts, fashioned from wood, had been cut and placed into position.

Unknown to Burlison, he and his escort were not the only visitors to Long Jawi during their two-day stay. Hiding in the village was a reconnaissance group from the Indonesian raiding force, which had been concealed by the villagers in the longhouse. Early on the morning of 28 September one of the Border Scouts left the new position on the hill and returned to the longhouse to visit his wife who was ill. On the way, however, he spotted the reconnaissance group, which by this time had been joined by the main body of the raiding force. Slipping away unseen, the scout returned to the hill and warned Cpl Tejbahadur that an attack was imminent. The latter quickly made his way to the school hut and warned the two PFF radio operators and his own signaller, who immediately began attempting to contact their respective headquarters. As they did so, Tejbahadur returned to his position, taking with him a case of No. 36 grenades.

No sooner had he reached the top of the hill than it came under fire from automatic weapons and 60mm light mortars positioned on an area of flat ground to the west of the village. Meanwhile, in the village below the hill, the three radio operators were frantically attempting to make contact when the school hut was raked with automatic fire. The Gurkha signaller, Rifleman Chandrabahadur Gurung, and one of the PFF operators were killed immediately but the remaining policeman, despite being wounded badly in the leg, succeeded in escaping and dragged himself to the position on the hill under covering fire from the Gurkhas and Border Scouts. After a while, however, the latter lost their stomach for a fight and slipped away down the blind side of the hill towards a stream to the south. Their attempt at escape failed, however, as they were intercepted by the Indonesians, who disarmed all but one of them and tied them up. The remaining Scout lost little time in heading back to the hill and the relative safety of its defensive positions.

During the following two hours Cpl Tejbahadur and his remaining four men put up a fierce resistance against overwhelming odds, with their LMG gunner, Rifleman Amarbahadur Thapa, engaging four enemy machine-guns to good effect. The Gurkhas did, however, suffer casualties: Rifleman Dhanbahadur Gurung was killed by a mortar bomb which exploded in a tree directly above him while Rifleman Kharkabahadur Gurung was wounded in the thigh by a bullet from a machine-gun. This left only Cpl Tejbahadur, Rifleman Belbahadur Gurung, Rifleman Amarbahadur Thapa and the Border Scout unwounded and fit to continue fighting.

By around 8 a.m., however, Tejbahadur and his men were down to a few rounds of ammunition each and he realised that there was no alternative but to abandon the post. Unseen by the enemy, who had suffered a number of casualties and were no longer pressing home their attacks with such vigour, they succeeded in withdrawing down the hill, dragging the wounded Rifleman Kharkabahadur with them. Crossing the stream to the south of the hill, they reached the cover of thick jungle and made their painful way to the top of another hill from where, an hour later, they were able to observe the enemy attacking the abandoned post.

The group remained on the hill throughout that night, during which it poured with rain. On the following morning Cpl Tejbahadur realised that his first priority was to reach the Border Scout outpost at Long Linau to raise the alarm. To do so, however, he would have to leave Rifleman Kharkabahadur behind. Having redressed the latter's wounds and ensured that he was well hidden in the thick jungle, Tejbahadur and his two remaining riflemen set off for Long Linau with the Border Scout leading the way.

Two days later they reached the village of Kampong Labuai – from where, on the following morning, they set off downriver to Long Linau, where they found that a Border Scout from Long Jawi, one of a small number who escaped from the Indonesians during the battle, had already arrived there and sounded the alarm. Without further ado Cpl Tejbahadur and his companions set off for the Border Scout headquarters at Belaga, where they arrived on the following day and gave a full report on the action at Long Jawi.

The Commandant of the 1st/2nd KEO Gurkha Rifles, Lt Col Clements, deployed Maj John Mole and a platoon of C Company to Long Jawi in three helicopters while working out the most likely withdrawal route to be taken by the raiders. A report from one of the Border Scouts who had escaped from the Indonesians indicated that the raiders had established a base camp 5 miles upriver from Long Jawi. By the time Mole

(*Overleaf*): Gurkhas being landed by a Royal Navy Wessex 3 helicopter during operations in Borneo.

and his platoon arrived at Long Jawi, Maj Muljono and his force had returned upstream to this camp.

On their arrival at Long Jawi Mole and his men found the village deserted and looted. Meanwhile Rifleman Kharkabahadur, still alive despite the ordeal of surviving several days alone in the jungle, observed the arrival of the helicopters bringing in the platoon. Leaving his hiding place, he crawled down the hill towards the village, being shot at by his fellow Gurkhas (who fortunately missed their target) until they recognised him.

On 1 October Clements deployed two more platoons of C Company by helicopter into ambush locations near Batang Balui, upriver of Long Jawi, on the Indonesians' most likely withdrawal route. Soon after being inserted, 11 Platoon, commanded by Lt (QGO) Pasbahadur Gurung, heard the sound of outboard engines and established an immediate ambush on the riverbank. Shortly afterwards two longboats, carrying twenty-six fully armed Indonesians, came into view. Waiting until they were at point-blank range, the platoon opened fire as the leading boat reached the upstream end of the killing area. One boat sank almost immediately while the other foundered on rocks on the far side of the river.

Few of the enemy survived the ambush but the strength of the current precluded any attempts to cross the river and search the stranded boat until the following day, when the Adjutant, Capt Digby Willoughby, flew in by helicopter and succeeded in crossing the river with the aid of toggle ropes. In the boat he found one dead Indonesian, a 60mm light mortar, a large quantity of mortar and small arms ammunition, and supplies of food and equipment looted from Long Jawi – which included the two radio sets from the signal hut.

In the meantime, acting on information provided by another Border Scout who had escaped from the Indonesians, Clements had deduced that Muljono's base camp was almost certainly on the far side of the Jalangai River, which flows into the Rajang 5 miles upstream of Long Jawi. Accordingly the platoon at Long Jawi was ordered to make its way to the area of the suspected enemy camp. Having crossed to the northern bank of the Rajan, Maj Mole and his men set off eastwards with a Border Scout named Bit Epa, one of those who had escaped from the Indonesians, leading the way. The terrain was very difficult, the platoon having to climb and descend a seemingly endless series of steep ridgelines, the going made all the more arduous by heavy rain. Having reached the Balui River, which also flows into the Rajang, the platoon was unable to find a crossing point and had to be ferried across by two helicopters. At this juncture Maj Mole was lifted out, suffering from exhaustion, and Capt Digby Willoughby assumed command of the operation.

The platoon reached the Sungei Jalangai on 12 October and shortly afterwards located the Indonesian camp on the far bank of the river. The depth of the water and the strength of the current, however, were such that it would have been impossible for fully equipped men to cross and so Willoughby and Bit Epa, dressed only in their underclothes and armed with knives, swam across, with the platoon in positions ready to give covering fire. On reaching the far bank Willoughby and his companion found the enemy camp deserted except for the decomposed bodies of the captured Border Scouts, who had subsequently been murdered. Nearby Willoughby also discovered a number of graves of Indonesians killed during the action at Long Jawi.

Shortly afterwards the platoon was ferried across the river in three longboats found near the enemy camp. Unfortunately one of these overturned, dumping its load of Gurkhas into the river. One man, Rifleman Bhimbahadur Thapa, drowned and a number of weapons were lost, although these were recovered soon afterwards by the Border Scout who dived several times to the river bed. Sadly Bhimbahadur's body was never found.

A week later the platoon was extracted and replaced by another, commanded by Capt (GCO) Narbu Lama, which continued the search along the Balui River. Meanwhile two more platoons had been deployed at the uppermost reaches of the Balui and the Aput. Three days later, however, it was realised that the platoon on the latter had been inserted in the wrong location, 5 miles down the Kliong River, a tributary of the Aput. Five helicopters were despatched to extract the platoon and reinsert it in the correct location, a task made difficult by the height of the trees, the small size of the landing zone and the depth of the valley in which it was situated.

Hovering over the area the five aircraft were spotted by a group of Indonesians, who despatched a three-man team armed with a Browning .50 heavy machine-gun to a position from which it could engage the helicopters. Half an hour earlier, however, another platoon of the 1st/2nd had been inserted at the junction of the Kliong and the Aput, where it laid an ambush. The three Indonesians entered the killing area, one man being shot dead; the other two were wounded but succeeded in escaping.

By the end of October it was apparent that the rest of Muljono's raiding force had escaped back across the border into Kalimantan, albeit a number were believed to have died in the jungle. The raid on Long Jawi, and in particular the murders of the Border Scouts, coupled with the swift and effective response by the 1st/2nd KEO Gurkha Rifles, resulted in the local population thereafter allying themselves firmly with the security forces and it was some time before the Indonesians appeared in the area again.

Following the raid on Long Jawi there were no major incursions during the following few months. It soon became apparent, however, that the Indonesians were switching their attention to Sabah and in particular the Tawau Residency, one of the most prosperous areas throughout Sawarak and Sabah. The inland areas of the Residency comprised estates devoted to the production of tea, rubber, cocoa, palm oil and hemp. A large timber logging centre was situated at Kalabakan, some 40 miles to the north-west of Tawau, with logging camps to the north of Kalabakan at Wellawatta, Mawan and Brantian, and another newly established on the Umas Umas River between Kalabakan and Tawau. All these camps were interconnected by a network of gravelled roads.

The area around Tawau itself comprised mangrove swamps and tidal rivers, which flowed into Cowie Harbour, at the eastern end of which lay Tawau. Across the harbour lay the island of Sebatik, the northern half of which belonged to Malaysia and the southern to Indonesia. At Wallace Bay, at the northern end of the island, was a major logging station only 4 miles from the border with Kalimantan.

The area to the north of Kalabakan comprises steep jungle-clad hills covered mainly with primary jungle, the remainder consisting of mangrove swamps or areas of secondary jungle. This was terrain cleared during logging that had become overgrown with thick undergrowth, almost impenetrable in places. Other than on the estates, the area was thinly inhabited with the majority of the population being concentrated near the rivers, the Serudong featuring two large villages at Serudong Laut and Serudong Ulu.

By October 1963 the Indonesians had established a number of training camps in East Kalimantan, with instruction being provided by army and KKO personnel. In mid-December 1963 a force of 128 IBT and 35 KKO crossed the border in four detachments and made their way via Serudong to a logging camp near Kalibakan which they reached on 28 December.

In addition to elements of Sabah's police force, the security forces in the Tawau Residency, under command of East Brigade, comprised the 3rd Battalion The Royal Malay Regiment (3 RMR), a company of The KOYLI and a detachment and four Ferret scout cars of the 2nd Federation Reconnaissance Regiment. The Royal Navy was also present in the form of a frigate based off Tawau on anti-piracy operations. Kalabakan featured a heavily fortified police post, manned by fifteen men of the PFF. Some 400 yards away on a ridge was a military outpost comprising two huts surrounded by trenches and occupied by a platoon and two sections of C Company 3 RMR. These two posts were the objectives of the Indonesian raiding force.

Following last light on 29 December the Indonesians moved into positions in two groups, the first moving along high ground to the north and down the ridge towards the 3 RMR outpost while the second moved to a position to the north of the police post. At 8.55 p.m. the first group launched its attack, throwing grenades into the 3 RMR positions and then subjecting them to very heavy fire which killed eight men, including the commander of C Company, and wounded nineteen. Ten minutes later the second group attacked the police post and a battle ensued, during which the attackers were repulsed, losing one man killed and four wounded. After two hours the raiders withdrew and headed north, press-ganging three local inhabitants to guide them to Brantian which lay some 10 miles to the north-east.

On 2 January 1964 the 1st/10th PMO Gurkha Rifles, commanded by Lt Col E.J.S. 'Bunny' Burnett, received orders to deploy to Tawau. By the following morning Burnett himself had arrived at Kalabakan, being joined there by last light on 4 January by B and C Companies. Acting on information received from a KOYLI patrol, which had discovered a camp recently used by a force of between twenty and thirty men who had headed north, he despatched a platoon to relieve a 3 RMR platoon at Brantian, where it was joined by a platoon of the KOYLI company. In the meantime steps were taken to deny all sources of food to the raiders, with villages being cleared of their occupants and their possessions.

Having decided that the first area in which they were likely to encounter the raiders was the triangular zone formed by Kalabakan, Mawang and Brantian, the 1st/10th deployed ambushes on the road between Wellawatta and Mawang, and then along the road to Brantian. These measures proved successful and a number of contacts took place which resulted in fifteen enemy killed and six captured by 17 January. Three of the four Indonesian detachments thereafter began heading back towards Kalimantan, two of them heading west for the Serudong River. The 1st/10th, however, deployed a company to the area of the Silimpopon River and another to the Serudong to cut them off. In the meantime the fourth detachment, 31-strong and commanded by an individual named Lasani, was heading for the Umas Umas.

By the end of February 96 of the 128-strong force had been killed or taken prisoner. A further 20 were known to have succeeded in reaching Kalimantan, while a further 12 remained unaccounted for inside Sabah. Of the 35 KKO marines that had accompanied the IBT, 21 had been either killed or captured, providing firm evidence of the involvement of Indonesian regular forces.

January 1964 saw the Indonesians continuing their efforts to carry out subversion and create unrest in Sarawak. Early in the month a group of fourteen, comprising an Indonesian sergeant and thirteen Malaysian communists from Sarawak, arrived at the estuary of the Rajang River with the task of arming and training members of two local communist organisations, the Borneo Communist Party (BCP) and the Barisan Pemuda Sarawak (BPS). It was not long, however, before news of the group's presence reached the ears of Special Branch and an operation was launched to round it up. The task of doing so was given to A Company 1st/7th DEO Gurkha Rifles, commanded by Maj Dennis O'Leary and based at Sarikei.

Warned that their presence had been detected, the Indonesian NCO divided his group into three: one seven-strong element hid on an island in a tributary of the Rajang while the other two headed upstream. It was not long, however, before the men on the island were discovered and on the afternoon of 7 January two platoons of A Company were landed on the western side under covering fire from Company Headquarters, which was embarked on a large launch, the *Jolly Bachelor*, lying off the island to the north. A fierce battle ensued, with the Gurkhas coming under fire from automatic weapons, resulting in a section commander and a rifleman being wounded. Seeing his two platoons being held up, Maj O'Leary landed from the *Jolly Bachelor* and led his men forward in an assault which resulted in three of the enemy being killed, two wounded and one taken prisoner. The seventh man made good his escape. An LMG, two Sten guns and two Armalite rifles were also captured. A Company's casualties amounted to three men wounded.

Approximately a week later the remaining seven guerrillas were apprehended. Spotted heading upriver in a stolen fishing boat, they were pursued by a small force of A Company and members of the PFF in another craft. After ignoring orders to heave-to, the boat was rammed and those aboard it surrendered without a fight.

On 25 January, following an appeal from the Secretary General of the United Nations for an end to hostilities, a ceasefire came into effect while the Foreign

Ministers of Malaysia and Indonesia met for talks in Bangkok. These failed, however, and the conflict resumed, the Indonesians launching a number of major incursions, particularly notable for the larger number of regular troops accompanying IBT groups. Furthermore infantry and RPKAD units also began taking part in operations.

One such incursion involving members of a regular unit took place in Sarawak's Second Division in early March 1964. Following information received from some Ibans about smoke seen rising from the jungle in the area of a hill on the Kling Kang Range, a 2,000ft-high feature running along the border, A Company of the 2nd/10th PMO Gurkha Rifles, commanded by Maj Ian Mayman, deployed its 2 Platoon under Lt (QGO) Karamdhoj Sunwar to establish two ambushes on tracks near the foot of the hill.

On the morning of 7 March Lt Karamdhoj reported to Maj Mayman that music and the sounds of radio traffic could be heard coming from the top of the hill. Ordered to carry out a close reconnaissance and to mount an attack if the enemy were in sufficiently small numbers, Karamdhoj despatched reconnaissance patrols up the hill. Two hours later these reported that a large enemy force was in positions on a large rocky outcrop. Unfortunately, however, the Indonesians had detected the presence of the patrols and were on the alert.

In the meantime 1 Platoon, commanded by Lt (QGO) Purandhoj Rai, had been moved forward by Maj Mayman, who accompanied it in an outflanking move designed to position the platoon between the enemy force and the border, thus cutting the Indonesians' withdrawal route. Meanwhile 2 Platoon was to hold the enemy's attention by launching a feint attack from the front.

Unfortunately, however, a contact took place before Mayman's plan could be put into effect. A section commander from 2 Platoon, Cpl Birbahadur Rai, and two riflemen had gone forward to observe the enemy positions but had been spotted. An Indonesian sentry positioned in a tree caught sight of them and opened fire, killing Cpl Birbahadur. The rest of his section moved up immediately, encountering a group of Indonesians, two of whom were hit by fire from the section's LMG gunner, Rifleman Panchabahadur Rai. The rest of 2 Platoon followed up swiftly, with 1 Platoon moving up behind in reserve, as a battle ensued in the thick jungle. Eventually the weight of fire from 2 Platoon forced the enemy to withdraw under covering fire from further positions on an escarpment above.

At this juncture Maj Mayman despatched 1 Platoon in an outflanking move to the right. Shortly afterwards, however, he discovered a ledge which provided a route to the left and set off along it with two sections. The Indonesian commander, realising that he was being outflanked, withdrew his force under covering fire from his own machine-guns. A Company pushed forward, hard on the Indonesians' heels, and inflicted a number of casualties. Eventually its advance became held up by covering fire from other enemy positions sited nearer the border.

By 4 p.m. the enemy had reached the border and withdrawn across it, taking their dead and wounded with them. It was later discovered that the entire force, numbering forty in all, had comprised members of the Indonesian 328th Raider Battalion. During the action it had suffered five killed and eight wounded.

Towards the end of March a 36-strong raiding force of the Indonesian Army's Black Cobra Battalion, commanded by Major Audy Patawari, crossed into the Second Division in the area of Lubong Tanah and headed north towards Jambu. It was not long, however, before it found itself being pursued by a force comprising the 2nd/10th PMO Gurkha Rifles (less A Company) and the Gurkha Independent Parachute Company, the latter commanded by Maj L.M. 'Phil' Phillips. On 5 April the Indonesians were located and the Commanding Officer of the 2nd/10th, Lt Col Fillingham, immediately deployed B Company into ambush positions north-west of Jambu and moved C and D Companies, together with the parachute company, into positions behind the enemy force, sealing off its withdrawal routes to the south and east. During the following two days helicopters carried out dummy insertions of troops and strafed areas not covered by the battalion.

On 7 April the enemy force began withdrawing and in doing so encountered 8 Platoon, which ambushed three scouts reconnoitring ahead of the main body, killing two and wounding the third. The remainder of the enemy fled, abandoning their packs and splitting up into small groups which headed north, joining up that evening at a pre-arranged emergency RV. Thereafter they attempted again to reach the border but were intercepted by the 2nd/10th, which deployed platoons into cut-off positions by helicopter.

During the following three days four more contacts took place during which seven more Indonesians were killed. A further six were killed and seven captured by twenty Iban tribesmen led by a PFF warrant officer. On 12 April a further contact took place when a corporal and a rifleman of the 2nd/10th shot dead four enemy who had ambushed them. A final contact took place when C Company killed two more near the border, bringing to 27 the total number of enemy accounted for out of the 36 who had crossed the border.

During the following month further attempts were made to bring an end to hostilities with the holding in Tokyo of a summit attended by Prime Minister Rahman, President Sukarno and President Diosdado Macapagal of the Philippines. Both before and during the summit, however, the Indonesians mounted a large number of incursions.

In mid-June, while the summit was still in progress, information was received by the security forces in the Second Division that a cock-fight was due to be held. This was a popular form of entertainment during which substantial wagers were placed and it was known that on a previous occasion Indonesian troops had come across the border in civilian dress to participate in the gambling. This information was passed to the 2nd/2nd KEO Gurkha Rifles, whose Commanding Officer, Lt Col D.F. 'Nick' Neill, tasked Maj Johnny Lawes's E Company, formed from the Bugle Platoon, MMG Platoon, Assault Pioneer Platoon and a section of 3-inch mortars, with taking the necessary action.

On the night of 12 June Lawes despatched the Assault Pioneer Platoon, commanded by Lt (QGO) Nandaraj Gurung, to Batu Lintang, from where it set off in the early morning of the following day to lay an ambush on one of two tracks leading from the border through an area of rubber and secondary jungle. It was not until 5 o'clock that afternoon, following a careful reconnaissance of the area, that the platoon moved into its positions. The weather conditions were appalling, with torrential rain making visibility difficult.

Lt Nandaraj and his men did not have long to wait as the Indonesians made their appearance only 50 minutes later. The latter were not, however, troops in civilian clothes coming across from Kalimantan for an evening's entertainment but a force of over fifty troops carrying out a major incursion. Preceded by two scouts, the leading section entered the ambush killing area at which point the Gurkhas opened fire at close range, killing one man and wounding another. The remainder of the enemy reacted swiftly, taking cover and fighting back.

By now it was dusk and visibility had deteriorated even further. One of the platoon's LMG machine-gunners, Rifleman Resambahadur Thapa, moved forward on his own and killed two of the raiders before returning to his position. At that point the Indonesians opened fire on the platoon's left flank with machine-guns and a light mortar prior to mounting a counter-attack. Recognising the threat, Lt Nandaraj redeployed his men, who brought heavy fire to bear just as the enemy attempted to rush their positions, Rifleman Resambahadur again using his LMG to good effect. This broke up the assault and the enemy began withdrawing, spurred on by artillery fire called down by Lt Nandaraj and fired by a troop of guns at Batu Lintang. Forty minutes later they broke contact and fled for the border, pursued by salvoes of shells.

The platoon remained on the alert in its positions during that night. On the following morning a search of the area revealed nine enemy dead, all of whom had been shot in the head. It later transpired that the Indonesians had suffered a total of thirteen killed and an unknown number wounded. As a result of this action Lt (QGO) Nandaraj Gurung was awarded the Military Cross while Rifleman Resambahadur Thapa received the Military Medal.

On 20 June the summit talks in Tokyo broke down and within 24 hours the Indonesians launched a major assault. This took place at Rasau, in the First Division. Here, on the evening of 21 June, two platoons of the 1st/6th QEO Gurkha Rifles returning from a patrol operation had occupied an abandoned jungle base, instead of establishing a temporary camp in the jungle for the night. No sooner had the Gurkhas settled in for the night than the base came under heavy fire from rocket launchers, mortars and machine-guns, a four-hour-long battle ensuing in which the Indonesians launched five attacks. By the time the enemy withdrew, five Gurkhas had been killed and five wounded.

In August Indonesia escalated the level of conflict by launching attacks on West Malaysia. In the early hours of 17 August a force of over 100 men, comprising RPKAD para-commandos, KKO marines and CCO guerrillas, landed on the coast of south-west Johore after crossing the Straits of Malacca in boats. Soon afterwards, however, they were intercepted by Malaysian troops, who killed or captured the majority during the following days, the remainder escaping into the jungle where the pursuit continued.

Two weeks later the Indonesians mounted an airborne operation. Some 200 paratroops of the Air Force PGT were embarked in four C-130 transports at Djakarta with the mission of dropping in Johore in the area of Labis, approximately 100 miles north of Singapore. One aircraft, however, failed to take off while another crashed into the sea while flying at low level to avoid detection by radar. The remaining two encountered an electric storm over Labis, their 'sticks' being scattered over a wide area. The security forces in the area, notably the 1st/10th PMO Gurkha Rifles, were swift to react. Joined by the 1st Battalion The Royal New Zealand Infantry Regiment (RNZIR), and supported by Wessex helicopters of 845 Naval Air Squadron which flew in from the commando carrier HMS *Bulwark*, the 1st/10th set to hunting down the raiding force and within a month had virtually wiped it out.

It was during this period that Maj Gen Walker received clearance from the Malaysian and British governments to carry out operations over the border inside Kalimantan, up to a depth of 3,000 yards. Codenamed Claret, the aim of these operations was to disconcert the Indonesians and throw them off balance. Initially they would be carried out by Gurkhas because of their extensive experience in jungle warfare. One of the early Claret operations was carried out by A Company 1st/2nd KEO Gurkha Rifles, commanded by Maj Digby Willoughby, which was tasked with attacking a platoon of the Indonesian Army's 518th Battalion based at the village of Nantakor, just over the border from Sabah, which had been abandoned by its previous inhabitants.

On 4 September a 45-strong force of A Company, comprising three 15-man platoons and the company headquarters, were moved by helicopter to an LZ near the border. On the following day, with Murut guides leading the way, Willoughby and his men set off for the border, making their way south over hilly, jungle-clad terrain into Kalimantan. By 8 o'clock on the morning of 6 September they had reached a position above and behind Nantakor, situated at a stream junction and astride a track leading north to the border with Sarawak. The enemy defensive positions comprised a screen of outposts facing north and two machine-gun positions on high ground, the main approaches to them being covered by anti-personnel mines.

Willoughby's plan was to deploy one of his platoons in stop groups to the south and east prior to mounting an attack with a second platoon and Company Headquarters, the third platoon being left in reserve in the company's firm base. Initially, however, he decided to send out small reconnaissance patrols – but shortly after the first had moved off it encountered a group of Murut tribesmen, who reported the presence of an enemy foraging party heading directly for the firm base. The platoon providing the stop groups set off immediately, while Willoughby and his assault group headed down a track for its start line, where machine-gun and rocket launcher teams moved to positions from which they would give covering fire for the assault.

At that point, however, an enemy soldier approached along the track and spotted a member of the assault group, L/Cpl Sherbikram Ale, and opened fire. The Gurkha NCO reacted swiftly, killing the Indonesian. Meanwhile, with the element of surprise lost, the rocket launcher teams and machine-gunners opened fire on a small *basha* (hut) some 50 yards away, this being the only position they could observe. Under covering fire from Company Headquarters, the assault group platoon, commanded by Lt (QGO) Manbahadur Ale, carried out a left flanking move to engage an enemy machine-gun that had opened fire on Company Headquarters, fortunately without causing any casualties. Hacking their way through thick undergrowth, Manbahadur and his men closed with the enemy, attacking the machine-gun.

Hearing the platoon opening fire, Willoughby led his headquarters group forward, joining Lt Manbahadur's team, who had by this time overrun the machine-gun position. From there Willoughby was able to observe two further enemy positions in secondary jungle down the hillside, one situated near a longhouse to the north-east, with another to the north-west covering the track to the border. Shortly afterwards the Indonesians launched a counter-attack from these positions under covering fire from two machine-guns. This was broken up by a machine-gunner, L/Cpl Hastabahadur Pun, who stood in the open with his GPMG supported on a tree stump, seemingly oblivious of the heavy enemy fire being directed at him.

In the meantime the stop groups platoon had redeployed and engaged the position by the longhouse. During the ensuing firefight L/Cpl Manbahadur Thapa, seriously wounded in the back by a mortar bomb exploding in the trees above him, continued to man his GPMG and succeeded in knocking out an enemy machine-gun. After about an hour the Indonesians withdrew with their wounded, leaving behind them five dead, among them their commander. A search of the longhouse indicated that at least twelve more enemy had probably been killed and a similar number wounded.

Four Gurkhas had also been wounded during the action and this posed a serious problem for Maj Willoughby as the rules for Claret operations dictated that no form of air support could be provided south of the border except in extreme emergency. Nevertheless he transmitted a request for evacuation of his casualties by helicopter, this being sent up the chain of command to Gen Walker, who gave his consent when told of the four wounded. When the aircraft arrived, Willoughby and his men were astonished and delighted to see the Commandant, Lt Col Johnny Clements, at the door of the aircraft, manning its LMG.

With its casualties evacuated, A Company turned its attention to destroying the enemy base, burning large amounts of stores and equipment, before setting off northwards to the border which was reached without incident. Subsequently Maj Digby Willoughby was awarded the Military Cross, with L/Cpls Hastabahadur Pun and Sherbikram Ale receiving the Military Medal.

The following month saw a Claret operation, codenamed Nelson's Eye, mounted by B Company 2nd/2nd KEO Gurkha Rifles under Maj Michael Joy. Following several incursions by enemy patrols into the company's area around Jambu in the Second

Division, Joy had received information concerning an Indonesian company base. Several reconnaissance patrols were despatched across the border and eventually the base was located 6,000 yards inside Kalimantan. Initial requests by the Commandant, Lt Col Neill, to attack the camp were refused by Maj Gen Walker. Neill, however, persisted and eventually persuaded Walker to allow him to harass the camp with small arms fire.

During the second week of October B Company, accompanied by the MMG Platoon with four Vickers .303 machine guns, was lifted by helicopter to an LZ close to the border. Thereafter Joy and his men carried out a long approach march, reaching a point some 1,500 yards from their objective. The MMGs, together with the company's 7.62mm GPMGs, were sited in positions at ranges of 1,200 yards and 800 yards respectively from the enemy camp.

Close reconnaissance of the camp revealed that it was occupied by only a small number of men and thus Joy was forced to wait until the evening of 13 October when enemy patrols were observed returning to their base. At first light on the following morning Joy struck, his MMGs and GPMGs bringing down a very heavy volume of fire on the camp where enemy troops could be seen running for cover as .303 and 7.62mm bullets hammered down on the entire area.

Ordering his men to cease fire, Joy gave the order to withdraw and the company made its way back to the border. Soon afterwards he returned to reconnoitre the remains of the camp, which by then had been abandoned by the Indonesians. He found several graves. It was subsequently confirmed that 37 Indonesians had been killed and a large number wounded by E Company's machine-guns.

In early January 1965 C Company 1st/2nd KEO Gurkha Rifles, based in the Ba Kelalan valley in the Fifth Division, carried out a major Claret raid. Commanded by Capt Bruce Jackman, the company was responsible for a 25-mile stretch of border; its headquarters and two platoons were based at a heavily fortified location in the Ba Kelalan valley, while the Assault Pioneer Platoon and a detachment of The RAF Regiment protected an airstrip at Long Semado, between 10 and 20 miles to the north.

In early 1964 the Indonesians had established a base at Long Medan in the Long Bawan Valley, which adjoined that of Ba Kelalan to the north. Some 5,500 yards over the border and occupied by sixty troops, it was sited on a hill and was surrounded by padi fields on three sides with jungle on the fourth. About 400 yards behind it was a river, a tributary of the Sungei Sembakung. Surrounded by a 4ft-high perimeter fence fashioned from bamboo, the base itself comprised a network of well-sited and well-prepared trenches, bunkers and support weapon pits.

There had been little activity in this sector of the border until late October 1964, when the Indonesians had crossed the border and attacked a longhouse just inside Sarawak and some 12 miles from Ba Kelalan. Capt Jackman received a visit from a deputation of Murut *pengulus* (headmen), who demanded that action be taken to prevent any repetition of the raid. At that stage he could do little but assure them that he would try his utmost to protect them. Shortly afterwards, however, 11 Platoon, commanded by Lt (QGO) Sukdeo Pun, ambushed a group of nine Indonesians, killing two and wounding three. While this delighted the *pengulus*, it did not remove the problem of the enemy at Long Medan, who that night responded to the ambush by attacking C Company's base with two rocket launchers. This proved ineffective, the rockets falling short, but the company's section of two 3-inch mortars responded, scoring direct hits on the launchers' position, one bomb landing on a stockpile of rockets which exploded in dramatic fashion. It was subsequently confirmed that three Indonesians had been killed.

Jackman had already asked for permission to launch a raid on Long Medan but it was not until 20 January 1965 that it was granted. By this time he had carried out a number of reconnaissances of the enemy base, during one of which he used an 8mm cine camera to film it. Throughout the following week C Company rehearsed the coming operation thoroughly and it was during one such rehearsal, on the afternoon of 28 January, that it was attacked by a small force of Indonesians armed with rocket launchers based in the position they had used previously. Fortunately their aim was bad and the situation was saved by Cpl Dhane Ghale who brought his 3-inch mortar into action single-handedly, firing ten bombs in less than a minute, these impacting with unerring accuracy on the enemy position, killing two Indonesians and, judging by the blood trails leading to the border, wounding at least four more.

That night 9 and 10 Platoons, commanded by Lt (QGO) Lalitbahadur Gurung and Sgt Rupsing Gurung respectively, secured the selected border crossing point, with 10 Platoon also establishing an OP to observe the Long Bawan valley. On the following afternoon, as the remainder of the company was moving down the Ba Kelalan valley towards the crossing point, a member of the OP party, Rifleman Dilbahadur Thapa, spotted three enemy approaching his position. Waiting until they were at point-blank range, he opened fire, killing the leading man. The other two enemy fled but the Indonesians responded swiftly by bringing down mortar fire on the OP, which moved to a new location. From here Capt Christopher Tofield, the artillery FOO attached to C Company, called for fire from a 105mm pack howitzer located at C Company's base. This had the desired effect, the enemy mortar team being forced to abandon its position.

Despite this preliminary action, Capt Jackman decided to proceed with his operation and on the afternoon of 29 January 148 men of C Company and 12 Platoon of D Company crossed the border and set off on a 7-mile approach march over high hills and through thick jungle, heavily burdened with ammunition, mortar bombs and 3.5-inch rockets. Jackman and his men marched all night and by first light on 30 January had reached a hill where the company's two mortars and machine-gun teams, together with 12 Platoon, were to take up positions from which they would provide supporting fire for the attack. Thereafter Company Headquarters and 9, 10 and 11 Platoons continued their march until, as dawn was breaking, they reached the assembly area where 9 and 10 Platoons shook out into assault formation while 11 Platoon prepared to 'shoot in' the attack with 3.5-inch rocket launchers.

At 5.45 a.m. 11 Platoon opened fire on the bunkers on the enemy base. As four rockets impacted on their targets, 9 and 10 Platoons charged the enemy positions, smashing their way through the bamboo perimeter fence as a second salvo of rockets hit the bunkers and the command bunker. A member of 9 Platoon, Rifleman Syambahadur Thapa, was hit by a burst from a machine-gun and fell dead while his comrades proceeded to attack the bunkers with their rifles and grenades. It soon became apparent to Capt Jackman, however, that there were fewer enemy than expected and he realised that the enemy had withdrawn from the base during the night, leaving only a small force to hold it.

At this juncture a 12.7mm heavy machine-gun (HMG) and two MMGs opened fire from positions across the river to the rear of the base, wounding Rifleman Amarbahadur Gurung in the leg and Rifleman Jagatman Gurung in the head. At the same moment an enemy 60mm light mortar began bringing down bombs, one of which exploded near Capt Jackman as he ran across the base with his orderly, signaller and mortar fire controller (MFC). Jackman was sent sprawling by the blast but was uninjured. His MFC, Cpl Birbahadur Gurung, ignoring the enemy fire, remained in the open as he called down fire from the company's 3-inch mortars on the enemy mortar position. Their second bomb was on target, and hit a pile of 60mm bombs, which exploded with a huge blast. Thereafter Cpl Birbahadur switched the mortars' fire to the enemy machine-guns which were subjected to a barrage of fifty bombs. The enemy HMG, however, survived unscathed and continued to subject C Company to heavy fire. Eventually, it was knocked out by a three-man rocket launcher team from 12 Platoon, which worked its way to within firing range and scored a direct hit with its first rocket.

The battle continued, with C Company pounding the enemy positions across the river until 7 a.m. when Capt Jackman ordered his men to cease fire. Half an hour later, having carried out a search of the base during which they found eight enemy dead and a number of wounded, the Gurkhas withdrew and made their way back to the border, carrying Rifleman Amarbahadur Thapa and the body of Rifleman Syambahadur Thapa; Rifleman Jagatman Gurung was fit enough to walk despite the wound in his head. The march was an exhausting one, all the more so since Jackman and his men had eaten nothing except biscuits and chocolate since 3 o'clock on the previous afternoon. At one point an enemy 120mm gun opened fire at random into the jungle in the area of the company but caused no casualties. Any follow-up by the enemy was discouraged by the FOO, Capt Tofield, who had remained in the OP, from where he was able to bring down fire to cover the company's withdrawal.

Eight hours after setting off from Long Medan C Company reached the border, where it was met by the Commandant, Lt Col Clements. The raid had been a total success and the Indonesians never reoccupied the base at Long Medan. It was learned later that 32 enemy had been killed in the raid, this representing approximately half of their total strength, and a large number were wounded. As a result of the success of the operation, Capt Bruce Jackman was awarded the Military Cross for his outstanding leadership while Cpl Birbahadur Gurung received the Military Medal.

Despite the undoubted effect of the Claret operations inside Kalimantan, the Indonesians continued to carry out incursions into Sarawak and Sabah. On 18 February 1965 a 14-strong patrol of the 1st/7th DEO Gurkha Rifles, based in the Bau district of the First Division, was tasked with reconnoitring a track along the border. Commanded by Capt (QGO) Bharat Rai, it was moving through thick jungle in torrential rain when the lead scouts reported the sound of voices. Moving stealthily forward, the patrol spotted five Indonesians crouched in a huddle, studying a map. As Capt Bharat realised that this was an Indonesian commander in the process of giving orders to his subordinates, he heard the sounds of a larger body of men moving in the jungle on either side of his patrol. While he was aware of the danger of being surrounded and cut off from his line of withdrawal, the target of an enemy commander and his O-Group was too important to miss and Bharat deployed his patrol silently into fire positions.

At that juncture the Indonesian commander stood up and stretched, at which point the patrol opened fire, killing him and three other members of the O-Group and wounding the fifth. The main enemy force reacted swiftly, bringing heavy fire to bear on the patrol from both sides. Despite this, Capt Bharat miraculously succeeded in extracting his men from their highly perilous situation, wounding three more enemy in the process. The Indonesians were unaware that the patrol had withdrawn and half an hour later could still be heard firing furiously into the area where they had last seen the Gurkhas.

March 1965 saw the departure of Maj Gen Walter Walker as Director of Borneo Operations. He was replaced by Maj Gen George Lea, who had commanded 22 SAS during the Malayan Emergency. By this time the conflict in Borneo was approaching its final stage. The Indonesians had abandoned their guerrilla tactics and were employing regular troops in attacks on British and Commonwealth security force bases and positions along the border. One such attack took place in the early hours of 2 April when a battalion of RPKAD para-commandos attacked the base of B Company 2nd Battalion The Parachute Regiment (2 PARA) at Plaman Mapu in the First Division. Most of the company, under Maj Jon Fleming, was out on patrol at the time and thus the base was defended only by an understrength platoon of young soldiers who had recently completed their basic training in England, the Company Headquarters and a section of 3-inch mortars.

The Indonesian attack began at 5 a.m. with the base subjected to a barrage of rockets and mortar bombs as well as small arms fire. Sappers blew gaps in the barbed wire defences with Bangalore torpedoes and shortly afterwards the enemy succeeded in overrunning one of the company's 3-inch mortar pits. A counter-attack was mounted by one of the platoon's sections, which drove off the enemy but lost three or four men wounded in the process. This was followed by another led by the Company Sergeant Major (CSM), WOII John Williams, and the platoon commander, Capt Nick Thompson. A second assault followed but was also beaten off by another section.

Under heavy supporting fire, the enemy then launched a third assault on the same sector of the base but this was broken up by B Company's remaining 3-inch mortar which, at maximum elevation, succeeded in dropping bombs on the enemy at a range of only 30 yards from its pit. At the same time 105mm pack howitzers at another 2 PARA base at Gunan Gajak responded to a call for supporting fire from B Company's FOO and shells began to fall among the enemy.

Thereafter the Indonesians began withdrawing and at dawn 2 PARA's quick reaction force company was flown in by helicopter. At the same time three platoons were deployed to block withdrawal routes likely to be used by the enemy, while two companies of Gurkhas were flown in to follow up. It was later learned that two RPKAD companies had carried out the attack, a third having set up a firm base for the operation. In the meantime a fourth company had been deployed in an ambush position on the Kalimantan side of the border to counter any attempt by the security forces to follow up.

Despite the ferocity of the enemy assaults, B Company's casualties numbered only two killed and seven wounded. The Indonesians, however, had suffered very heavily, with many killed, although no bodies were ever found, and an unknown number wounded. The absence of bodies was eventually explained ten years later when an Indonesian officer who had taken part in the action attended a course in Britain. He said that, during the withdrawal, the dead and severely wounded had been thrown into a nearby river flowing back into Kalimantan.

Claret missions continued during the second half of 1965. One major operation comprised a series of strikes across the border by A Squadron 22 SAS, which worked in close cooperation with the 2nd/2nd KEO Gurkha Rifles. The first of these missions, codenamed Kingdom Come, involved six large-scale ambushes by the 2nd/2nd on the Koemba and Sentimo rivers, while two troops of A Squadron were tasked with stirring the enemy into action. Atrocious weather conditions resulted in four of the ambushes being unsuccessful. The remaining two, carried out by A and Support Companies (the latter having replaced E Company in the battalion), under Maj Len Lauderdale and Capt Christopher Bullock respectively, resulted in fourteen enemy being killed. Kingdom Come was followed by Blood Alley, in which C Company, commanded by Maj Geoff Ashley, and a troop of A Squadron accounted for six Indonesians in an ambush on a tributary of the Koemba, and then another twenty-one in an action following the appearance of a larger force of enemy.

On 28 August, while the SAS mounted another operation, Jack Sprat, along the Sentimo and its tributary, the Sungei Ayer Hitam, Support Company set off on Operation Hell Fire. Its task was to ambush a convoy of boats, which, as reported by Special Branch sources, would be carrying reinforcements and supplies up the Sungei Sentimo to an Indonesian base at Berjongkong during the following week. Accompanying Capt Bullock and his men was the squadron sergeant major (SSM) of A Squadron 22 SAS, WOII Lawrence Smith, who had visited the area previously during an SAS reconnaissance sortie and whose task it was to help Bullock find the Sentimo.

On the morning of 28 August the approximately 70-strong company was airlifted from the 2nd/2nd's base at Lundu to a hill feature known as 'Kandai', the site of a

Gurkha soldiers pictured during a river patrol. The front soldier is armed with a Bren gun. These waterborne patrols provided the flexibility to get deep into jungle areas which would have taken days to reach by foot.

radio relay station and firebase into which a 105mm pack howitzer and two sections of 81mm mortars were also flown to provide supporting fire for the operation. This would be called down by an FOO, Capt John Masters of the Royal New Zealand Artillery, who was accompanying Capt Bullock and his men.

Making its way over the border, Support Company headed off on a long approach march of 10,000 yards to its objective, the stretch of the Sungei Sentimo along which ran the Indonesian line of communications between a base at Babang Baba and another south of Berjongkong. Prior to the start of the operation, Bullock had been warned by the Commandant, Lt Col Neill, to keep well clear of the village of Aachen, which was occupied by a company of Indonesian troops supported by mortars. Thus Bullock headed north-west, WOII Smith accompanying the Assault Pioneer Platoon in the lead, and followed a route which took him and his men to a point north of

Aachen, following which they turned south-west and headed for the Sungei Sentimo. On the afternoon of the second day the company reached the Sungei Aachen, which was crossed via a bridge constructed by the Assault Pioneers from a felled tree.

The following day found the company searching for the Sentimo but hampered in its efforts by heavy rain and an area of treacherous swamp. Establishing a base camp on a hill, Capt Bullock and WOII Smith, accompanied by a 12-man patrol of the Anti-Tank Platoon, set off to find the elusive river but without success. The next day the weather improved and the company set off once more, and later that morning came upon a river. A reconnaissance by Capt Bullock, WOII Smith and Cpl Bhagtasing Gurung, the commander of the Assault Pioneer Platoon, confirmed that it was the Sentimo.

Having established a firm base about 1,000 yards from the river, on the small hill where the company had spent the previous night, Bullock, again accompanied by WOII Smith, reconnoitred the area and selected the sites for his ambush.

On the following day, 1 September, the company moved into its positions. The Anti-Tank Platoon, commanded by Lt (QGO) Deoparsad Gurung, provided the main killing group covering the river over a frontage of some 25 yards while the Reconnaissance Platoon, commanded by Sgt Chabilal Rana, was deployed on the right to give flank protection covering a track which ran along the riverbank, the Assault Pioneers doing likewise on the left. Both flanks and the rear of the ambush position were also covered by Claymore mines. To the rear of the ambush was a checkpoint manned by a group comprising the CSM, WOII Hariparsad Gurung, Bullock's signaller, a medical orderly, Capt Masters and his Gurkha signaller, L/Cpl Tekbahadur Thapa. The latter was in radio contact with the 105mm pack howitzer and two sections of mortars at Kandai, which would provide fire support during the company's withdrawal. Behind the checkpoint, on an area of ground protected on either side by two fallen trees, was a strongpoint or RV through which the ambush group would withdraw before making its way back to the firm base. Trenches had been dug to strengthen the position should the enemy attempt to outflank. Further to the rear was the company's firm base manned by fifteen men, including the company second in command, Capt (QGO) Surendraman Gurung, and WOII Smith, who was suffering from a cough and fever, and so was not with the ambush group.

That afternoon two boats appeared carrying twelve fully armed Indonesians. Using long poles rather than paddles or outboard engines, their approach was silent and by the time the early warning group had signalled their presence, both craft had passed through the killing area before Bullock and his men could react. Withdrawing after last light the ambush group made its way back to the firm base.

The morning of 2 September found Bullock and his men back in their ambush positions. When the Indonesians did appear, however, it was not in boats along the river as expected but on foot along the track from the right flank. Numbering over a hundred, they were spotted first by a Reconnaissance Platoon LMG gunner, Rifleman Ramparsad Pun, who waited until the leading enemy were within his arc of fire before opening fire and killing the leading four men with his first burst.

The enemy were well trained and reacted swiftly, launching an attack. This was beaten off by the Reconnaissance Platoon, who killed twelve men, L/Cpl Birbahadur Pun knocking out a machine gun with a Claymore mine before standing up and inflicting further casualties with his SMG and grenades. As the battle continued the Indonesians attempted to carry out a left flanking attack in an attempt to move round to the rear of the ambush but this failed, thanks to the stout resistance of the Reconnaissance Platoon. At this juncture an enemy rocket launcher team opened fire from the other side of the river and was engaged by the Anti-Tank Platoon.

Aware that he and his men were in danger of being outflanked, Capt Bullock ordered the Assault Pioneer Platoon to withdraw to the strongpoint/RV. As he did so, a salvo of enemy mortar bombs landed in the area. As soon as the Assault Pioneers had occupied the trenches at the strongpoint, Bullock ordered the Reconnaissance Platoon to withdraw by bounds, following it shortly afterwards with the Anti-Tank Platoon, which had been involved in a fierce battle with the enemy on the other side of the river.

Taking two GPMG teams from the Anti-Tank Platoon, Bullock then despatched the remainder of that platoon and the Reconnaissance Platoon to the firm base. By this time the enemy were bringing down heavy small arms and mortar fire on the area and at this point Cpl Bhagtasing Gurung reported that four members of the checkpoint party, Capt John Masters, his signaller, the medical orderly and WOII Hariparsad Gurung, had not come through the RV. Bullock then left the RV and went forward to look for the missing men, shouting the name of his CSM. As he did so, however, he was confronted suddenly by three Indonesians. He was saved by a member of the Assault Pioneer Platoon, Rifleman Hariprasad Gurung, who had followed him on his own initiative and opened fire on the three enemy, sending them diving for cover.

No sooner had Bullock and Hariprasad regained the strongpoint than the Indonesians launched an attack, but were beaten off by the Assault Pioneers. Realising that it was imperative that he withdraw before being cut off, but at the same time worried about his missing men, Bullock established radio contact with Battalion Headquarters and spoke to Lt Col Neill, who ordered him to withdraw to the firm base without delay. Bullock and the Assault Pioneer Platoon made their way into the area of swamp which lay between the strongpoint and firm base, their withdrawal covered by an LMG gunner, L/Cpl Reshambahadur Thapa. As the last man entered the swamp, however, a number of enemy appeared at the strongpoint. Seeing them, Reshambahadur immediately turned back, firing his weapon from the hip and discharging a complete magazine to good effect before following his comrades into the swamp.

Fifteen minutes later Capt Bullock and his men reached the firm base, where the rest of the company was manning the trenches. Bullock discovered that one of the four missing men, the medical orderly, had succeeded in reaching the firm base after becoming separated from the rest of the checkpoint party.

The absence of his FOO meant that Bullock had been unable to call for supporting fire from the 105mm pack howitzer and mortars at Kandai. Fortunately, however,

WOII Smith had produced an artillery fire plan and now put it into effect, bringing down fire on the enemy. Shortly afterwards Capt Bullock made radio contact again with Battalion Headquarters and was ordered by Lt Col Neill to withdraw without delay.

An hour later Support Company left the firm base and began heading swiftly for the border. En route Bullock received a radio message from Battalion Headquarters informing him that Capt Masters' signaller, L/Cpl Tekbahadur Thapa, had succeeded in avoiding capture and had made his own way 10,000 yards back to the border and the firebase without the aid of a map or compass. By late afternoon, having taken just six hours to march the distance previously covered in the five days of the approach march, Bullock and his men approached the border. As they did so, they heard two shots fired near the Kandai hill feature. An hour's search of the area, however, revealed nothing and the company continued its march to the firebase, reaching it just before last light.

On reaching Kandai, Bullock discovered that the shots had been fired by Capt Masters, who had appeared at the firebase that afternoon. It transpired that the checkpoint had been attacked by a group of Indonesians, who had succeeded in working their way round to the rear of the ambush. Masters and WOII Hariparsad Gurung had returned their fire but the latter had been hit in the leg by five bullets from a submachine-gun, which rendered him incapable of walking. Deciding to head for the strongpoint, Masters had called to his signaller to help him carry Hariparsad but L/Cpl Tekbahadur had been unwilling to leave the checkpoint. Before Masters could order him to do so, a number of Indonesians had appeared, these being engaged by Masters and Tekbahadur, who killed one each. One of the Indonesians promptly collapsed on top of Tekbahadur, covering him in blood. In the ensuing confusion Tekbahadur had become separated from Masters and Hariparsad and, somewhat disorientated, had headed back towards the border.

During the following hours Masters had carried WOII Hariparsad for a distance of 6,000 yards. Eventually, overcome with exhaustion, he realised that he would have to leave the wounded Gurkha in order to reach the border and return with a rescue party. Placing him in a carefully concealed position and having given him all his food and his water bottles, Masters had set off for the border to fetch help, heading for the sound of the 105mm pack howitzer covering Support Company's withdrawal. Shortly after reaching Kandai, he had gone back over the border with D Company, commanded by Maj Piers Erskine-Tulloch, which, accompanied by the 2nd/2nd's medical officer, Capt Howard Manuel, had been flown to the firebase to search for the missing men.

Capt Bullock realised that D Company, which was not familiar with the area, had little chance of finding his missing CSM and that the latter's only chance of survival lay in Bullock himself joining a search party going back over the border to look for him. On the following morning, accompanied by Capt (QGO) Surendraman Gurung, WOII Smith and eighteen Gurkhas, including two trackers, L/Cpls Ramparsad Gurung and Birkabahadur Gurung, he set off back over the border. By 8.30 a.m. he had caught up

with D Company and thereafter his two trackers led the search. It took them an hour
before they found Capt Masters' tracks and began backtracking them into Kalimantan.
They found Hariparsad in the late afternoon, by which time he had lost a considerable
amount of blood and was at risk of losing his wounded leg through gangrene.
A request for a helicopter was transmitted to Battalion Headquarters and Lt Col Neill,
ignoring the rules governing the use of helicopters over the border, immediately
despatched the RAF Whirlwind attached permanently to the battalion.

Flown by Flt Lt Brian Skillicon, the helicopter appeared two hours later, by which
time D Company had felled sufficient trees to make a hole in the jungle canopy large
enough for a stretcher to be winched down from the aircraft. In torrential rain the
helicopter was guided in by WOII Smith using a search-and-rescue radio beacon
(SARBE), and Skillicon carefully manoeuvred his aircraft over the hole while his
crewman lowered the stretcher. No sooner had the wounded Gurkha been lashed on to
it than the helicopter climbed vertically away, the stretcher swinging beneath it. It later
transpired that Lt Col Neill himself had been aboard the aircraft. Flown to a hospital
where he underwent immediate surgery, WOII Hariparsad Gurung subsequently made
a full recovery, albeit he was left with a slight limp.

Capt Christopher Bullock received the MC for his outstanding leadership during this
operation. In recognition of his actions, which saved WOII Hariparsad Gurung's life,
Capt John Masters was also awarded the MC and was made an honorary life member
of the 2nd KEO Gurkha Rifles as a sign of their gratitude, while L/Cpl Birbahadur Pun
received the DCM and Rifleman Ramparsad Pun the MM for their actions during the
battle. In due course it was learned that enemy casualties inflicted during Operation
Hell Fire amounted to sixteen killed and several wounded.

Two months later another Claret operation took place which resulted in a Gurkha
receiving the highest decoration for gallantry that can be awarded to a member of the
British and Commonwealth armed forces.

The 2nd/10th PMO Gurkha Rifles, commanded by Lt Col Peter Myers, had
returned to Borneo in August, relieving the 3rd Battalion The Royal Australian
Regiment in the First Division. In November information was received that the
Indonesians were constructing a base in the area of Bau and C Company, under Capt
Kit Maunsell, was tasked with locating and destroying it.

The terrain in which the enemy base was situated comprised razor-backed ridgelines
and dense secondary jungle leading to hills covered in primary jungle. It was on the top
of one of the latter that the Indonesians had sited the base, which was occupied by a
platoon. The position posed formidable problems for any attacker, the slopes of the hill
being very steep and the approaches to it being along three very narrow ridgelines. Two
of these, and the deep valleys between them, were covered in thick secondary jungle.
Situated 500 yards down a ridgeline to the west was another position held by a company.

An initial reconnaissance was carried out on 19 November by Lt (QGO) Ranjit Rai,
the commander of 7 Platoon, who located the enemy position. On the following day
Capt Maunsell, accompanied by the commander of 8 Platoon, Lt (QGO)

Baghatbahadur Rai, conducted his own reconnaissance while despatching Lt (QGO) Puransing Limbu, the commander of 9 Platoon, to reconnoitre the area from another direction.

On 21 November C Company, accompanied by the 2nd/10th's Reconnaissance and Assault Pioneer Platoons, set off across the border on its approach march. Some 800 yards from the southernmost ridgeline leading to the enemy position Maunsell set up a firm base manned by the Assault Pioneers and the FOO attached to the company. Pressing on, he established an RV point secured by his CSM and a section of 9 Platoon. Thereafter Maunsell himself, together with three Gurkhas, slowly and silently cut a 400-yard route with secateurs through the dense undergrowth covering the ridge leading to the enemy base. Following behind came the rest of C Company.

The task took until 1.30 p.m. when Maunsell and his lead scouts found themselves just 60 feet below the base. The enemy, however, had cleared the immediate area surrounding their positions, felling a number of trees which now formed a barrier blocking the 5ft-wide ridgeline. Maunsell and his men were about to start clearing these when they heard the sounds of someone working on a second similar barrier a few yards beyond. Minutes later the Indonesian could be heard walking away and shortly afterwards he appeared on the position above before walking out of sight. The Gurkhas began silently clearing the trees from their path and, as soon as they had done so, moved on to the second barrier. They had just cleared it when another Indonesian appeared above them. As he unslung his rifle from his shoulder, he was shot dead and C Company immediately launched its assault.

Quickly 7 Platoon moved to the left, with 8 Platoon going to the right, the ridgeline being only wide enough for the Gurkhas to charge up it four abreast. Lt (QGO) Ranjit Rai led the way, suppressing the fire from an enemy machine-gun with several hand grenades and storming a hut whose occupants were all killed. Capt Maunsell then ordered Lt (QGO) Bhagatbahadur Rai and 8 Platoon to attack from the right and clear the next line of positions from which the enemy had now begun directing a heavy volume of fire on to C Company, who took cover. One Gurkha attempted to charge a trench but was killed, while another was seriously wounded. Capt Maunsell crawled forward to him and dragged him to safety below the crest of the hill, whereupon Lt Bhagatbahadur and his men charged and stormed the enemy positions, overrunning them.

Meanwhile on the left flank an NCO of 9 Platoon, L/Cpl Rambahadur Limbu, together with his section's two-man LMG group, was dealing with an enemy machine-gun which was causing problems. Charging across open ground under fire, he killed the machine-gunner with a grenade before taking cover with his two companions in a nearby trench. Moving forward once more, the three Gurkhas headed for the cover of a large fallen tree. As they did so, they passed a trench into which one of Rambahadur's companions dropped a grenade. Before it detonated, however, an Indonesian in the trench fired a burst from an automatic weapon, wounding both members of the LMG group. A split-second later the grenade exploded, killing the occupant of the trench.

With his LMG group out of action, and unable to contact his platoon commander, L/Cpl Rambahadur decided that his first priority was to move his two men under cover. Springing to his feet, he ran to the first man, picked him up and carried him to the shelter of the hut stormed earlier by Lt (QGO) Ranjit Rai. Having placed him under cover, he returned for the second Gurkha and carried him back, ignoring the heavy fire being directed at him. He then ran forward a third time and, retrieving the LMG lying on the ground, immediately charged the enemy positions, firing the weapon from the hip and silencing the enemy machine-guns, killing at least four enemy while doing so.

By this time the two forward enemy positions on the hill had been taken, leaving a third in depth still occupied by the enemy. Lt (QGO) Ranjit Rai brought up the rest of 7 Platoon and, moving through the area secured by 8 Platoon, launched an assault which quickly overran the remaining trenches. With the entire feature now held by C Company, Capt Maunsell's immediate concern was that the Indonesians would launch a counter-attack from the company position on the western ridgeline. In fact the attack came from the route along which the company had approached the objective. Unable to see the enemy but observing the smoke from their weapons, one of C Company's machine-gunners fired 150 rounds from his GPMG into the area. This obviously had a salutary effect on the Indonesians, whose counter-attack was halted in its tracks.

The Reconnaissance Platoon, commanded by Lt (QGO) Bhuwansing Limbu, and elements of 9 Platoon then took up positions along the approach ridge ready to deal with any further counter-attack from that direction. Seconds later two enemy appeared on the ridge to the south-west of the base and came under fire, and were killed. Almost immediately afterwards three more were observed and suffered the same fate. The Indonesians then resorted to opening fire on the Reconnaissance Platoon with mortars whose bombs began falling only yards away. The Gurkhas responded with their own 2-inch mortar to good effect and shortly afterwards the enemy ceased firing.

Further desultory attempts at counter-attacks were followed by a more serious effort when a force of over seventy Indonesians approached along one of the ridgelines. Capt Maunsell, however, radioed his FOO and requested supporting fire. The guns were swift to respond and a salvo of ten 105mm shells impacted shortly afterwards, albeit a bit short and somewhat too close for comfort for Maunsell and his men. A correction was transmitted, resulting in the second salvo being on target, stopping the enemy counter-attack dead in its tracks.

At this point Capt Maunsell gave the order to withdraw. During the 90-minute battle the base had been destroyed and at least twenty-four enemy killed. C Company had suffered three killed, two of them being the Gurkhas rescued by L/Cpl Rambahadur Limbu, who had died of their wounds almost immediately afterwards. One Gurkha had been seriously wounded while another had been only slightly so and was able to walk.

Carrying the three dead and the seriously wounded man, C Company set off back towards the border, with 8 Platoon leading the way, followed by 7 Platoon, the

Reconnaissance Platoon, Assault Pioneer Platoon and finally 9 Platoon. As soon as the company was clear of the area Capt Maunsell called down 105mm and 5.5-inch artillery fire on to the enemy base.

Following this action Capt Kit Maunsell and Lt (QGO) Ranjit Rai both received the MC. It was the award of the VC to L/Cpl Rambahadur Limbu, however, which made the headlines, attracting public attention to the hitherto unknown conflict in Borneo. Such was the secrecy covering Claret operations, however, that the citation was carefully worded so as to give the impression that the action had taken place inside Sarawak. The first Victoria Cross to be won by a member of the 10th PMO Gurkha Rifles, it was the thirteenth awarded to a Gurkha. The twelfth had been awarded twenty years previously in 1945 to Rifleman Lachhiman Gurung of the 4th/8th Gurkha Rifles. By coincidence, Lachhiman's company commander then was one Maj Myers, who, as a lieutenant colonel, was now Rambahadur's Commanding Officer.

On 1 October 1965 there was an attempted coup in Indonesia, attributed to communists headed by a Revolutionary Council involving the Chiefs of Staff of the Air Force and Navy, Gen Omar Dani and Rear Admiral Martadinata, and Dr Subandrio, the First Deputy Prime Minister. The coup began in the early hours, with six generals, including Maj Gen Achmad Yani, the Commander of the Army, being abducted and taken to an air force base at Halim, where they were later tortured and murdered. The C-in-C of the Armed Forces, Gen Nasution, the communists' chief opponent, escaped capture and, within five hours of the coup being announced by the rebels over Radio Djakarta, declared that it had been crushed. Sukarno, who had also been taken to the Halim air force base, and who claimed to be 'neutral' in his sympathies, was taken to his country residence at Bogor, about 40 miles to the south of Djakarta.

During the following ten days the rebellion spread to Central Java where the army commander, Colonel Suhirman, sided with the communists, and to the Celebes where the army beat off an attempt to take control. The coup having failed, the communists turned to terrorism and during the following three weeks murdered 170 people in Central and Eastern Java. The PKI, numbering some three million members, posed a potent threat but the army, now led by Gen Suharto, exercised a considerable degree of restraint during this period, albeit it arrested and imprisoned 5,000 communists.

By this time Sukarno had returned to Djakarta but his presidential powers had been reduced dramatically by Nasution and Suharto. In early February 1966 he broadcast a statement defending the PKI, claiming that the communists had sacrificed the most in the struggle for Indonesian independence. This was followed by a broadcast by Gen Nasution condemning the communists and stating that they should be punished for the terrorism and other crimes in which they had been involved. Two days later he was removed from office by Sukarno, who now advocated rehabilitation of the communists.

Shortly afterwards Sukarno dissolved the National War Council, replacing it with a new body, the Crush Malaysia Command. He had achieved by political means that which the coup had failed to do by force: the removal of Nasution and others who were obstacles to Indonesia becoming a communist state which would form an axis

Gurkha VCs. Left to right: Rambahadur Limbu VC, Gaje Ghale VC, Agansing Rai VC, Ganju Lama VC, Bhanbhagta Gurung VC.

with China and create an organisation to rival the United Nations: the Conference of the New Emerging Forces (CONEFO) for which North Korea and North Vietnam had already pledged support.

In early March 1966 gathering resentment at Sukarno's increasingly pro-communist stance, coupled with rising unrest at Indonesia's growing economic problems, exploded into riots in Djakarta. Sukarno ordered his guards to open fire on a crowd of students outside his presidential palace and several of them were killed. On 12 March the army took control of the country and Sukarno was forced to hand over power, retaining only his title as president. Thereafter the country was governed by a triumvirate of Gen Suharto, the Sultan of Jogjakarta, who was appointed Deputy Premier for Economics, and Dr Adam Malik, who became Foreign Minister. Gen Nasution, meanwhile, was appointed Deputy Supreme Commander.

The weeks following the army's assumption of power saw a purge of the PKI during which between half a million and a million communists died. In early July communism was outlawed and Sukarno, who had been refused contact with his ministers without permission and whose speeches and interviews were carefully monitored, was stripped of his title of President for Life. In early August Tun Abdul Razak, the Malaysian Deputy Prime Minister, accompanied by five other ministers, flew to Djakarta for talks with Gen Suharto and his fellow ministers. Shortly afterwards a peace agreement between Malaysia and Indonesia, known as the Bangkok Accord, was signed in the Thai capital by Tun Abdul Razak and Dr Adam Malik. On 11 August the Borneo Confrontation officially came to an end.

The end of 1965 saw the Indonesians withdrawing their forces to a distance of 10,000 yards from the border and thereafter their incursions into Sarawak and Sabah decreased. In June 1966, however, it was reported that a raiding force of some fifty men, commanded by a Lt Sumbi, was heading towards the border with the Fifth Division. Reports indicated that its objective was the Brunei Shell Oil Company installations at Seria in western Brunei and it was thought that Sumbi planned to cross the border via a ridgeline between Ba Kelalan and Long Semado. As recounted in detail in Chapter 8, a patrol of the Gurkha Independent Parachute Company picked up Sumbi's trail, the pursuit being joined by the 1st/7th DEO Gurkha Rifles and other units. Eventually, during an operation which lasted almost three months, Sumbi and his men were tracked down and eliminated or surrendered themselves to the security forces.

The Borneo Confrontation lasted three years and nine months. At the height of the campaign some 17,000 British and Commonwealth troops, naval and air force personnel were deployed in Sarawak, Sabah and Brunei. The infantry battalions of The Brigade of Gurkhas had played a major role, both in the conduct of Claret cross-border operations inside Kalimantan and in the interception and destruction of Indonesian raiding forces in Sarawak and Sabah. British and Commonwealth losses during the campaign numbered 114 killed and 181 wounded while Indonesian casualties were officially stated as being 590 killed, 222 wounded and 771 captured, these latter figures excluding the large numbers killed and wounded inside Kalimantan during Claret operations.

CHAPTER 8

GURKHA AIRBORNE TROOPS

In India during 1941 the decision was taken to create a parachute formation and in October of that year 50 Indian Parachute Brigade was formed. Commanded by Brig Bill Gough, it comprised: 151st Parachute Battalion, a British unit under Lt Col Martin Lindsay; 152nd Indian Parachute Battalion, commanded by Lt Col B.E. 'Abbo' Abbott; 153rd Gurkha Parachute Battalion under Lt Col Freddy Loftus-Tottenham; and 411th (Royal Bombay) Parachute Section Indian Engineers under Capt Michael Rolt.

At that time there was no parachute training facility in India, so the Airlanding School (ALS) was established at Willington Airport, New Delhi, under Wg Cdr J.H.D. Chapple, assisted by a Chief Instructor, Flt Lt Bill Brereton, and seven RAF and army parachute jumping instructors (PJI) sent from No. 1 Parachute Training School (PTS) at Ringway in Britain. The aircraft allocated to the ALS comprised initially two, and subsequently five, elderly Vickers Valencia biplanes. The main problem facing Chapple was a serious shortage of parachutes and associated equipment such as helmets. The ALS was equipped with only fourteen canopies, which Flt Lt Brereton and his instructors had brought with them from No. 1 PTS.

The first parachute descents were made on 15 October by Brereton and two officers of 50 Indian Parachute Brigade, Capts Abbott and Hopkinson. In spite of the shortage of parachutes and equipment for ground training, Wg Cdr Chapple and his staff began training the officers and men of the new brigade. In February 1942 the first exercise was carried out, the airborne element consisting of a stick of ten men while the remainder of the brigade was taken to its dropping zones (DZ) by trucks prior to being deployed. By the end of the following month the parlous situation regarding parachutes and equipment had not improved significantly, only 200 out of an order for 2,200 parachutes having been received from Britain. Attempts were made at local manufacture but these proved unsuccessful owing to a lack of suitable materials and technical expertise. Moreover, the five Valencias had been withdrawn to assist in the evacuation of refugees from Burma and the lack of aircraft for parachute training caused major problems for the ALS. Six Hudson light bombers had also been promised from Britain but these had not materialised.

Eventually the situation became so serious that the C-in-C India, Gen Sir Archibald Wavell, sent a signal to the Prime Minister in Britain, Winston Churchill, in which he drew the latter's attention to the problem. A reply from the Secretary of State for India revealed that a consignment of parachutes destined for India had mistakenly been delivered to the Middle East and that two of the six promised Hudsons had crashed on the way. Shortly afterwards, however, the lack of parachutes was remedied by the installation of a factory at Khanpur by the American parachute manufacturer Leslie Irvin, which by June 1942 was producing 300 parachutes per month, its target being 1,750.

Meanwhile 50 Indian Parachute Brigade continued its training with a ceaseless programme of exercises, taking part in July in combined operations exercises at Kharakvasla near Poona. July also saw the first operational deployment by the brigade when a company of 152nd Indian Parachute Battalion was dropped from Valencias over an area in Sind Province in an operation against Hur tribesmen, who had attacked and derailed a mail train two months earlier.

The second operation, codenamed Puddle, was carried out by a group of 153rd Gurkha Parachute Battalion. Commanded by Capt Jimmy Roberts, it comprised three VCOs, four Gurkhas and three British signallers, and was tasked with gathering intelligence behind enemy lines in Burma. The British were keen to discover whether the enemy were constructing any airfields in the area of Myitkina and it had thus been decided to drop a small group of parachutists into the area. Roberts was also to ascertain the extent of the Japanese progress northwards along the routes between Fort Hertz and the Hukawng Valley. On completion of its tasks, the group was to make its way to Fort Hertz from where it would be extracted by air.

Training for the operation was conducted with maximum secrecy, Roberts and his men learning to jump from a Lockheed Lodestar which involved an exit via a door in the side of the fuselage rather than through an aperture in the floor as was the case with the Valencia and the Hudson.

On 24 June the men were flown to Dinjan where they waited to be despatched on their mission. A week later, on the afternoon of 3 July, they embarked on an aircraft which an hour later dropped them and seven containers over the padi fields of the Ningchangyang Valley in the Kachin Hills. On the following day Roberts made radio contact with his base at Dinjan and that afternoon moved his group to a local rest house where he established a base. Shortly afterwards he despatched two patrols, each of two Gurkhas and a Kachin guide, to reconnoitre the areas around Myitkina and Tiangzup. The Myitkina patrol returned on 8 July, having been unable to cross the Mali Hka River because of Japanese troops guarding the ferry. The other patrol appeared on the following day and reported a similar lack of success.

By this time Roberts had lost radio contact with Dinjan. It had been arranged before the start of the operation that in this event a Lysander aircraft would be despatched to look for the group. No aircraft appeared, however, and Roberts thus decided to head for Fort Hertz. This entailed a 150-mile march via narrow twisting tracks through very dense jungle. It was the monsoon season and the torrential downpours of rain made the going very difficult, the tracks becoming slippery and treacherous. Six of the group were already suffering from malaria and it was not long before the remainder also succumbed.

After seven days the group reached Kajitu, where Roberts was told that a Blenheim bomber had flown over the area twice, looking for him and his men. There was no sign of the aircraft on the following day and so he decided to press on towards Nbyem. That afternoon, however, the Blenheim was spotted over Kajitu and its attention was eventually attracted with Very flares. Communication was established by laying out messages on the ground, and the aircrew responded by dropping a message saying that the aircraft would return on the following day with supplies of food. During the following two days, however, there was no sign of it and so Roberts and his men resumed their march towards Nbyem. As they did so, they came upon the dead and wounded of the Chinese Fifth Army, which was then retreating into China via the Hukawng Valley.

In the meantime concern at Headquarters 50 Indian Parachute Brigade was mounting and eventually Maj Paul Hopkinson, the Brigade Major, was despatched to Assam to establish contact with Roberts. By this time the monsoon rains had rendered the airstrip at Fort Hertz unusable, so he was only able to overfly the area in a Hudson, spotting Roberts and his men. Returning to Assam, the aircraft loaded up with supplies which were dropped to Roberts that same day. Meanwhile preparations were under way to drop a force at Fort Hertz to repair the airstrip. On 13 August Capt Jack Newland of 153rd Gurkha Parachute Battalion, accompanied by a VCO and four Gurkhas, Lt Bob McLune of 411th (Royal Bombay) Parachute Section IE and four other ranks from the brigade headquarters, parachuted into Fort Hertz. The airstrip was repaired and on 20 August a company of infantry, a detachment of Burma Levies, a number of sappers and several medical personnel were flown in. That same day Capt Roberts and his men, all of whom were very sick, were evacuated back to India.

In December 1942 a new unit joined 50 Indian Parachute Brigade, replacing 151st Parachute Battalion. This was the 3rd Battalion 7th Gurkha Rifles which had been converted to the parachute role. It was initially commanded by Lt Col Hugh Parsons of the 2nd KEO Gurkha Rifles but in February 1943 he broke a leg while on his parachute course and was replaced by Lt Col George Bond of the 1st KGO Gurkha Rifles. Shortly afterwards the battalion was redesignated 154th Gurkha Parachute Battalion.

By early 1943 there had been considerable progress with regard to parachute training in India, the ALS being redesignated No. 3 PTS. The aircraft allocated for parachute training still consisted of Valencias and a single Hudson, until 215 Sqn RAF arrived with its Wellington bombers. This unit was joined in April by 99 Sqn RAF with more Wellingtons, these being replaced in turn a month later by 62 Sqn equipped with Hudsons. In June, however, the first C-47 Dakota transport arrived and was in use by the end of July. More followed later in the year, replacing the Wellingtons and Hudsons.

In the meantime 50 Indian Parachute Brigade underwent expansion, each battalion being allocated a support company comprising platoons of 3-inch mortars and Vickers

.303 medium machine guns. In addition the brigade was also allocated an MMG company, a pathfinder platoon and a brigade headquarters defence platoon. Its engineer element was increased from a section to a squadron, and its medical support increased to a field ambulance.

In late 1943 the commander, Brig M.R.J. 'Tim' Hope-Thomson, was warned that the brigade would be taking part in Operation Bulldozer which involved the capture of Akyab, a town on the coast of Burma 200 miles north of Rangoon, by an amphibious assault to be carried out by 36th Infantry Division with 50 Indian Parachute Brigade in support.

A period of intensive training began in preparation for Bulldozer, carried out at the Indian Army's Jungle Warfare School at Raiwala. 153rd Gurkha Parachute Battalion, along with the brigade headquarters and its signals section, arrived by parachute. Transported in thirty-two Dakotas, the entire force flew 400 miles across the Punjab and conducted the largest drop carried out so far by the brigade. By the end of 1943 the brigade had completed its training and was at a high state of readiness. Thus the announcement that Bulldozer had been cancelled caused considerable disappointment.

At the end of February 1944 the brigade, less 154th Gurkha Parachute Battalion, which was carrying out parachute training, moved 1,500 miles from its base at Cambellpur to Assam by rail and steamer. Its new location was at Chakabama, 10 miles to the east of Kohima, and its area of responsibility was the Jessami–Ukhrul sector to the south-east. Under command of the brigade was the 1st Battalion Assam Rifles and two companies of the Shere Regiment, a native state unit. The brigade itself was under command of 23rd Indian Division which, with 17th and 20th Indian Divisions in the Chin Hills and Kabaw Valley respectively, formed part of IV Indian Corps based at Imphal, which, as described earlier in Chapter 4, was a major Japanese objective.

Following intelligence reports that the Japanese were preparing for an offensive in Assam, the commander of the Fourteenth Army, Gen Sir William 'Bill' Slim, realised that the main threat faced IV Indian Corps and decided to fight a defensive battle in the area of Imphal. Consequently on 14 March 17th and 20th Indian Divisions were ordered to withdraw but the Japanese moved swiftly and attacked the 17th at two locations in its rear. Thus 23rd Indian Division was ordered to send forward two of its formations, 49 Indian Infantry Brigade and 50 Indian Parachute Brigade, to cover the withdrawal of 17th Indian Division.

On 10 March the commander of 23rd Indian Division, Maj Gen Ouvry Roberts, ordered 50 Indian Parachute Brigade Group to take over the vast area of mountainous jungle south of Kohima, bounded by the Kohima–Imphal road and Chindwin River to the east, and as far south as a number of tracks linking Litan, Sangshak, Finch's Corner and Sheldon's Corner. Its task was to patrol the area and prevent enemy infiltration. The next day 152nd Indian Parachute Battalion set off, reaching the village of Litan on the following day. Three days later it marched 15 miles to Sangshak, passing through Finch's Corner to Sheldon's Corner where it relieved the 4th Battalion 5th Mahratta Light Infantry.

The battalion position at Sheldon's Corner was intended to block the approaches along a number of tracks from the Chindwin to a road running from Imphal to Ukhrul. It comprised a forward company base at Point 7378 and another at 'Gammon Hill'. Two miles from Point 7378, on the northern side of a feature known as 'Badger Hill', was a hide position occupied by the remainder of the battalion, which would launch a counter-attack against any enemy advance, the two forward positions acting as pivots on which any manoeuvre would be based. The positions at Sheldon's Corner, however, had been designed for a battalion with four rifle companies but, like all the battalions in the brigade, 152nd Indian Parachute Battalion only possessed three. It was thus unable to man both the forward positions and provide a counter-attack force while also defending the hide position on Badger Hill.

On 16 March troops of the Japanese 15th Division crossed the Chindwin and advanced on Imphal along an axis via Myothit, Sangshak and Litan. Meanwhile the 31st Division crossed the river further to the north, heading for Ukhrul and Kohima.

On the morning of 19 March a patrol of 152nd Indian Parachute Battalion encountered a force of 200 enemy. Shortly afterwards the Commanding Officer, Lt Col Paul Hopkinson, and his tactical headquarters on Badger Hill observed eighty Japanese of the 3rd Battalion 58th Regimental Group, commanded by Maj Gen Miyazaki, swarming up a track from the direction of the village of Pushing. Throughout that day C Company on Point 7378 was subjected to a series of attacks, which were beaten off. A Company and a company of the 4th/5th Mahrattas were sent to its aid but failed in their attempts to fight their way through. On the following morning C Company was overrun, with only one subaltern officer and a small number of other ranks succeeding in escaping and making their back to the battalion that night. Meanwhile B Company, on Gammon Hill, was subjected to probing attacks, all of which were beaten off.

By this time the Japanese were approaching Ukhrul itself and there was an increasing risk of the force at Sheldon's Corner being outflanked. Thus during the early hours of 21 March 50 Indian Parachute Brigade received orders to withdraw under cover of darkness west to Sangshak, where it was to form a defensive box. In the event of the Japanese passing it by, it was to harass and cut their lines of communication as part of the operations to defend Imphal. At 2 a.m. on the following day 152nd Indian Parachute Battalion and the Mahrattas withdrew, making their way along a track through the jungle to Kidney Hill, where a patrol from 153rd Gurkha Parachute Battalion, which had arrived at Sangshak on 20 March, reported that the track leading to Sangshak was clear but that a large enemy force was heading along the road from Ukhrul to Sangshak. The two battalions pressed on to Sangshak, which had been occupied by the rest of the brigade on the previous evening.

Sangshak was far from ideal as a defensive position. A Naga village with the road from Finch's Corner running along its southern side to Sheldon's Corner and on to the Chindwin, it was in a commanding position dominating several major track junctions. The ridgeline on which it was situated offered little cover, while the slopes approaching it were clad in thick jungle right up to the brigade's perimeter. There were no anti-personnel mines, explosives or barbed wire available, making it virtually impossible for the defenders to construct obstacles to prevent the enemy from reaching the forward positions or to channel them into covered approaches. Moreover a thick layer of rock prevented trenches being dug any deeper than 3 feet and in some places outcrops of rock prevented any digging whatsoever. Finally the only available supplies of water were from sources outside the perimeter.

In addition to its two parachute battalions, the brigade had under command the Kalibahadur Regiment (a Nepalese Army unit) less two companies; D Company 4th/5th Mahratta Light Infantry; 15th Mountain Battery RIA; 582nd Jungle Mortar Battery RIA; and 74th Field Company IE.

153rd Gurkha Parachute Battalion defended the western sector of the perimeter and part of the southern, while the Kalibahadur Regiment was allocated the eastern sector and part of the northern. 152nd Indian Parachute Battalion took up positions along the north-west sector, which included a small Baptist mission church, while the Mahrattas, together with 74th Field Company and the brigade headquarters defence platoon, assumed responsibility for the rest of the southern sector. 15th Mountain Battery and the brigade's mortars were positioned on a plateau in the north-west corner of the area.

At 1.30 a.m. on 23 March the Japanese began their first assault on Sangshak, launching an attack on the Mahrattas and also probing the southern and south-western sectors. A fierce attack on the area of the church was broken up by the brigade's MMG company and mortar battery, which mowed down large numbers of screaming Japanese as they launched themselves against the perimeter. The attacks nevertheless continued throughout the day and the following night, with the defenders beginning to run short of ammunition, rations and medical supplies. On 24 March the Japanese brought up a force of 400 reinforcements and a number of 75mm artillery pieces which at 2 p.m. began bringing down fire on the brigade headquarters and 152nd Indian Parachute Battalion, this being followed by a strong attack which was only beaten off after some very fierce fighting. Two hours later air support for the beleaguered garrison arrived in the form of Hurricane fighter-bombers, which attacked the Japanese – although they were hampered in their pinpointing of targets by the thick jungle. The bitter fighting continued throughout the rest of that day, an attack during the evening taking some of the forward positions in the area of the church before the enemy were driven off by a counter-attack.

By this time the situation was becoming very grim. Efforts at resupply had failed almost completely, with only one Dakota succeeding in dropping its containers at low level inside the perimeter on each occasion; it was later learned that this aircraft had been flown by a crew who had transported and dropped units of the brigade during their training. The Japanese had cut all the tracks around Sangshak and a reconnaissance patrol sent out from the village reported a large build-up of troops and the establishment of a large administrative base area.

In the early morning of 26 March the enemy launched another major assault, bringing down a heavy concentration of artillery fire on 152nd Indian Parachute Battalion, followed by an attack by three companies of infantry. Eventually they succeeded in taking the area of the church, which dominated the brigade's main positions, and from it attacked the positions of 15th Mountain Battery and 582nd Jungle Mortar Battery.

Counter-attacks by 152nd Indian Parachute Battalion and the Mahrattas failed to recapture the positions by the church and at 9 p.m. that night Brig Hope-Thomson ordered 153rd Gurkha Parachute Battalion to retake the area, the task being given to Maj Jimmy Roberts's A Company. The Gurkhas stormed the positions, led by Roberts blowing a hunting horn, and the Japanese were routed.

By now it was apparent that the situation was hopeless and it was only a matter of time before Sangshak was overrun. During the late afternoon of 27 March Hope-Thomson received orders by radio that the brigade was to fight its way out to the south and then move westwards. Following last light, equipment, stores and documents were destroyed, the noise being masked by diversionary bursts of machine-gun fire and the noise of enemy shelling. At 10.30 p.m. the withdrawal began, the brigade carrying as many of its wounded as possible on makeshift stretchers, the others hobbling along on improvised crutches. The column of men made their way in the darkness through the Mahrattas' positions on the southern sector, which was not covered by the Japanese, who had found the steep slopes unassailable during their first attack. On reaching the jungle, the column split up into small groups, all of which had been ordered to head south until 6 a.m. when they were to turn west towards Imphal, 30 miles away.

Initially the going was relatively easy as all the ridgelines ran north–south. On turning west, however, the groups of exhausted men were confronted with a seemingly endless series of steep ascents and descents over the crests of ridgelines. Although armed, almost all were without ammunition and grenades, while others were either too exhausted or too badly wounded to be able to carry their weapons. There was little or no food and caution had to be exercised as the groups stumbled their way through the jungle; the Japanese had occupied most of the Naga villages and columns of their troops were moving along the tracks, heading for Imphal and Sangshak. For the wounded the journey was an appalling ordeal and eventually it became impossible to carry them any further through the thick jungle or over the steep ridgelines. Those who could not walk were left in the care of friendly Naga tribesmen.

Eventually, on the sixth day of the withdrawal, the leading groups, including those led by Maj Harry Butchard of 153rd Gurkha Parachute Battalion and Col 'Abbo' Abbott, the brigade's Deputy Commander, encountered patrols of the 17th Dogra Regiment, who directed them to the road between Imphal and Yaingangpokpi, along which they made their way to Imphal itself.

Many feats of survival and endurance came to light once 50 Indian Parachute Brigade had regrouped at Imphal. Among them was that of Lt Kynoch Shand of 153rd

Gurkha Parachute Battalion, who reappeared miraculously after having been given up for lost. He had been captured by the Japanese, who, having stripped him of most of his clothes and boots, had led him by a rope with his hands bound behind his back. During the night, however, he had escaped by launching himself down the side of a ridgeline and rolling several hundred feet to the valley below. Thereafter he had wandered barefoot through the jungle until he met a Naga who cut his bonds, enabling him to make his way to Imphal.

Following a short period spent regrouping and refitting, 50 Indian Parachute Brigade came under command of 17th Indian Division and took part in the defence of Imphal. The only battalion in the brigade which was in reasonable condition following the battle at Sangshak was 153rd Gurkha Parachute Battalion, which was assigned to a defensive box with the codename Oyster, while the remainder of the brigade, reinforced by a company of the 1st Battalion The West Yorkshire Regiment, assumed responsibility for Catfish. The brigade tactical headquarters, together with a company of 152nd Indian Parachute Battalion and the West Yorkshire company, formed a mobile counter-attack force while a mobile reserve was produced from another West Yorkshire company mounted in Bren carriers, a company of the 7th Baluch Regiment and a detachment of 129 Field Battery RA. Dubbed 'Abforce', this latter force was commanded by Col Abbott.

On the night of 20 May the Japanese 33rd Division, commanded by Lt Gen Yanagida Tanaka, launched an attack on 17th Indian Division and cut off its headquarters from its forward brigades. Two days later Brig E.G. 'Lakri' Woods took over command of 50 Indian Parachute Brigade and immediately was tasked with clearing the enemy from the divisional headquarters area with a composite force formed from units at his disposal.

Meanwhile the rest of the brigade had been deployed on operations to harry the Japanese, who were withdrawing via Ukhrul. 153rd Gurkha Parachute Battalion, which had been placed with 152nd Indian Parachute Battalion under command of 20th Indian Division, was deployed around Mung Ching. The enemy were resisting fiercely any attempts to dislodge them from the area south of Ukhrul and were particularly active to the east of Imphal, in the area of Tangkhul Hundung. C Company, under Maj John Saunders, was given the task of forming a column that would include detachments of the Assam Rifles and 'V' Force, a locally recruited intelligence-gathering unit led by British officers. Designated 'Sancol', its mission was to monitor Japanese activity in the area, to engage enemy forces and destroy or capture them, and to interdict enemy escape routes between Kamjong and Humine.

Sancol set off on its mission on 25 June. The remainder of 153rd Gurkha Parachute Battalion meanwhile formed part of a larger column. Called 'Tarforce' and commanded by Lt Col G.L. Tarver of the Baluch Regiment, it also comprised 152nd Indian Parachute Battalion, a company of the 1st Battalion The Devonshire Regiment and a company of the 4th Madras Regiment.

By now the Japanese had been routed and were in full retreat, hampered by the monsoon rains and lack of air support. As they streamed back down the tracks towards the Chindwin, they discarded their equipment and abandoned their wounded, leaving the dead where they fell. Tarforce and Sancol meanwhile carried out a large number of ambushes, inflicting heavy casualties. Despite their desperate situation, the Japanese refused to surrender when cornered and in every case fought hard to the end.

By 23 July the two columns had completed their tasks and on 26 July both parachute battalions returned to Imphal. Two days later 50 Indian Parachute Brigade left Burma and returned to India, in early August arriving at Secunderabad where it was joined by 154th Gurkha Parachute Battalion. Subsequently, however, it was discovered that the airfields in the area were unable to accommodate Dakotas and so by October the brigade had moved to the area of Rawalpindi. The brigade headquarters was based at Chaklala while 152nd Indian Parachute Battalion and 153rd Gurkha Parachute Battalion were located at Sangjani, and 154th Gurkha Parachute Battalion took up residence at Kahuta.

The following period saw an expansion of the Indian Army's airborne forces with the formation of 9th Indian Airborne Division, commanded by Maj Gen Eric Down, which shortly afterwards was redesignated 44th Indian Airborne Division. Meanwhile 14 (Long Range Penetration) Brigade, which had operated in an airlanding role during the second operation carried out by the Chindits of Maj Gen Orde Wingate's Special Force, was redesignated 14 Air Landing Brigade. In January 1945, following the disbandment of Special Force, 77 Infantry Brigade was converted to the parachute role and redesignated 77 Indian Parachute Brigade.

In the meantime, on 18 December 1944, authorisation had been given for the formation of The Indian Parachute Regiment and this came into effect on 1 March 1945. The insignia of the new regiment was the same as that of The Parachute Regiment of the British Army but with the word 'India' inscribed at the base of the parachute. This was worn on the maroon beret, which replaced the broad-brimmed Gurkha hat previously worn by all Indian and Gurkha parachute battalions.

With the formation of the new regiment, the parachute battalions were renumbered and in some instances reorganised. 152nd Indian Parachute Battalion was divided to form two new units, the 1st and 4th Indian Parachute Battalions, the 1st Battalion being Hindu and the 4th Muslim. Meanwhile 153rd and 154th Gurkha Parachute Battalions were renumbered the 2nd and 3rd respectively. The 1st Indian and 3rd Gurkha Parachute Battalions were allocated to 50 Indian Parachute Brigade, while the 2nd Gurkha and 4th Indian Parachute Battalions went to 77 Indian Parachute Brigade. In the meantime two British parachute battalions, the 15th and 16th, had been formed in India from the 1st Battalions of The King's Regiment and The South Staffordshire Regiment, and these were allotted to 77 and 50 Indian Parachute Brigades respectively.

During this period the campaign in Burma had been continuing apace and two airborne operations had been planned as part of Gen Slim's Fourteenth Army strategy for the recapture of the country, one to seize the Yeu-Shwebo Plain and the other to

(*Opposite*): An image of a Gurkha paratrooper dropping into action during the assault on Rangoon in 1945, taken a second after he exited the aircraft.

take Rangoon. A third operation had also been under consideration for the capture of Kalewa and Kalemyo. All three operations, however, were cancelled owing to Slim's unwillingness to divert much-needed transport aircraft from supplying his forward formations, and because of the successes and swift progress of Fourteenth Army, which had advanced south and taken Kalewa and Kalemyo. The Yeu-Shwebo Plain had been taken a month ahead of schedule but an unexpected enemy counter-offensive had slowed down the advance to Rangoon, which had to be captured before the arrival of the monsoon.

An amphibious operation, codenamed Dracula, described previously in Chapter 4, had been planned for the capture of the Burmese capital and at the end of March it was decided to proceed with it, albeit in a modified form. It comprised landings by 26th Indian Division, with naval and air support, on both banks of the Rangoon River south of the city and midway between Elephant Point and the Bassein Creek. The river had been mined by the Japanese, as well as by Allied aircraft, and thus minesweepers would be required to precede the warships and landing craft carrying the division. Furthermore the enemy had sited coastal defences on the west bank of the river and these would have to be silenced before the minesweepers could enter the river mouth. The task of dealing with them would be carried out by a parachute battalion on 1 May, the day before the landings.

When 44th Indian Airborne Division was given details of the operation, it was in the midst of reorganisation. Furthermore a number of its officers were in Britain on leave, and a proportion of the men of the two Gurkha battalions were likewise in Nepal or, in the case of the 3rd Gurkha Parachute Battalion, in the process of transferring to 77 Indian Parachute Brigade. Consequently a composite battalion, commanded by Maj Jack Newland, was formed from the two Gurkha battalions for the operation. Moving to Chaklala, it was joined by two teams of pathfinders, a section of 411th (Royal Bombay) Parachute Squadron IE, a detachment of 80th Parachute Field Ambulance and detachments from the signals and intelligence sections of Headquarters 50 Indian Parachute Brigade. On completion of its training at Chaklala, the battalion was transferred on 14 April to Midnapore where it remained for ten days, preparing its equipment and rehearsing for the operation. On 29 April it flew to Akyab, on the coast of Burma, 200 miles north of Rangoon, where it was joined by a 200-strong reserve force under Maj Maurice Fry.

At 2.30 a.m. on 1 May 1945 two Dakotas took off from Akyab with two pathfinder teams, forward air controllers (FACs), a group of personnel from Force 136 and a platoon to secure and hold the DZ. Thirty minutes later the main force took off in another thirty-eight Dakotas and at 5.45 a.m. the battalion dropped over Tawhai.

Having suffered only light casualties during the drop and rallying swiftly in the pouring rain, Maj Newland and his men advanced the first 2½ miles towards their objectives before they were forced to halt and wait for Liberator bombers of the USAAF to carry out a bombing raid on Elephant Point. Although the battalion was 3,000 yards from the nearest of the bombers' targets, and despite the fact that some officers and men wore yellow recognition panels on their backs and carried orange umbrellas, C Company was bombed and strafed from the air, losing 15 men killed and 30 wounded. Consequently one of the FACs called a halt to any further bombing except when ordered.

Thereafter the battalion continued its advance over flooded terrain and at 4 p.m. came under fire from an enemy bunker and some small craft on the river. The latter were silenced by aircraft called in to do so before the bunker was attacked by a company supported by flamethrowers. Of the 37 Japanese inside it, only one survived but the battalion suffered 41 casualties in this action.

Maj Fry and his 200-strong reserve force, accompanied by a field surgical team, dropped at 3.30 p.m. and half an hour later a resupply drop was carried out. Meanwhile the rain continued unabated and the tides that night were so high that the battalion's positions were under three feet of water, the paratroops being forced to perch wherever they could find any dry ground. Next morning the battalion continued its task of searching and clearing the bunkers in the area; as it did so the convoy of vessels carrying 26th Indian Division headed up the Rangoon River.

On the following day the battalion moved to Sadainghmut and two days later marched on to Rangoon, where it was employed on anti-looting patrols and searches for enemy stragglers. It remained in the city until 16 May when it departed by ship for India, arriving ten days later at Bilaspur, where it rejoined the rest of 44th Indian Airborne Division.

On 11 August 1945 the war with Japan ended. The end of the conflict inevitably meant demobilisation on a large scale for the Indian Army, which had swelled from a peacetime strength of 194,373 to some 2,500,000 by the time hostilities ended. Shortly afterwards all British elements of 2nd Indian Airborne Division, as 44th Indian Airborne Division had been redesignated, were withdrawn and formed into 6 Independent Parachute Brigade Group under command of the division which by this time was commanded by Maj Gen Charles Boucher. In the meantime 14 Air Landing Brigade was converted to the parachute role.

This was the end, for the time being, of Gurkha airborne troops as shortly afterwards the 3rd and 4th Gurkha Parachute Battalions were withdrawn from The Indian Parachute Regiment and transferred to Gurkha regiments. On 26 October 1945 The Indian Parachute Regiment itself was disbanded, the infantry element of India's airborne forces thereafter being provided by parachute battalions of the Indian Army's infantry regiments, among them the 1st Parachute Battalion 12th Frontier Force Regiment and the 4th Parachute Battalion 6th Rajputana Rifles (Outram's).

* * *

Following Partition between India and Pakistan in August 1947 and the formation of Britain's Brigade of Gurkhas in 1948, there were no Gurkha airborne troops in the British Army's order of battle until January 1963, when the Gurkha Independent

Parachute Company was formed. The rebellion in Brunei in December 1962 and the initial tactical airlanding operations carried out at Brunei Town, Anduki and Seria by the 1st/2nd KEO Gurkha Rifles and the 1st Battalion The Queen's Own Highlanders had highlighted the requirement for a parachute unit to be based in the Far East with the role of seizing an airfield into which troops could be flown thereafter. It was subsequently decided to form such a unit and the task of doing so was given to The Brigade of Gurkhas.

Formed on 1 January 1963, the company comprised men drawn from all eight infantry battalions and the corps units. Parachute training was conducted in Malaya, a selection course having been established at Johore Bahru under Capt Bruce Niven of the 10th PMO Gurkha Rifles, who had already undergone parachute training in Britain. Commanded by Maj Peter Quantrill, the company was initially employed in an infantry role but shortly afterwards was deployed to the First and Second Divisions of Sarawak, where its members were formed into small groups of two and three tasked with training and leading sections of Border Scouts.

This, however, did not prove successful and it became apparent that the Gurkhas were not happy working with the Scouts. Their role was an unenviable one: the conduct of surveillance over large areas of the border with Kalimantan while trying to train and lead groups of indigenous tribesmen about whom they knew little, and who were unused to military discipline and at times proved temperamental, and of whose loyalty they were uncertain. The Gurkhas' misgivings about the Scouts appeared justified to a certain extent following the action at Long Jawi, an account of which is given in Chapter 7.

At this point command of the company was assumed by Maj L.M. 'Phil' Phillips of the 10th PMO Gurkha Rifles. The Director of Borneo Operations, Maj Gen Walter Walker, had decided that the company was to be regrouped and used in a 'fire brigade' role, being deployed wherever it was needed at short notice. During the first six weeks of his command, Phillips walked the length and breadth of the First and Second Divisions, visiting his men and restoring their morale with news of the company's impending new role. In due course the unit was concentrated in Kuching, where it was based for the time being. From there it carried out a number of quick reaction tasks in support of units based in the Lundu area.

In early 1964 the company returned to the Malaysian mainland where it was based at the Jungle Warfare School at Johore Bahru. Shortly afterwards, however, Maj Phillips was summoned to Maj Gen Walker's headquarters on the island of Labuan, where he was informed that the company was to operate henceforth in the long-range reconnaissance patrol role in Borneo, augmenting the SAS squadrons and the Guards Independent Parachute Company. With the assistance of 22 SAS, the unit underwent reorganisation from three platoons into sixteen five-man patrols plus a headquarters and logistic support element. Each patrol consisted of a commander, a medic, two

(*Opposite*): Members of the Gurkha Independent Parachute Company pictured during training in Malaya in the 1960s. These soldiers had the benefit of reserve parachutes which were only introduced after the Second World War.

assault pioneers and a signaller. The rationale behind the adoption of the five-man patrol, as opposed to the four-man patrols used by the SAS squadrons and the Guards Independent Parachute Company, was that the company's primary role continued to be that of airfield assault and its established strength of 128 all ranks was based on the operational requirement for that role. Moreover there were only sufficient radios available for sixteen patrols and the company headquarters, plus a small stock of spare sets.

Following a short period in which the weaker members of the company were weeded out and a number of new recruits selected and trained for the new role, the company underwent a period of training at Johore Bahru under instructors from 22 SAS. Patrol medics then underwent training at the British Military Hospital in Singapore.

By August 1964 all training had been completed and the company was once again concentrated at Johore Bahru. During the latter half of the month it took part in operations with the 1st/10th PMO Gurkha Rifles in Central Malaysia to hunt down Indonesian paratroops who had been dropped in the area of Labis, as recounted in Chapter 7. In the event none of the company's patrols made contact with the enemy but the operation proved of value in helping to prepare for its coming deployment.

Towards the end of October the company returned to Borneo, where it relieved the Guards Independent Parachute Company at Sibu in the Third Division, deploying twelve patrols, the remaining four being attached to a Gurkha battalion in the Fifth Division. One of those deployed on the border in the Third Division was commanded by Lt Mike Callaghan of the 10th PMO Gurkha Rifles, based at Long Banai, a village inhabited by a nomadic Punan tribe. After reading a book compiled by a university expedition to Borneo prior to the Second World War, Maj Phillips began to doubt the location of the patrol's base, which had been taken over from the Guards Independent Parachute Company. He became convinced that it was not on the border but a considerable distance from it. Enlisting the aid of the Fleet Air Arm helicopter detachment at Nangga Gaat, Phillips flew on the next fortnightly resupply mission. Leaving Long Banai, he then flew further eastwards until he spotted the escarpment that followed the line of the border. Accordingly Lt Callaghan's patrol was moved to a new location on the border, being followed soon afterwards by the Punan from Long Banai, who were already missing the food and tobacco dispensed by the patrol. The tribesmen soon proved invaluable in providing information concerning Indonesian activities over the border.

Over the next six months the company was on operations in the Third Division, the longest period in the jungle being twelve weeks. Patrols were rotated to allow them to rest and recuperate at periodic intervals at the company's base at Sibu. During this period there were no contacts with the enemy in the Third or Fifth Divisions, although some of the company's patrols did carry out unauthorised forays across the border into Kalimantan. Despite a request from Maj Phillips, Maj Gen Walker had refused to authorise the company to take part in Claret operations, as described in Chapter 7.

In April 1965 the company handed over to C (Independent) Company 2 PARA and returned to the Malaysian mainland, where it moved to a new base at Kluang. Shortly afterwards Phillips handed over command to Maj John Cross. During the following five months the company underwent a period of stringent retraining while also adding further men to its ranks; a new and stricter selection procedure was introduced for potential recruits as the parachute course generally had proved to be easy for Gurkhas, the majority of whom possessed a very high standard of physical fitness. While parachuting posed no problems for them, however, the same could not be said for the standards of navigation and the other skills required for the patrol company role. Tests were thus introduced which assessed each Gurkha's suitability for this type of work and his ability to master it.

In September the company deployed to Borneo, this time finding itself in the Fifth Division of Sarawak. During this second tour of operations the company carried out Claret missions into Kalimantan, one being led by the company commander, Maj John Cross. Two patrols under him were inserted by helicopter to a location a mile inside Sarawak, from where they climbed through the jungle until they reached the unmarked border on a 4,000ft-high ridgeline. Crossing over into Kalimantan, Cross and his men broke track and took up positions for the night as last light approached. On the following day both patrols continued heading south to carry out their task of reconnoitring a designated area to check for any sign of Indonesian activity, subsequently discovering a recently abandoned camp.

On another occasion Cross led four patrols from the company on a task to reconnoitre a track running parallel to the border. There was an enemy base 3 miles to the west, accommodating up to 500 men, from which the Indonesians had been mounting raids into the Fifth Division. Cross's task was to determine whether the track was in use as a route via which such incursions were being launched. His four patrols were to spend four days reconnoitring in four different directions, thereafter concentrating at an RV and laying an ambush on the track, for which all four patrols were equipped with Claymore mines.

Cross and his men crossed the border without incident but, just before separating to carry out their respective reconnaissance tasks, they encountered a local inhabitant approaching from the direction of the enemy base. After some deliberation Cross let him continue on his way but decided that the patrols would spend only that day reconnoitring before returning to the RV that evening. Thereafter he led his own patrol eastwards, following the local, who had revealed that there were enemy tracks in the area and that a longhouse nearby was inhabited by a number of Indonesian troops.

When the time came to head for the RV, however, Maj Cross found that he was lost and there was no sign of the tracks referred to by the local. During the afternoon he and his three Gurkhas passed by the longhouse and, on climbing a rise nearby, came upon a tree with the letters 'RPKAD', the initials of the Indonesian Army's para-commando regiment, and the previous day's date carved on its trunk. While he was unable to determine his precise location, Cross was sure that he was between the enemy base and his planned ambush location. By this time, however, last light was fast approaching and thus, rather than risk walking into his own ambush, he moved his patrol into a lying-up position under cover of darkness. That evening he sent a message by radio to his other three patrols, ordering them to move to his location by 8 o'clock the next morning.

First light on the following day revealed the patrol's LUP as being in a clump of trees surrounded by a large expanse of open terrain. By 10 a.m. there was no sign of the other patrols and Cross was becoming increasingly anxious. Eventually, at the suggestion of one of his men, he resorted to making cuckoo calls, a ruse he had used eighteen years before during the Malayan Emergency, after discovering that there were no cuckoos in Malaya! The calls proved successful and 20 minutes later the three patrols appeared, having been waiting half a mile away. They had guessed that Cross would use the cuckoo call and had been waiting for it.

Without delay Cross moved his small force into the cover of the jungle nearby, where he decided to reconnoitre the longhouse his patrol had passed on the previous afternoon. Approaching it with great caution, he found it inhabited by a small group of elderly locals, who made the Gurkhas welcome.

On the following day Cross and his men began the long march back to the border. During the late afternoon they camped on a ridgeline overlooking an area that had been the scene of an action between the Indonesians and elements of the 1st/2nd KEO Gurkha Rifles some months previously and which featured a large and apparently well-maintained LZ. As the four patrols were eating their evening meal, however, an Indonesian helicopter, escorted by fighters, suddenly flew overhead in the direction of the LZ. From the change in the noise of the aircraft's engines, Cross could tell that it had landed and guessed that it was disembarking troops. A few minutes later it reappeared and flew away. In the meantime the four patrols had stood-to and were ready to engage any enemy who appeared. In the event none did so and Cross led his men back to the border without any contact taking place.

June 1966 saw the official affiliation of the Gurkha Independent Parachute Company to The Parachute Regiment, all members thereafter wearing the maroon beret and the badge of the regiment, the latter worn on a backing of rifle green bearing the colours of The Brigade of Gurkhas.

As mentioned briefly in Chapter 7, that same month saw a force of Indonesians under Lt Sumbi crossing the border between the villages of Long Semado and Ba Kelalan in the Fifth Division. The battalion in whose area Sumbi's possible crossing point lay was the 1st/7th DEO Gurkha Rifles. Deployed forward of its positions were patrols of the Gurkha Independent Parachute Company and on 29 July it was one of these, commanded by Cpl Singbahadur Gurung, that picked up the Indonesians' trail when Rifleman Dharmalal Rai spotted a small piece of silver paper that smelt of coffee. As there were no British or Commonwealth troops in the area and in view of the fact that the Gurkha ration pack did not contain coffee, Singbahadur and Dharmalal assumed that the paper had been dropped by an Indonesian.

A careful search of the area revealed the tracks of three men heading north into the Fifth Division. The patrol followed up, tracking the Indonesians for the next two days and nights and not camping or cooking any food for fear of alerting the enemy to its presence. Their persistence paid off as on the third day Cpl Singbahadur and his men discovered three pairs of discarded jungle boots and pieces of hessian used by 45 men who had secured them over their boots to disguise their tracks.

The initial reaction to the patrol's report was one of disbelief and Cpl Singbahadur was ordered to backtrack to ensure that the tracks originated in Kalimantan. This having been confirmed, there was no doubt that the tracks belonged to Sumbi's raiding force.

Together with elements of the 1st/7th DEO Gurkha Rifles and other units, five more of the company's patrols joined the pursuit. Two platoons of the 1st/7th were inserted by helicopter on 20 August into a remote area of mountains to the east of Bukit Pagon, a 6,000ft-high peak straddling the border between Sarawak and Brunei, while a third made an approach on foot, accompanied by two of Sumbi's group who had been captured. These led the platoon to where they had last seen the rest of the raiders. Two weeks later a number of contacts took place, during which 24 of Sumbi's men were either killed or captured, while others either died of starvation or surrendered themselves to the security forces. Of the total force of 50, 46 enemy were accounted for by the 1st/7th Gurkha Rifles. Lt Sumbi himself was captured on 3 September, three weeks after the signing of the Bangkok Accord. It was later discovered that he had attended a course at the British Army's Jungle Warfare School, where his performance had earned him a 'B' grading.

In 1968 the company reverted to the organisation of a conventional rifle company and resumed its role of parachute assault on to an airfield. Based at the Jungle Warfare School, it also performed the duties of demonstration company. In 1971 The Brigade of Gurkhas withdrew from Malaysia to Hong Kong, where no role was envisaged for a parachute unit. Consequently on 31 October that year the Gurkha Independent Parachute Company was disbanded.

Thereafter there was a gap of twenty-five years during which there was no parachute element within The Brigade of Gurkhas, albeit some members of the UK-based Gurkha battalion, which formed part of 5 Airborne Brigade at that time, underwent parachute training. In 1996, however, as a result of a shortage of manpower in The Parachute Regiment, the decision was taken to form a Gurkha parachute company as reinforcement for one of the regiment's battalions. Along with two other Gurkha reinforcement companies, C (Gurkha) Company 2 PARA, commanded by Maj Angus Forbes, was formed from men drawn from the 2nd and 3rd Battalions The Royal Gurkha Rifles (2 and 3 RGR) at Knook Camp, on Stanford Practical Training Area in Norfolk, on 17 November 1996. Following a month of build-up training, the company formally became part of 2 PARA under Lt Col David Benest. It was not until May 1997, however, following a period of intensive jungle training in Belize, that the company joined the battalion, which had been in Northern Ireland.

Gurkhas serving with C (Gurkha) Company 2 PARA take the opportunity to enjoy a break during Tactical Air Landing Operations (TALO) training.

The years 1997 and 1998 saw C (Gurkha) Company on overseas exercises in France and the United States, all members being awarded their French and US parachute wings. In January 1999, with the remainder of 2 PARA back in Northern Ireland, the company, now commanded by Maj Simon Gilderson and reinforced by a platoon of 1 RGR, was despatched to Bosnia on Operation Palatine, a six-month operational deployment as part of the NATO forces supporting the Dayton Peace Accord. Deployed in the Banja Luka area, it was employed on a number of operations, which ranged from intelligence gathering, inspecting sites at which arms were stored under the terms of the Accord, and carrying out community relations projects.

April 2000 found C (Gurkha) Company, by this time commanded by Maj Tristan Forster, moving with 2 PARA from Aldershot to Colchester to join the newly formed 16 Air Assault Brigade, which replaced 5 Airborne Brigade as the British Army's airborne element. On 5 May 1 PARA was deployed to the strife-torn West African state of Sierra Leone. The battalion was accompanied by 7 and 8 Platoons of C (Gurkha) Company, commanded respectively by Lt (QGO) Bhuwani Limbu and Lt Umesh Pun, and reinforced by some members of 9 Platoon, which assisted in defending the British forces' main base at Lungi Airfield as well as patrolling the nearby jungle and surrounding areas.

By March 2001 the company, under Maj Dan O'Donnell, was back in Belize. Accompanied by the Reconnaissance Platoon and two platoons of D Company 2 PARA, it carried out six weeks of jungle warfare training, culminating in a five-day company exercise. August saw C (Gurkha) Company deployed overseas with 2 PARA in Macedonia on Operation Bessemer, whose aim was the collection and disposal of weapons and ammunition handed in by the National Liberation Army (NLA). The company's role was the provision of protection teams forming part of Task Force Harvest, the NATO formation responsible for disarming the NLA. Covered by members of these teams, British military personnel made contact with members of the NLA, subsequently gaining their agreement to hand over their weapons. Such operations were of a highly sensitive nature and took place in areas of high tension.

By this time 2 PARA was fully up to strength and, following the company's return from Macedonia, the decision was taken to disband C (Gurkha) Company, despite the Parachute Regiment's desire to retain it, and to return its officers and men to 2 RGR. The date for disbandment was set for 16 November 2001 but, two days beforehand, it was announced by the Commanding Officer of 2 PARA, Lt Col James Bashall, that the battalion was to take part in Operation Fingal, the deployment of British troops to

C (Gurkha) Company 2 PARA pictured on parade during the presentation of new colours to The Parachute Regiment, 19 June 1998.

Gurkhas running around the deck of the *QE2* during their passage to the Falklands and subsequent deployment with 5 Infantry Brigade.

GURKHAS IN THE FALKLANDS

In 1982, the 1st/7th DEO Gurkha Rifles formed part of 5 Infantry Brigade, along with the 2nd Battalion Scots Guards and 1st Battalion Welsh Guards, when it was deployed to the South Atlantic with 3 Commando Brigade RM. This was the first time that a Gurkha unit had seen active service since the Borneo Confrontation campaign in the mid-1960s and the Commandant, Lt Col David Morgan, who had seen service in Borneo, was delighted that his battalion had been given the opportunity.

The Gurkhas' reputation, however, preceded them to the Falklands, the British press and other media making much of their fighting reputation, in particular highlighting their skill with their razor-sharp kukris. This was no doubt part of the British psychological warfare campaign aimed at undermining the morale of the Argentinian occupation forces on the islands.

The 1st/7th travelled south aboard the QE2, cross-decking to another liner, the Canberra, at South Georgia for the final leg of the journey to San Carlos where 5 Infantry Brigade was to land. Thereafter, the battalion took part in the advance east towards Port Stanley but by the time it carried out an attack on the objective allotted to it, Mount William, the enemy had fled on hearing of the Gurkhas' advance. The latter were understandably disappointed at being robbed of the opportunity to fight, not a shot being fired or a kukri drawn as they captured Mount William from which they were able to see the white flags of surrender flying over Port Stanley.

Men of the 1st/7th DEO Gurkha Rifles digging in after landing at San Carlos from the *Canberra*, having been cross-decked from the *QE2* in South Georgia.

Gurkhas of C (Gurkha) Company 2 PARA wait to embark on a C-130 Hercules aircraft following a multi-national exercise in Poland.

Gurkhas take part in Tactical Air Landing Operations (TALO) training.

Gurkhas being airlifted by RAF Chinook helicopters during an airmobility exercise in the UK.

Members of C (Gurkha) Company 2 PARA pictured in Macedonia during their deployment on Task Force Harvest in September 2002.

A Gurkha enjoying his *bhat* (meal) during operations in Macedonia.

Afghanistan as part of the International Security Assistance Force (ISAF), and that the Gurkha company would go with it.

On 1 January 2002 two members of the company, Cpl Dillikumar Rai and Rifleman Anup Chamling, attached as Hindi interpreters, flew with 2 PARA's advance party from Britain to the Afghan capital Kabul. Accompanied by Maj O'Donnell and part of his headquarters, 7 and 9 Platoons arrived on 21 January, followed by 8 Platoon and the rest of Company Headquarters on 8 February.

Members of 7 and 9 Platoons were attached to 2 PARA's other three companies, providing Hindi speakers for each, while 8 Platoon was deployed on patrolling duties. Company Headquarters meanwhile was tasked with the training of an Afghan National Guard battalion.

Given the previous history of Gurkha regiments serving in Afghanistan, where five of the twenty-six Victoria Crosses awarded to Gurkhas and their British officers were won in the past, Kabul was of particular interest to the members of C (Gurkha) Company. Areas of the war-torn city were in a state of devastation after years of conflict, with many buildings appearing to be on the verge of collapse. The Gurkhas' ability to speak Hindi, a language understood by the majority of Afghans, enabled them to establish a good relationship with the local inhabitants and in particular with the Hazaras, an ethnic group from central and western Afghanistan who are of Mongolian origin and clearly identified themselves with the Gurkhas.

Subsequently the company's three platoons were deployed to different locations in Kabul, their tasks rotating between patrolling, guarding camps and providing quick reaction forces (QRF). Patrols were inserted by vehicle into certain sectors in the city, patrolled for up to six hours and then met their vehicles at pre-arranged RVs from which they were extracted and returned to base. It was during one such patrol that 9 Platoon, commanded by Capt Richard Hakes, came under fire at close range after inadvertently stumbling upon a robbery by a group of bandits taking place in a building. Returning fire, the platoon advanced swiftly on the building which, along with the surrounding area, was subsequently cleared and secured by a section commanded by Cpl Yakcharaj Limbu. The efficient manner in which this was carried out undoubtedly deterred any further activity on the part of the bandits, who fled.

Meanwhile Company Headquarters was hard at work training the 630-strong Afghan National Guard battalion. Manned solely by volunteers, it was ethnically balanced in that it comprised majority groupings of Pakhtuns and Tajiks while also incorporating Hazara, Uzbek, Nuristani and Turkmenistani elements. Initial instruction consisted of weapon training, navigation, first aid and physical fitness. Thereafter the troops underwent training in internal security (including riot control and urban operations), patrolling, unarmed combat, live firing and additional physical fitness training. In the meantime a team of Afghans were also being trained as instructors to provide further training while others, who would form the headquarters staff of the new unit, underwent instruction in administration and documentation procedures. Eventually a passing-out parade was held for the new

A member of C (Gurkha) Company 2 PARA monitors the registration of Afghan men for service with the Afghan National Guard.

Two members of C (Gurkha) Company 2 PARA pictured in Kabul during Operation Fingal in February 2002.

A member of C (Gurkha) Company 2 PARA, seen here armed with an L7A1 7.62mm GPMG.

unit, attended by Hamid Kharzai, the leader of Afghanistan's new interim government.

2 PARA remained in Afghanistan for eight to ten weeks until relieved by the 1st Battalion The Royal Anglian Regiment, returning to Britain over the period from 10 March to 7 April.

On 25 May 2002 C (Gurkha) Company 2 PARA was disbanded at a formal parade held as part of the annual Airborne Forces Day. Two days later all ranks moved to Shorncliffe in Kent, where they joined the 2nd Battalion The Royal Gurkha Rifles. Thus, for the third time in sixty years, the connection between The Brigade of Gurkhas and The Parachute Regiment was terminated again. Given the suitability and success of Gurkhas as parachutists in the past, it can only be hoped that they will rejoin the ranks of the British Army's airborne forces at some point in the future.

(Opposite): Members of C (Gurkha) Company 2 PARA pictured on Airborne Forces Day 2002 at Wattisham, in Suffolk.

CHAPTER 9

THE GURKHA CORPS UNITS

THE QUEEN'S GURKHA ENGINEERS

Following the transfer of the four Gurkha infantry regiments, each of two battalions, to the British Army in 1947 and the formation of The Brigade of Gurkhas in Malaya, the decision was taken in 1948 to form a Gurkha engineer regiment for 17th Gurkha Division. In December of that year the Gurkha Training Squadron, Royal Engineers (RE), was formed at the Engineer Training Centre at Kluang, in the south Malayan state of Johore. Commanded by Maj Jack Thornber, it comprised 6 British officers, 2 KGOs, 2 British NCOs and 34 Gurkha warrant officers, NCOs and sappers.

In order to avoid having to train raw recruits as infantrymen before turning them into trained sappers, it was decided to seek recruits for the first squadron from former members of the Gurkha infantry regiments. The first draft of 100 men assembled in November 1948 with another arriving shortly afterwards. In addition to engineer training, however, the trainee sappers were required to provide detachments for operations against the communist terrorists (CT). Inevitably this resulted in their not being fully trained in engineer skills by the end of the unit's first year of existence, when, on 1 October 1949, it was redesignated 67 Field Squadron (Gurkha) RE. In August of the following year a second Gurkha sapper unit, 68 Field Squadron (Gurkha) RE was also formed under the command of Capt Graham Sandeman. A new training squadron had meanwhile been formed from a cadre of 67 Field Squadron.

In the meantime both battalions of the 7th Gurkha Rifles had been converted to artillery regiments, with cadres of Royal Artillery officers and NCOs being posted in to train them. Like the Gurkha sappers, however, both the 1st/7th and 2nd/7th found themselves being deployed as infantry on operations against the terrorists, which inevitably hampered their conversion to the artillery role. In 1950 the decision was taken to halt the programme and the 7th Gurkha Rifles thus reverted to being an infantry regiment.

In mid-1950 both field squadrons were transferred to Hong Kong where, together with 54 Field Squadron RE, they were employed in the infantry role, taking the place of British units of 27 Infantry Brigade despatched as reinforcements to Korea. During the following year 50 Field Engineer Regiment RE was established as the parent unit for both squadrons with the first Commanding Officer, Lt Col F.M. 'Paddy' Hill, assuming command on 5 July 1951. In addition to the two Gurkha field squadrons, it subsequently also incorporated 75 Malayan Field Squadron and 78 Malayan Field Park Squadron RE which operated under the watchful eye of the second in command and the RSM, who remained in Malaya.

The year 1952 saw the two Gurkha field squadrons concentrating on engineer training while retaining their infantry role, completing a number of engineer tasks in the New Territories of Hong Kong where they constructed tracks leading to forward positions on the border with China.

In 1954 50 Engineer Regiment, commanded by Lt Col John Carver, left Hong Kong for Malaya where subsequently it was split into two units: 50 Field Engineer Regiment RE, incorporating the two Gurkha field squadrons; and 51 Field Engineer Regiment RE, comprising the two Malayan squadrons and a newly formed sub-unit, 1st Federation Field Squadron. In November the regiment, now known as 50 Gurkha Field Engineer Regiment, moved to its new base at Sungei Besi, a few miles south of the Malayan capital Kuala Lumpur, where it took up its new role as the divisional sapper unit of 17th Gurkha Division.

One of the initial requirements facing the regiment was to train all its personnel in jungle warfare while at the same time providing a small detachment for an operational deployment lasting ten days, during which it constructed a number of helicopter LZs. Its first major engineer task began in February of the following year when 67 and 68 Gurkha Field Squadrons, commanded by Maj Jimmy Radford and Maj Murray Dunne respectively, commenced the initial stages of the construction of a road between Gemas and Rompin in Johore. The area was inhabited by a large number of terrorists but the security forces were hindered by the 70 miles of road between the two towns. A new, more direct route was to be cut through the jungle, crossing the Sungei Gerau, Gemenche and Muar rivers, and reducing the route to 13 miles. The two Gurkha field squadrons were tasked with cutting an operational route to the Muar and with bridging all three rivers. The road was opened on 6 August, with the Muar bridge being completed on 3 September.

The end of September marked an important milestone for the Gurkha sappers as on the 29th they became an integral part of The Brigade of Gurkhas. Hitherto 50 Gurkha Engineer Field Regiment and its two field squadrons had been units of the Royal Engineers, the sappers being enlisted in the four Gurkha infantry regiments from which they were attached permanently to the Royal Engineers.

In 1956 the regiment's establishment was increased to include a third field squadron, which was not formed for the time being, and a field park squadron. At the same time its pipes and drums, whose members had hitherto been held on the strengths of the two field squadrons, were officially included in the establishment of the regimental headquarters.

During this period the regiment provided engineer support for 17th Gurkha Division on operations against the CT, its two field squadrons undertaking eight months of deployment in the field, followed by four months of recuperation and retraining at the regiment's base at Sungei Besi. One major task undertaken during 1956 was the construction of a 15-mile road between Ayer Hitam, in Negri Sembilan, and Kemayan on the border of Pahang. Lasting eight months, this task was carried out by 68 Gurkha Field Squadron, commanded by Maj Bill Branford, reinforced by a troop of 67 Squadron, 11 Independent Field Squadron RE and 410 Plant Troop. Meanwhile 67 Gurkha Field Squadron, under Maj J.H. 'Bill' Spencer, performed a series of tasks in Johore, including the construction of a road between Sedenak and Tek Wah Heng, which was completed in three months. Stretching 6 miles and crossing three rivers, each of which had to be bridged, the road was cut through extremely difficult terrain covered in thick jungle.

By 1958 the CT threat in Malaya had declined considerably and during the first two months of 1959 Negri Sembilan, Johore and Selangor were all declared safe areas. By March emergency restrictions had been lifted throughout most of Malaya, with only the mountains of Perak and the area of the border with Thailand being occupied by terrorist groups. During this period both field squadrons of 50 Gurkha Field Engineer Regiment were committed to the Kedah Roads Project, the last operational deployment carried out by the Gurkha sappers during the Malayan Emergency. The project consisted of the construction of 65 miles of road connecting the roads and tracks that provided approaches to the border with Thailand in the northern state of Kedah.

The first to deploy was 67 Gurkha Field Squadron, supported by 74 Field Park Squadron and a civilian labour force of 20 civilian plant operators and 200 labourers. The squadron's tasks were threefold: to complete 6 miles of road between Jeniang and Gajah Puteh, for which a pilot track had already been cut by a Malayan sapper unit; to build a new road 4 miles long from Gaah Puteh to Kampong Kura; and to cut a 7-mile-long access track to link up with a Public Works Department road at Kampong Bahru. These three tasks, which incorporated the construction of two reinforced concrete bridges and more than forty concrete culverts, were completed in September, in time for the start of the monsoon, at which point 67 Squadron returned to Sungei Besi. In January 1959 68 Gurkha Field Squadron took its place on the project, which was completed in May.

The period following the end of the Malayan Emergency saw 67 and 68 Gurkha Field Squadrons formally allocated to 99 and 63 Gurkha Infantry Brigades respectively, with the CO, Lt Col Bill Jackson, also holding the post of Commander Royal Engineers (CRE) 17th Gurkha Division.

During 1959 50 Gurkha Field Engineer Regiment was faced with its largest task so far. This took place in North Borneo (later Sabah) where a training area in the north-west corner of the state, in the area of Kota Belud, had been selected for use by Britain in training its Strategic Reserve, a new formation intended for deployment worldwide by air and sea. The area, however, was accessible only via a narrow road from the capital Jesselton, some 60 miles to the south, the last 23 miles of which was effectively a jeep track, or via the Sungei Abai, across whose estuary was a bar preventing access by seagoing vessels.

The initial phase of constructing a road was given to 50 Gurkha Field Engineer Regiment, which allocated the task to 67 Gurkha Field Squadron, commanded by Maj John Allen. Work commenced in May, with plant being landed from ships at Usukan Bay and a road built across the isthmus to the estuary of the Sungei Abai, up which a ferry transported troops, plant and materials to a base camp established at Kota Belud.

The new road led east from Kota Belud to the training area, a low-level causeway being constructed across the Sungei Tempasuk, with a powered close-support raft being used when water levels rose above it. A second smaller river, the Sungei Gunding, was spanned using a 70ft Bailey bridge. 67 Squadron remained employed on this task until November, when 68 Squadron, under Maj Jimmy Radford, took over. Despite very heavy rain the road was open by the end of May 1960, by which time the training area was operational, the Gurkha sappers having equipped it with two camps designed to accommodate a major and minor unit respectively, a medical centre, workshops, water supply, fuel and stores compounds, and all other necessary support facilities. Further engineering tasks on the area remained and for the following twelve months these were carried out by Commonwealth and Malayan sappers. In July 1961 67 Gurkha Field Squadron, under Maj Mike Wright, returned to the area and remained there until January 1962, when it handed over to 75 Malayan Field Squadron.

In the meantime, on 2 April 1960 50 Gurkha Field Engineer Regiment had formed 70 Gurkha Field Park Squadron, commanded by Maj Douglas Miller, which replaced 74 Field Park Squadron RE. On the same day the regiment itself was disbanded as the divisional sapper unit for 17th Gurkha Division and replaced by Headquarters The Gurkha Engineers.

In February 1961 the decision was taken to substitute three independent Gurkha infantry brigades for 17th Gurkha Division. 48 and 99 Gurkha Infantry Brigades were to be based in Hong Kong and Malaya respectively, with 63 Gurkha Infantry Brigade (subsequently redesignated 51 Infantry Brigade) being stationed in the United Kingdom. 67 Gurkha Field Squadron would remain in Malaya, forming part of 99 Gurkha Infantry Brigade, while 68 Squadron would accompany 63 Gurkha Infantry Brigade to Britain. On 1 April the cadre of a third sub-unit, 69 Gurkha Field Squadron, was raised under Maj Tony Cronk, the squadron itself being formed in April of the following year. On 22 September 1962 all three squadrons were redesignated as 67, 68 and 69 Gurkha Independent Field Squadrons and during the following month 67 Squadron moved from Malaya to Hong Kong to join 48 Gurkha Infantry Brigade. Maj Tony Cronk subsequently moved from 69 Squadron to 68, taking the latter to the United Kingdom and commanding it throughout its tour there.

In January 1963, following the outbreak of the Brunei Rebellion in early December of the previous year, 69 Gurkha Independent Field Squadron, commanded by Maj Dick Francis, moved to Brunei, from where its A and B Troops, commanded by Lt Bruce Abernethy-Clark and Lt Mike Stephens respectively, were deployed to Bangar and Limbang in support of 42 Commando RM while C Troop, under Lt Dominic

Verschoyle, was flown to Long Seridan in the Fifth Division of Sarawak to upgrade an airstrip so that it could accommodate RAF Twin Pioneers and Beverley transports.

During the following months 69 Squadron carried out a number of tasks which included opening up 17 miles of road between Brunei Town and Limbang, building a jungle fort for the Border Scouts and constructing helicopter LZs. In September the squadron, less B Troop, returned to the Gurkha Engineers base at Kluang in Malaya. In December 68 Gurkha Independent Field Squadron, commanded by Maj Hank Bowen, arrived from Britain for a seven-month tour of operations at the end of which, in July 1964, it moved to Kluang for a period of rest and retraining. During that month a permanent Gurkha Engineers squadron base, named Salkeld Camp, was established at Seria in Brunei, from which the resident squadron, 69 Gurkha Independent Field Squadron, commanded by Maj R.D.P. 'Billy' Brown, provided support for 51 Infantry Brigade, which had been deployed to Borneo from Britain and was responsible for the Central Brigade area of operations. Tasks varied from constructing forward bases in border areas, each designed to accommodate an infantry company, to establishing radio relay sites on mountain peaks. On one occasion in March 1965 C Troop 69 Gurkha Independent Field Squadron, commanded by Lt David Roberts, was tasked with clearing anti-personnel mines, including Claymores and booby-traps, laid around the perimeter of the base at Long Seridan. The task was made all the more risky by the fact that successive units had kept no record of the mines' locations and thus the entire area had to be cleared using methods normally employed in breaching a minefield. The task was completed successfully with no casualties incurred and no explosions caused.

The year 1966 saw 67 Gurkha Independent Field Squadron, commanded successively by Maj Gil Roach and Maj Tony Rickets, and 68 Gurkha Independent Field Squadron, under Maj Hank Bowen, succeeded by Maj Philip Rich, deployed in Borneo.

In August 1965, following the assumption of power in Indonesia by Gen Suharto, the Borneo Confrontation ended and The Gurkha Engineers, who had expanded rapidly during the campaign, now faced, along with the rest of The Brigade of Gurkhas, the prospect of reductions in manpower. During the following year lengthy deliberations took place concerning the reductions in the strength of the brigade and in 1967 it was announced that The Gurkha Engineers would be reduced from 1,500 men to 600. During the latter part of that year all three field squadrons were reduced by a troop to two field troops and a support troop each. 68 Gurkha Independent Field Squadron subsequently transferred its C Troop to 69 Squadron, bringing the latter up to operational strength and itself being reduced to cadre strength of a field troop and a support troop.

During the summer of 1967 civil disorder erupted in Hong Kong with anti-European demonstrations taking place in Kowloon on 6 May. These were orchestrated by communist elements supported by China, which at that time was in the throes of the Cultural Revolution. The demonstrations were followed by a wave of riots, strikes and bombing incidents that culminated in a confrontation on 24 June in the New Territories, at the town of Sha Tau Kok, where a mob of 200 Chinese attacked a Royal Hong Kong Police post, being beaten off with the aid of CS gas. On 8 July the situation deteriorated when the post was attacked again, on this occasion with firearms. Five policemen were killed and eleven wounded in the incident, following which the Hong Kong government requested military assistance. Troops of the 1st/10th PMO Gurkha Rifles, supported by armoured cars, relieved the police, who thereafter handed over the entire border to the army.

Elements of 69 Gurkha Independent Field Squadron were deployed to Sha Tau Kok, where they improved facilities at the police station so that it would accommodate a company of infantry, and to Lo Wu, where special gates were constructed to block the rail border crossing point there. During the ensuing eight months of disturbances the squadron provided sapper support throughout the colony, including the provision of demolition parties for the Royal Hong Kong Police during raids on known communist strongholds and premises in Kowloon and on Hong Kong Island.

By this time the decision had been taken to disband 69 Gurkha Independent Field Squadron as part of the reductions imposed on The Gurkha Engineers. The squadron, with C Troop 68 Squadron under command, however, was fully up to strength, while 68 Squadron itself consisted of only a small cadre. It was thus decided to redesignate 69 Squadron as 68 Gurkha Independent Field Squadron, and in January 1969 69 Gurkha Independent Field Squadron was formally disbanded.

March 1970 saw the move of 67 Squadron to Hong Kong, followed by the transfer of 70 Squadron to Singapore in May, the latter being disbanded on 26 June the following year. Two months later Headquarters The Gurkha Engineers at Kluang was closed and RHQ The Gurkha Engineers moved to Hong Kong. Lt Col Gil Roach remained as Commandant but with Lt Col John Booth as CRE at HQ Land Forces Hong Kong. In September 1970 Lt Col Tony Rickets took over as Commandant and CRE.

During the early 1970s 67 Gurkha Independent Field Squadron provided sapper support for 51 Infantry Brigade, the latter being based on Hong Kong Island and in Kowloon with its third infantry unit, a Gurkha battalion, being located in Brunei, while 68 Squadron did likewise for 48 Gurkha Infantry Brigade in the New Territories. In February 1973 Lt Col John Edwards took over as Commandant from Lt Col Tony Rickets. Following the handover of command, the two squadrons exchanged brigades in order to avoid the risk of stereotyping. In addition to performing engineer tasks in Hong Kong, both carried out projects and exercises in Brunei, Fiji, Australia, the Solomon Islands and elsewhere.

The March 1975 defence review by the Labour government in power in Britain at the time announced a further cut of 1,000 men in The Brigade of Gurkhas, reducing it to a total strength of 6,000. Consequently 51 Infantry Brigade was disbanded while 48 Gurkha Infantry Brigade was redesignated the Gurkha Field Force. Fortunately, however, The Gurkha Engineers were spared any further reductions and indeed were

Internal security training at Fanling police station in Hong Kong.

required to form a field park element within RHQ to take on support functions, including the provision of trade training, which hitherto had been performed by 54 (Hong Kong) Support Squadron RE, a victim of the cuts. This element was later reorganised and reformed as 70 Gurkha Support Squadron.

On 21 April 1977 The Gurkha Engineers received a royal accolade when the title of the regiment was changed to The Queen's Gurkha Engineers, this honour being conferred in recognition of the loyal and distinguished service rendered by Gurkha sappers over the previous thirty years.

From the mid-1970s onwards Hong Kong suffered from a large influx of refugees from China, whose numbers increased steadily during the latter part of the decade. The closing of the border, which was sealed off through the use of high wire fences and infantry patrols, forced illegal immigrants to make the crossing into the colony via the sea. In 1979 The Queen's Gurkha Engineers formed a boat troop, comprising men of both field squadrons under Lt Hamish McLeod. Equipped with Gemini inflatables and Rigid Raider dories, and trained by Royal Marine instructors, the troop operated under 67 Squadron, commanded by Maj Dermot Stack, supporting the three Gurkha battalions deployed in areas such as the Tolo Peninsula and other outlying areas,

Members of the 7th DEO Gurkha Rifles on the Hong Kong border at Tau Kau Ling in 1981.

An illegal immigrant being apprehended at Tau Kau Ling on the Hong Kong border in 1981.

whose coasts had to be patrolled to intercept refugees crossing from the Chinese mainland. Once arrested, the refugees were handed over to the Royal Hong Kong Police and subsequently repatriated to China.

Such were the demands on the regiment that in October 1980, as Lt Col Mike Stephens handed over as Commandant to Lt Col John Worthington, it was announced that 69 Gurkha Independent Field Squadron would be reformed in the following year under command of Maj Bill Chesshyre. This duly took place on 4 May 1981 and immediately afterwards 69 Squadron departed for the United Kingdom where it moved to its new base at Kitchener Barracks at Chatham in Kent, coming under command of 2 Infantry Brigade on 1 January 1982. At that juncture Maj Bill Chesshyre handed over command to Maj John Baker.

In August 1982, following the Falklands conflict, 69 Squadron found itself deployed to the Falkland Islands, where it formed part of a force of 1,200 sappers carrying out a large number of tasks ranging from extending and resurfacing the airfield at Mount

Pleasant to enable it to accommodate RAF Phantom fighters, to clearing Argentinian minefields and booby traps. The squadron remained on the Falkland Islands for six months, returning to Britain in January 1983. Four months later, less one troop which remained in Britain, it was despatched to Belize where it carried out an emergency six-month tour during which its tasks included the construction of blast-wall-protected hides for the detachment of four RAF Harriers based in the country.

Throughout the rest of the 1980s 69 Gurkha Independent Field Squadron continued to deploy troops and detachments on tasks in the United Kingdom and overseas, the latter including Belize, Cyprus, Canada and Kenya. In 1985 the entire squadron deployed to the Falkland Islands, where its primary task was airfield damage repair, ensuring that the runway at Mount Pleasant was fully operational at all times.

Meanwhile the remainder of The Queen's Gurkha Engineers continued to provide support for the Gurkha Field Force in Hong Kong. The first half of the 1980s saw Perowne Barracks, near Castle Peak in the New Territories, undergoing a complete rebuild and refurbishment as the new base for the regiment whose three Hong Kong-based squadrons had hitherto been accommodated at three separate locations. By mid-1985, however, the regiment was finally concentrated in its new home. Throughout the decade it was heavily involved in community projects in Hong Kong, the largest being on the island of Lantau where a new military training facility, Erskine Camp, was constructed on a remote peninsula. Over a period of almost two years Gurkha sappers were involved in the construction of a 54-metre reinforced concrete bridge and 1.5 kilometres of concrete road, the latter requiring the blasting and clearing of some 15,000 tonnes of rock. Each year, meanwhile, the regiment despatched squadrons and troops on exercises and tasks overseas to a number of countries including Brunei, the Cook Islands, Fiji, Malaysia, New Zealand, Papua New Guinea, the Solomon Islands, Thailand and the United States.

Following the collapse of the Soviet Union in 1991 the Conservative government in Britain saw an opportunity of exploiting the so-called 'Peace Dividend' to reduce defence expenditure and initiated an ill-conceived programme of severe defence cuts which were to have long-lasting and adverse consequences on the British Army as a whole. On 25 July 1991 it was announced that The Brigade of Gurkhas was to be reduced further to a total strength of 2,500, this comprising two infantry battalions, a squadron each of the three Gurkha corps, a small headquarters and two demonstration companies, the latter being based at the RMA Sandhurst and the School of Infantry NCOs Tactics Wing at Brecon.

The rundown from a full regiment to a single field squadron commenced in late 1992 following the arrival of Lt Col Peter Blundell, who took over as Commandant in September. In April 1993 it was announced that the sole Gurkha field squadron to be retained was to number only 100 all ranks and not 250 as had previously been stated. That same month saw 69 Gurkha Independent Field Squadron lose its independent status and come under the command of 36 Engineer Regiment RE, commanded by Lt Col 'Robbie' Burns and based at Maidstone in Kent. On 18 December 68 Gurkha

Independent Field Squadron and 70 Gurkha Support Squadron were disbanded, two-thirds of their strengths being absorbed by 67 and 69 Squadrons, with others being transferred to the Gurkha infantry regiments and the remainder returning to Nepal on pension or redundancy.

May 1994 saw the closure of the regiment's training wing in Hong Kong, all combat engineer training for Gurkha sappers thereafter being conducted in the United Kingdom at the Royal School of Military Engineering (RSME) at Minley. On 31 October RHQ The Queen's Gurkha Engineers became non-operational, Lt Col Blundell returning to the United Kingdom in mid-December.

The following year saw the temporary establishment within RHQ 36 Engineer Regiment of a small manning cell, comprising Maj (QGO) Judbahadur Gurung and a clerk, to oversee the disbandment of 67 Gurkha Independent Field Squadron, which was scheduled to take place during the second half of 1996. In June 1995 the Commanding Officer of 36 Engineer Regiment, Lt Col Burns, was also appointed Commandant The Queen's Gurkha Engineers, being succeeded in both posts in August by Lt Col Bob Hendicott.

In July 1996, following the realisation that the Commandant would require the services of a Gurkha major and a small staff to handle Gurkha matters, the decision was taken to reform RHQ The Queen's Gurkha Engineers within the headquarters of 36 Engineer Regiment. On 1 October 67 Gurkha Independent Field Squadron, commanded by Maj Alistair Sheppard, became non-operational and was formally disbanded in Hong Kong on 31 December 1996, being the last British Army sapper unit to serve in the colony prior to its handover by Britain to China in the following year. Half of the squadron's strength flew to the United Kingdom to join 69 Gurkha Field Squadron, the remainder returning to Nepal on pension or redundancy.

In March 1996 69 Squadron was deployed to Bosnia as part of 36 Engineer Regiment providing support for 1st UK Armoured Division. Arriving there three months after the Dayton Peace Accord, it was employed on tasks on both sides of the Inter-Entity Boundary Line and in the three ethnic areas inhabited by Serbs, Croats and Muslims. These ranged from construction of accommodation for units of the United Nations Implementation Force to bridging and maintenance of supply routes blocked all too often by snow, ice and rocks.

The Strategic Defence Review carried out by the Labour government in 1998 recognised the key role played by sappers and the decision was thus taken to form a fifth engineer logistics squadron, to be manned by Gurkhas. Initially the new unit was to be formed in 2002 but operational pressures resulted in this being brought forward by two years. Thus it was that the new millennium saw an increase in the strength of The Queen's Gurkha Engineers with the reformation, for the third time, on 17 July 2000 of 70 Gurkha Field Support Squadron, commanded by Maj Jim Crawford, as part of 36 Engineer Regiment RE.

Based at Invicta Park at Maidstone in Kent, and with a total strength of 126 all ranks, the squadron is organised on the same lines as the four other engineer support squadrons within the Royal Engineers. It comprises a squadron headquarters incorporating signals and clerical support; a resources and workshop troop; a support troop, possessing plant and transport assets; and an echelon providing stores and catering support. Its role is the supply of equipment and material, including boats, bridging and construction stores, and construction plant, and the provision of equipment support for RE-controlled equipment, using specialist repair facilities and secondary depot holdings of spares. In addition it provides local manufacture and infrastructure support, using RE workshops and local purchase, as well as route maintenance and plant support.

A month after its formation the squadron deployed for seven months to Kosovo, remaining there until February 2001 as part of 26 Engineer Regiment Group. In November it accompanied British forces to Oman, following which elements of the squadron accompanied the British element of the International Security Assistance Force (ISAF) deployed to Afghanistan on Operation Fingal, returning to the United Kingdom in mid-2002.

THE QUEEN'S GURKHA SIGNALS

It was in 1921 that Gurkha signallers first appeared in the ranks of the Royal Signals when 'G' Divisional Signals, then based at Rawalpindi in the Punjab in western India (now Pakistan), absorbed Gurkha personnel who hitherto had been serving in other signals units. Shortly afterwards the unit moved to Kohat in the North West Frontier Province, where it was responsible for the maintenance of communications in the area of Fort Lockhart. In 1923 trouble broke out in Waziristan and sections of 2 and 3 Companies were transferred to Tochi while two others were deployed with brigades operating in Razmak and Razani. The unit's headquarters meanwhile was located at Bannu. Following the end of operations the unit regrouped at Kohat. During the following year it was announced that no further Gurkhas would be recruited, those in the unit serving out their time. Among them was Capt (VCO) Tejsing Gurung, who held the post of Subedar Major of the Signal Training Centre at Jubbulpore for many years.

In July 1948, following the formation of 17th Gurkha Division in Malaya, Maj George Cox of The Royal Signals was tasked with raising Gurkha-manned signal units for it. In November a cadre was formed from eight Royal Signals personnel and seven Gurkha soldiers transferred from the infantry regiments, the latter being rebadged as Royal Signals. A Gurkha Signal and Training Wing (GSTW) was established in Kuala Lumpur and throughout 1949 and 1950 Gurkhas were recruited and trained in three signalling trades: Operator Wireless & Line (OWL), Lineman, Dispatch Rider (DR) and the general duty trade of Driver. In August 1950 the Gurkha Independent Signal Squadron was formed and in December became operational, providing communications for 48 Gurkha Infantry Brigade at Kuala Lipis in Pahang, under the command of Maj Lionel Gregory, Royal Signals.

In November 1951 the GSTW output of tradesmen enabled the formation of K Troop and its despatch to 63 Gurkha Infantry Brigade at Seremban. On 1 January 1952 the GSTW was disbanded and the Signal Training Squadron (STS) was established by Maj Ian Parkinson at The Brigade of Gurkhas Recruit Training Centre at Sungei Patani. Trade training was expanded to include Operator Switchboard, Technical Storeman, Driver Electrician and Clerk. In May 1952 I Troop was formed, expanded to independent squadron strength and deployed in support of 26 Gurkha Infantry Brigade in Kluang; simultaneously the Independent Signal Squadron was reduced in strength, redesignated J Troop and moved to Ipoh with Headquarters 48 Gurkha Infantry Brigade. In June L Troop joined 99 Gurkha Infantry Brigade in Johore Bahru.

In January 1952 Regimental Headquarters Gurkha Signals was established at Maxwell Road Camp (later renamed Lamjung Camp) under the command of Maj Gregory, with Maj Parsuram Gurung, formerly of the 2nd KEO Gurkha Rifles, as Gurkha Major.

By the end of October 1953 1 Squadron had been formed and had taken up its duties with Headquarters 17th Gurkha Division. By the end of the year 17 Gurkha Divisional Signal Regiment had been formed under the command of Gregory, now a lieutenant colonel, comprising RHQ, 1 and 3 Squadrons, the Independent Gurkha Signal Squadron and the Signal Training Squadron. Although consisting of individual establishments, the whole of Gurkha Signals functioned as a regiment comprising divisional and training elements with an independent unit. 1 Squadron provided both static and mobile communications for Headquarters 17th Gurkha Division and support troops while 3 Squadron comprised three brigade signal troops and a small squadron headquarters. The overall establishment for the regiment was 22 British officers, 18 QGOs, 96 British and 809 Gurkha other ranks, most of the latter being recruited and trained by the end of 1955.

On 23 September 1954 the regiment was presented with its own Gurkha Signals cap badge by the Major General Brigade of Gurkhas, Maj Gen Lance Perowne. This comprised two kukris in saltire surmounted by Mercury (or 'Jimmy' as he is known throughout The Royal Signals), surmounted in turn by the royal crown, and 23 September was thereafter adopted as the official birthday of the regiment.

In 1954 the first Gurkha Signals unit left Malaya when the Independent Gurkha Signal Squadron accompanied Headquarters 48 Gurkha Infantry Brigade in its move to Hong Kong, its place in 26 Gurkha Infantry Brigade being filled by J Troop.

In 1955, following the example of the 6th, 7th and 10th Gurkha Rifles in forming bonds with Scottish regiments, the regiment became affiliated to the 51st Highland Division Signal Regiment Royal Corps of Signals (TA), that same year also seeing the formation of the regiment's pipes and drums with permission for the nine pipers and seven drummers to wear the Grant tartan. Their first performance took place in September, in which month an amendment to the Corps Warrant was published in Army Orders, incorporating the Gurkha Signals in The Brigade of Gurkhas. On 21 April 1956 Her Royal Highness The Princess Royal, Colonel-in-Chief of The Royal

Corps of Signals, presented her pipe banner to The Gurkha Signals at an audience held at St James's Palace in London.

During this period the regiment underwent a number of changes in its title. Initially called Royal Signals Gurkha, this was altered to Gurkha Royal Signals. By 1 January 1956, however, when Lt Col Gregory handed over command to Lt Col 'Tadge' Griffiths, the Royal title had been lost, the regiment thereafter being designated The Gurkha Signals.

During the Malayan Emergency Campaign, described in detail in Chapter 5, Gurkha Signals provided and maintained the static and mobile communications within 17th Gurkha Division and for higher formations. The regiment utilised road, rail and air for the Signals Dispatch Service (SDS), the Malayan Telecoms service for telephone and teleprinter circuits and generic equipment for command and control high frequency (HF) radio networks at brigade and divisional levels. HF radio communications were particularly difficult to establish and maintain owing to interference, fading and noise being caused by distance, climatic and atmospheric conditions; most of the traffic was cleared by morse code. Providing reliable voice communications on command nets between brigade and battalion was rarely possible. In addition to their primary communications role, brigade signal units were responsible for testing the proficiency of battalion signals platoons and for the first line repair of their radios. The regiment's squadrons and troops were also tasked with headquarters defence and convoy escort duties as well as occasionally providing personnel for ambushes during major operations.

In 1957 The Gurkha Signals moved from Kuala Lumpur to Seremban in Negri Sembilan, where the regiment set up its new home in Sikamat Camp. It was joined there by 250 Gurkha Signal Squadron (Training), which moved from Sungei Patani. Two years later, in 1959, in line with a new army policy concerning the designation of signals units and sub-units, the three brigade signal troops left 17 Gurkha Divisional Signal Regiment and were reorganised as independent signals squadrons, with K and L Troops being redesignated 247 and 248 Gurkha Signal Squadrons respectively. The Independent Gurkha Signal Squadron, which since 1954 had formed part of 48 Gurkha Infantry Brigade, was redesignated 246 Gurkha Signal Squadron. Unfortunately, as the Malayan Emergency was drawing to a close, the regiment suffered its first loss when J Troop was disbanded along with 26 Gurkha Infantry Brigade. In 1960 the regiment itself was redesignated 17 Gurkha Signal Regiment.

In March 1962 247 Gurkha Signal Squadron, commanded by Maj John Ridge, left Malaya for the United Kingdom with 63 Gurkha Infantry Brigade, which was redesignated 51 Infantry Brigade on its arrival. Based at Tidworth in Hampshire, the Gurkha element of the brigade comprised the 1st Battalion 6th QEO Gurkha Rifles, 68 Gurkha Independent Field Squadron, 247 Gurkha Signal Squadron, 30 Company Gurkha Army Service Corps and 63 Gurkha Provost Company Gurkha Military Police. The following months saw the squadron retraining for warfare in Central Europe and in February 1963 it moved to Hubbelrath in West Germany to provide communications for 4 Guards Brigade Group, being the first Gurkha unit to serve in Germany since the First World War. Later that year the squadron returned to Britain and Tidworth before travelling with 51 Infantry Brigade to the Far East in February 1964 where it was deployed in Brunei to take part in the Borneo Confrontation.

In the meantime other elements of The Gurkha Signals had already been sent to Borneo. The Brunei Rebellion of December 1962 saw the deployment of 248 Gurkha Signal Squadron in support of 99 Gurkha Infantry Brigade which, following the suppression of the revolt, was deployed to West Sarawak, the squadron and brigade headquarters being located in Kuching. 51 Infantry Brigade was based in Brunei where the brigade headquarters and 247 Squadron took up residence at Bolkiah Camp on the outskirts of Brunei Town.

As in Malaya, the topography and climatic conditions in Brunei posed problems for the maintenance of radio communications. Moreover each brigade's tactical area of responsibility (TAOR) was huge, 51 Infantry Brigade's being the size of Scotland. The distances between the brigade headquarters at Bolkiah Camp and the battalions' forward company bases were between 80 and 140 miles. Roads were non-existent and all movement within the brigade's area was by air, boat or on foot. Initially radio communications within the brigade were via HF skywave signals using the C11/R210 set. Because of the distances and conditions involved, it was thought that this was the only means of maintaining voice communications during daylight hours. As had proved to be the case during the Malayan Emergency, interference reached a peak during the late afternoon and early evening, the period when brigade command nets were at their busiest, and this often made communications impossible. On occasions changing frequency eased matters but often, particularly at night, operators were forced to switch to the use of CW (morse).

The solution to such problems was the use of VHF, which would guarantee voice communications by day or night with little interference. However, the limited range of the army's VHF sets and the mountainous terrain made such a proposal impracticable. At this juncture 247 Squadron's commander, Maj Hamish Paterson, considered the possibility of installing radio relay stations on the tops of mountains. No sooner had he done so, however, than he learned that 248 Squadron was one jump ahead of him: Lt Max Young's troop had installed such a site on Gunong Serapi, a 3,000ft-high feature in West Sarawak.

Not to be outdone, Paterson selected two features, Gunong Murud and Gunong Mulu, whose summits were at heights of 7,000 and 8,000 feet, as possible sites. A party of ten Gurkha signallers, commanded by 2nd Lt (later Maj Gen) Sam Cowan, was tasked with establishing a station which consisted of 1,500lb of equipment including C42 radio sets, an A13 HF radio, antennae, batteries and a small generator.

Access to both sites was possible by helicopter only. The first attempt to land the party and its equipment from two Westland Scout light helicopters on the jungle-covered summit of Gunong Murud failed owing to air turbulence. Cowan and his men were thus landed on an LZ already cut some 4 miles down a ridge from the summit.

After six days of hacking their way up through thick jungle, they abandoned the attempt and were extracted by helicopter.

A few days later Cowan and his party were landed on the summit of Gunong Mulu by Wessex helicopters of 845 Naval Air Squadron and five hours later were on air, testing their equipment. Three radio links were established successfully but the fourth was screened by a mountain ridge, which included Gunong Murud. Maj Tony Hazel, who had just replaced Maj Hamish Paterson as commander of 247 Squadron, was a keen climber and was determined to see a relay site installed on Gunong Murud's summit.

A second attempt was launched, with Cowan and his party of Gurkha signallers being flown to the mountain in Wessex helicopters. Once again, however, air turbulence prevented the insertion of the party on the summit and eventually Cowan and his men, along with some of their equipment, were roped down into the valley, where they established a base camp and cleared an LZ. Almost immediately afterwards the weather conditions deteriorated and the helicopters were prevented from bringing in the remainder of the equipment. Five days passed before the weather improved sufficiently for the aircraft to return with the rest of the equipment for the relay station. In the meantime Cowan and his Gurkhas had hacked their way up from the valley to the summit, where they had constructed an LZ, enabling the helicopters to collect the equipment from the valley and fly it up to the summit. One such flight nearly ended in disaster when a Wessex bringing in the party's packs and personal equipment was caught in air turbulence which swept the aircraft's tail round against a tree, damaging the tail rotor. Fortunately the pilot was able to regain control and flew down the mountain to an LZ some 5 miles away, where he succeeded in landing safely. Two more Wessexes were despatched from Bario, collecting the party's equipment from the crippled helicopter and subsequently dropping it from a height of 60 feet on to the LZ on Gunong Murud's summit.

Cowan established his relay site without further problems and VHF communications were provided to almost every part of 51 Infantry Brigade's area, working at ranges of up to 130 miles. Communications were also established with army aircraft and an air safety operational net was set up, enabling pilots to maintain communications with the brigade headquarters at Bolkiah Camp and to report on their positions no matter where they were flying.

Conditions on these mountaintop sites were very difficult, the weather being unpredictable and frequently cold and wet. Moreover, limitations on range posed major problems. The standard army VHF set, the C42, was unable to cover the necessary distance of 50–60 miles. The Gurkha signallers realised that as the situation required point-to-point communications they could use directional antennae and thus concentrate all their sets' power in the required direction rather than dissipate it omnidirectionally. The army, however, did not possess any such antennae for the frequency range on which the C42 operated. Undaunted, the two squadrons proceeded to construct their own from F sections of normal antennae and designed special adaptors for connection to their sets. Unfortunately each antenna could only be adapted to a single frequency and there were a considerable number of frequencies to be covered. There were insufficient F sections in the stores and thus the squadron quartermaster sergeants were ordered to write sections off as having been lost or damaged irreparably, enabling them to indent for replacements.

As recounted in Chapter 8, the Gurkha Independent Parachute Company was converted to the long-range reconnaissance role in June 1964. It was soon acknowledged that it could not provide enough signallers of sufficient expertise for the number of patrols it would be deploying in its new role and thus The Gurkha Signals were approached to form a troop of signallers who would not only become members of patrols but also train other members of the company up to a sufficiently high standard of proficiency.

Commanded by Capt Paddy Verdon, with Lt Mike Walker as his second in command, the troop initially comprised twenty-nine Gurkha signallers, half of them already parachute-qualified, while the remainder underwent parachute training at RAF Changi in Singapore. Having joined the company, Capt Verdon and his men were put through a course of training which included map reading and navigation, immediate action drills, RV drills and tactics.

In late October 1964 the troop deployed with the company to Borneo, returning to the Malaysian mainland in March the following year. The troop remained as an integral part of the company, being commanded successively by Capt Keith Ryding and Capt Johnny Fielding, until 1968, when Gurkha Signals personnel were phased out of the company following its reversion to the organisation and role of a conventional rifle company.

As recounted earlier in this chapter, the end of the Borneo Confrontation in 1966 brought with it reductions to all elements of The Brigade of Gurkhas. It was announced that 17 Gurkha Signal Regiment would be disbanded and the total strength of the Gurkha Signals reduced from 1,170 all ranks to 415.

In July 1970, as part of the withdrawal of British forces from Malaysia, 17 Gurkha Signal Regiment moved from Sikamat Camp at Seremban to Nee Soon Camp in Singapore. On 19 April 1971 in Hong Kong the Commanding Officer of 27 Signal Regiment assumed the additional appointment of Commander Gurkha Signals. On 31 July, 17 Gurkha Signal Regiment was disbanded in Singapore. That same month saw the reformation in Hong Kong of 248 Gurkha Signal Squadron which thereafter was based in Kowloon where it assumed the role of providing field radio and other communications tasks for 51 Infantry Brigade and Headquarters Land Forces. Other elements of the Gurkha Signals which survived the reductions in The Brigade of Gurkhas comprised: 48 Gurkha Infantry Brigade Headquarters and Signal Squadron (as 246 Gurkha Signal Squadron had been redesignated in 1969), based at Sek Kong in Hong Kong's New Territories; a small RHQ Gurkha Signals and Trade Training Troop formed at Sek Kong in October 1971; five battalion rear link signal troops; a troop attached to the Headquarters British Gurkhas Nepal at Dharan in Eastern Nepal; the

Brunei Signal Troop located with the British garrison in Brunei, where, on 15 August 1969, it had taken over responsibility from The Royal Signals for the operation of the communications centre there; and a small number of personnel on Extra Regimental Employment (ERE).

In 1974, following the Turkish invasion of northern Cyprus, the 1st/10th PMO Gurkha Rifles were deployed from their base at Church Crookham in Hampshire to defend the British Sovereign Base Area at Dhekelia. The Gurkha Signals rear link signals troop attached to the battalion accompanied it on its year-long tour of duty, following which it returned to Church Crookham.

Two years later, on 15 December 1976, 48 Brigade Headquarters and Signal Squadron was redesignated Gurkha Field Force Headquarters and Signal Squadron. The following year brought further changes for The Gurkha Signals when 248 Gurkha Signal Squadron and the remnants of 27 Signal Regiment, which had been disbanded, were amalgamated into a new unit, The Hong Kong Gurkha Signal Squadron. At this time all Royal Signals personnel in the Far East became part of The Gurkha Signals and thus the squadron included Gurkha, British and Chinese personnel in its ranks.

In 1977, the year of Her Majesty The Queen's Silver Jubilee, The Gurkha Signals were honoured with a royal title, thereafter being named The Queen's Gurkha Signals. The new name was officially bestowed on 20 April, a formal retitling parade being held six months later on 21 September at Gun Club Barracks in Kowloon. Three years later, at Buckingham Palace, the Princess Royal, Colonel-in-Chief of The Royal Corps of Signals, presented her pipe banner to the Commander of The Queen's Gurkha Signals, following the example set by her predecessor twenty-seven years earlier.

During 1982 four members of the regiment saw active service when elements of the rear link detachment attached to the 1st/7th DEO Gurkha Rifles accompanied the battalion to the South Atlantic as part of the task force despatched by Britain to recapture the Falkland Islands.

On 16 May 1983 the regiment underwent a major reorganisation. The Hong Kong Gurkha Signal Squadron was redesignated 248 Gurkha Signal Squadron while 247 Gurkha Signal Squadron was reformed and the Gurkha Field Force Headquarters and Signal Squadron was redesignated 246 (Gurkha Field Force) Signal Squadron. In addition to the Nepal Signal Troop and the Brunei Signal Troop, the regiment also comprised six signal troops specifically allocated to the Gurkha infantry battalions: 526 Gurkha Infantry Battalion Signal Troop (2/2 GR); 528 Gurkha Infantry Battalion Signal Troop (2/7 GR); 531 Gurkha Infantry Battalion Signal Troop (6 GR); 534 Gurkha Infantry Battalion Signal Troop (1/2 GR); 541 Gurkha Infantry Battalion Signal Troop (1/7 GR); and 581 Gurkha Infantry Battalion Signal Troop (10 GR).

In 1987, following the disbandment of the 2nd/7th DEO Gurkha Rifles, 528 Gurkha Infantry Battalion Signal Troop was disbanded and 246 (Gurkha Field Force) Signal Squadron was redesignated 246 Gurkha Signal Squadron (48 Gurkha Infantry Brigade).

The 1990s started well for The Queen's Gurkha Signals when on 1 June 1990 250 Gurkha Signal Squadron, commanded by Maj Neil Couch, Royal Signals, was

BRITISH BASE

ΒΡΕΤΤΑΝΙΚΗ
ΒΑΣΙΣ

İNGİLİZ ÜSSÜ

reformed in Britain as part of 30 Signal Regiment, based at Blandford in Dorset, which provides the army's out-of-area communications. This was new ground for Gurkha signallers as 250 Squadron was the first of The Brigade of Gurkhas' corps units to be based permanently in the United Kingdom as an integral part of a British unit.

Only two months after the squadron's reformation 30 Signal Regiment deployed to Saudi Arabia as part of the British contribution to Coalition forces assembled in response to the Iraqi invasion of Kuwait. A total of 44 members of 250 Squadron accompanied the regiment and remained there during the initial stage of the conflict, with detachments being deployed to Riyadh, Tabuk, Muharraq, Dharan, Seeb, Al Jubayl and ultimately Kuwait. Thereafter individual members of the squadron were rotated on a roulement basis, being replaced and returning to Britain before being sent back to Saudi Arabia. In addition to these, a further twelve men were deployed as radio operators with 28 Squadron Gurkha Transport Regiment, providing ambulance support for 1st UK Armoured Division.

In 1994, as part of the reductions in Hong Kong's garrison prior to the handing over of the colony by Britain to China in 1997, The Queen's Gurkha Signals underwent a major reduction in strength. On 28 June that year 246, 247 and 248 Gurkha Signal Squadrons were amalgamated into the reformed Hong Kong Gurkha Signal Squadron, which was thereafter based at the Prince of Wales's Barracks on Hong Kong Island. On 1 July, following the amalgamation of the four Gurkha infantry regiments into The Royal Gurkha Rifles (RGR), 534 and 581 Gurkha Infantry Battalion Signal Troops were disbanded, the remaining three troops being retained to support the three battalions of the new regiment (1, 2 and 3 RGR). By October Headquarter Squadron had disbanded at Sek Kong while RHQ The Queen's Gurkha Signals moved to the Prince of Wales's Barracks. Once again the Hong Kong-based element of the regiment included Gurkha, British and Chinese signallers in its ranks. Meanwhile an All Arms Training Troop, providing signals trade training for Gurkha signallers in Hong Kong, remained at Sek Kong until 1995 when its responsibilities were transferred to The Royal School of Signals at Blandford.

On 1 April 1996 command of The Queen's Gurkha Signals was transferred from Hong Kong to Britain. In Hong Kong Lt Col Jeremy Ellis handed over command to the Commanding Officer of 30 Signal Regiment, Lt Col Paul Oldfield, at Gamecock Barracks at Bramcote in Warwickshire, the latter assuming the appointment of Commander Queen's Gurkha Signals. RHQ The Queen's Gurkha Signals was established at Gamecock Barracks by the Gurkha Major, Maj (QGO) Karnasher Tamang. Thereafter the rundown of the Hong Kong-based element continued under Lt Col Ellis and Maj (QGO) Silajit Gurung. On 1 November 1996, following the disbandment of 3 RGR, 531 Gurkha Infantry Battalion Signal Troop also disbanded and the remaining two troops were redesignated Rear Link Detachments 1 and 2 RGR.

At midnight on 30 June 1997, after a continuous period of forty-three years, The Queen's Gurkha Signals ceased to have a presence in Hong Kong. Thereafter the regiment comprised RHQ; 250 Gurkha Signal Squadron, as an element of 30 Signal

(*Opposite*): A rifleman of the 10th PMO Gurkha Rifles on duty in Cyprus during the 1974 emergency.

Regiment; Nepal Signal Troop; Brunei Signal Troop; and Rear Link Detachments 1 and 2 RGR.

The beginning of the new millennium, however, saw an improvement in the fortunes of The Queen's Gurkha Signals. On 1 November 2001 246 Gurkha Signal Squadron was reformed as an integral element of 2 Signal Regiment in the United Kingdom, increasing the total strength of The Queen's Gurkha Signals to 550 all ranks.

Throughout its life the regiment has successfully adapted its organisation and the skills of its soldiers to meet the varied communications tasks it has been directed to undertake. It continues to live up to the watchword contained in the address by the Major General Brigade of Gurkhas, Maj Gen Lance Perowne, at the Badge Presentation Parade on 23 September 1954: 'By your badge men shall know you. By your loyalty, by your behaviour and by your technical skill they will judge you as men and measure your efficiency as soldiers.'

THE QUEEN'S OWN GURKHA LOGISTICS REGIMENT

The Queen's Own Gurkha Logistic Regiment is the junior element of The Brigade of Gurkhas. Raised in 1958 in Malaya as The Gurkha Army Service Corps (Gurkha ASC), it became The Gurkha Transport Regiment (GTR) in 1965, following the reorganisation of the army's logistic services, and in 1992 it was granted the royal title of The Queen's Own Gurkha Transport Regiment (QOGTR). In 2001 its title was changed again to The Queen's Own Gurkha Logistic Regiment (QOGLR), reflecting the regiment's wider role in providing logistic support to the Field Army. During their existence units of the regiment have been stationed in Malaya, Singapore, Brunei, Hong Kong and the United Kingdom and have served on operations in Malaya and Singapore, Brunei, Borneo, the Persian Gulf, Cyprus, Bosnia and Kosovo.

On the transfer of the four regiments of Gurkha Rifles from the Indian Army to the British Army and the formation of The Brigade of Gurkhas in 1948, the role of the Gurkhas was expanded beyond that of infantrymen. In addition to meeting the recruiting requirements of the newly raised Gurkha units of the Royal Engineers and Royal Signals, Gurkhas were enlisted for The Royal Army Ordnance Corps (RAOC), Royal Electrical and Mechanical Engineers (REME), Royal Military Police (RMP) and The Army Catering Corps (ACC). However, there were difficulties in the assimilation and administration of the small numbers of Gurkhas in the RAOC, REME and ACC. It was thus decided to disband the Gurkha elements of these Corps units and absorb them into the establishments of the Gurkha infantry regiments and the Gurkha squadrons of the Royal Engineers and Royal Signals in the trades in which they had been trained.

In 1957 the government announced the suspension of conscription and the phasing out of national service by 1960. The impact of ending the latter was to create a crisis of manpower in the regular army which eventually led to the decision to raise The Gurkha ASC to replace Royal Army Service Corps (RASC) units in the Far East. The new corps was to consist of four companies for service in Malaya, Singapore and

Hong Kong and was to be manned by British officers and NCOs seconded from the RASC and by QGOs and Gurkha other ranks, initially transferred from the four Gurkha infantry regiments.

The cadres of the first two companies, 28 and 30 Companies Gurkha ASC, were formed on 1 July 1958, a number of their members being transferees from the motor transport (MT) platoons of the Gurkha infantry regiments. Over the next three months the QGOs and senior NCOs underwent training at the RASC School in Singapore in all aspects of driver instruction and transport management to prepare them for their new appointments. They in turn became the instructors to the junior NCOs of the companies. While the cadres were under training, the first RASC British officers and NCOs to be seconded to the Gurkha ASC attended Gurkhali language courses at the Training Depot Brigade of Gurkhas in Malaya and underwent familiarisation tours with Gurkha infantry battalions.

By June 1959 the cadres of 28 and 30 Companies had completed their training and had moved to their respective camps in Malaya to prepare for the arrival of the main body of Gurkha other ranks being transferred from the battalions. The two companies formed up in the first week of August 1959 and immediately began driver and supply training which continued until July 1960. At the same time the cadres for the second two companies, 31 and 34 Companies Gurkha ASC, were formed and assembled at the RASC School and thereafter followed a similar training cycle.

In November 1959 the first of the annual intake of recruits and former boy soldiers were posted to the Gurkha ASC directly from the Training Depot Brigade of Gurkhas. Like the other Corps units, recruits for the Gurkha ASC were drawn from both East and West Nepal.

On 1 July 1960 Headquarters RASC 17th Gurkha Division/Overseas Commonwealth Land Forces was redesignated Headquarters Gurkha ASC and assumed command of 28, 30, 31 and 34 Companies Gurkha ASC. On completion of their initial training, 28 Company sailed for Hong Kong while 30 and 31 Companies became Gurkha infantry brigade companies based in Malaya and Singapore. Meanwhile 34 Company moved to Kluang, which also became the home of Headquarters Gurkha ASC, in the general transport role. It later assumed responsibility for driver and trade training for the Gurkha ASC.

Initially officers and soldiers of the Gurkha ASC wore the badges and accoutrements of the RASC pending the design and approval of their own which, along with other regimental accoutrements, were approved during 1960 and worn from the end of 1961. The cap badge comprised a silver eight-pointed star, bearing a scroll inscribed Gurkha Army Service Corps, issuant therefrom a wreath of laurel all in gold, overall a pair of kukris in saltire, the blades silver, the hilts gold, ensigned with the Royal Cypher in gold. Over the next forty years the badge was to change four times, reflecting the varying role and title of the regiment. During these formative years Her Majesty The Queen also approved the affiliation of the Gurkha ASC to the RASC and the appointment of the Colonel Gurkha ASC.

The Gurkha ASC companies now began to settle into their new roles and environments as part of the order of battle of the British Army and The Brigade of Gurkhas. 28 Company, which had arrived in Hong Kong in September 1960, was destined to serve continuously in the colony for the next thirty years, its primary role being to provide transport support to the Hong Kong garrison and aid to the civil authorities. It also took over the tank transporters for the movement of the colony's stockpile of Centurion tanks between Kowloon and the New Territories, the sight of them travelling loaded along the colony's narrow and twisting roads being an awe-inspiring one.

The company's role of support to the civil authorities was put to the test in 1962 when it was involved in the transportation of a massive influx of illegal immigrants who had entered the colony from mainland China, and provided assistance after Typhoon Wanda had struck the colony. The latter was the most severe storm to hit Hong Kong for twenty-five years, causing 150 deaths and making 78,000 people homeless.

In May 1962 30 Company deployed from Malaya to the United Kingdom, along with the 1st Battalion 6th QEO Gurkha Rifles, a squadron each of The Gurkha Engineers and Gurkha Signals and a detachment of The Gurkha Military Police, as part of 51 Infantry Brigade. The latter formed part of 3rd Division, the United Kingdom's Strategic Reserve, and 30 Company trained and exercised both in the air-portable role and for general war in north-west Europe. This was the first time that Gurkha units had served in the United Kingdom and it proved to be a great, if short-lived, success. In early 1964, as a result of increasing confrontation between Indonesia and Malaysia, the United Kingdom tour of 51 Infantry Brigade, including 30 Company, was cut short when it returned to the Far East to take part in the Borneo Confrontation campaign. It was to be another thirty years before units of the Gurkha ASC once again served in the United Kingdom.

Meanwhile 31 Company had moved to Singapore in November 1961, on completion of its initial training, to join 99 Gurkha Infantry Brigade. In addition to supporting the brigade, it provided transport for internal security duties and administrative support to the Singapore garrison. In December 1962 the company became the first unit of the Gurkha ASC to be deployed on active service when, following the outbreak of the Brunei Rebellion, it was deployed to the islands of Labuan and Brunei. It established the main resupply base for the operation on Labuan while a forward detachment was set up in Brunei for the distribution of supplies to units. Although the rebellion was suppressed by the end of December, mopping-up operations continued, being followed by the start of the Borneo Confrontation with Indonesia, resulting in elements of 31 Company remaining on Labuan until they were withdrawn in November 1963. However, there was to be little respite as the company was redeployed to Borneo in January 1964. The Confrontation was to dominate the lives and activities of 30, 31 and 34 Companies for the next three years.

Early in 1964 30 Company returned from the United Kingdom to Singapore and, having re-equipped and reacclimatised, deployed to Borneo in June that year. For the next five months, from platoon bases centred on Brunei Town and Seria in Brunei, Tawau in Sabah, Kuching in Sarawak and on Labuan, it operated resupply points, distributed stores and undertook troop lifts. At the end of November 1963 30 Company completed its first operational tour in Borneo and returned to Singapore for rest and retraining.

For 31 Company 1964 had begun with elements being deployed on operations and ended with the company once again on active service in Borneo, having taken over from 30 Company in November 1964. This cycle of 30 and 31 Companies replacing each other in Borneo every six months was to continue until the end of the Confrontation in 1966. The Gurkha ASC provided the bulk of the road transport in Borneo during the campaign and both companies were to serve a total of seven operational tours between 1962 and 1966. Although the brunt of the operational commitment in Borneo fell on 30 and 31 Companies, both 28 and 34 Companies provided reinforcements to help ease the burden. Additionally 34 Company was itself committed to operations following a landing by Indonesian paratroops in Johore in Western Malaysia in 1964.

In 1965 the army's logistic services were reorganised. The RASC became The Royal Corps of Transport (RCT) with responsibility for the army's transport and movements, while The RAOC took over the army's supply functions. As a result of this change The Gurkha ASC was redesignated The Gurkha Transport Regiment (GTR) on 16 October 1965. Companies became squadrons, each retaining its number, and platoons became troops. British officers and NCOs were now seconded from the RCT while The RAOC provided British officers and NCOs for the Combat Supplies Troops. Regimental accoutrements also changed, the badge design remaining the same but now bearing the title Gurkha Transport Regiment.

28 Squadron was next to be committed to operations when the Chinese Cultural Revolution spilt over into Hong Kong. In May 1967 the squadron was recalled from field training to its barracks in Kowloon where widespread rioting had broken out. The violence quickly escalated and troops were deployed both on the streets of Kowloon and along the Sino–Hong Kong border. Over the next few months the squadron was fully engaged in providing transport in support of internal security operations on Hong Kong Island and Kowloon and to the battalions on the border.

By the end of 1966 the strength of the GTR, including those soldiers on Extra Regimental Employment (ERE), numbered over 1,200 all ranks. With the ending of the Borneo Confrontation, however, it was announced that The Brigade of Gurkhas would be reduced to a strength of 10,000 men by 1969. For the GTR this meant over 400 Gurkha officers and other ranks being made redundant during the next three years and the disbandment of 30 Squadron. The latter began to draw down during 1967 and at the regiment's 10th Anniversary Parade, held in Singapore in August 1968, 30 Squadron slow-marched through the ranks of the other squadrons to disbandment, ten years after its cadre had been formed in Singapore. In 1968 the government announced the withdrawal of British forces from Malaysia and Singapore by the end of 1971 and a further reduction in The Brigade of Gurkhas to 6,000 men. This was to result in the relocation of the GTR to Hong Kong, an increase in the number of soldiers being sent on redundancy and the disbandment of a second squadron, 34 Training Squadron, which had assimilated the Gurkha MT Wing from the Far East Training Centre in Singapore, thereafter becoming responsible for both the All Arms driver training for units of The Brigade of Gurkhas and the trade and regimental training and education within the GTR. By the end of the reductions in 1972 the regiment, which had shrunk to one-third of its size of 1966, consisted of a headquarters and 28 and 31 Squadrons.

In 1970 RHQ and the Training Wing of 34 Squadron moved to Hong Kong while the remainder of the squadron was disbanded. The following year 31 Squadron bade farewell to Singapore and also moved to Hong Kong, taking under its command the Training Wing – now designated the Gurkha MT School. For the first time since 1960, when 28 Company had sailed for Hong Kong, the regiment was together once more, with a troop serving with the Gurkha battalion in Brunei and a detachment with the Gurkha battalion in the United Kingdom. RHQ and 28 Squadron were co-located in Kowloon while 31 Squadron was based in the New Territories. 28 Squadron retained its field force role while 31 Squadron assumed responsibility for administrative transport to units in the New Territories and for running the Gurkha MT School. Hong Kong was to remain the home of the GTR for the next twenty-five years.

There now followed a period of adjustment and consolidation as the regiment settled down in Hong Kong. While its primary role was the provision of transport for operations, training and administrative duties, it was kept increasingly busy supporting colony exercises and providing detachments for overseas training, ceremonial parades, community projects, and military skills and sporting competitions, with a healthy rivalry developing between the two squadrons.

Annual ceremonial parades for Gurkha units had been introduced by the Major General Brigade of Gurkhas in 1971 and the GTR's first parade in Hong Kong was held in 1972. The occasion was used to reintroduce the attestation of recruits on joining the regiment. The ceremony, known as Kasam Khane, had first been conducted in 1962 but had lapsed during the Borneo Confrontation and the subsequent rundown period. The parade also attracted the attention of the world's press, as it was reported to be the last occasion on which the renowned Gurkha olive green starched shorts were to be worn on parade. Many photographs of knees were taken and pictures appeared in the local and world newspapers. During the following year the regiment paraded in the new stone-coloured tropical No. 6 Dress of jacket and trousers.

During 1975 the GTR was tasked with providing one of the platoons for a tour of duty with the Korean Honour Guard. This was the first occasion that a Gurkha corps unit had found the 30-strong platoon as part of the United Nations Honour Guard Company in South Korea. The duties of the platoon were mostly ceremonial and required it to adopt highly complicated US Army foot and arms drill and to have its uniforms specially tailored with a number of embellishments for the two-month tour.

The regiment went on to find platoons for the Korean Honour Guard on a regular basis until 1992.

Following the 1975 Defence Review the size of the Hong Kong garrison was reduced. This resulted in the withdrawal of some British units and the disbandment of the GTR's sister RCT unit, 31 Regiment RCT. The surviving RCT transport squadron and maritime troop, 29 Squadron RCT and 415 Maritime Troop RCT (which comprised locally enlisted Hong Kong Chinese soldiers), were transferred to the GTR. The regiment now had two Gurkha squadrons, a Chinese transport squadron and a maritime troop, and was the sole surviving transport unit of the British Army serving east of Suez. The withdrawal of British units meant that the regiment was able to move into better accommodation both in Kowloon and in the New Territories. 28 Squadron also swapped its field force role for that of providing garrison transport, although this loss was partly compensated for when the squadron took over a fleet of Saracen armoured personnel carriers (APCs) from the departing squadron of the 16th/5th Queen's Royal Lancers, for internal security duties.

Until 1977 the GTR had been the only regiment in The Brigade of Gurkhas without a band. Earlier attempts to form a pipe band had been thwarted, although the companies and squadrons had managed to retain the occasional piper transferred from one of the Gurkha infantry regiments. In 1977 a concerted effort was made by the GTR to form its own Pipes and Drums with transferees from the 6th QEO, 7th DEO or 10th PMO Gurkha Rifles and the reroling of soldiers within the regiment to the dual trade of Piper and Driver. The band made its debut with the regiment's Korean Honour Guard contingent in 1980 and thereafter performed on a regular basis. In 1985 two pipers were despatched to Tokyo at the request of Her Majesty's Ambassador to Japan and played at the embassy in the presence of His Majesty the Emperor of Japan. Later that same year the Pipes and Drums performed in the United Kingdom and Germany.

In 1979 there was a dramatic increase in the number of illegal immigrants entering Hong Kong from mainland China, which led to a major deployment of British forces along the border to try to stem the flow. Over the next year the regiment provided not only transport support but also reinforcements to the hard-pressed battalions, as well as helicopter handling teams for the despatch of defence stores by helicopter to the border areas and searchlight teams to illuminate the marshes through which illegal immigrants were trying to enter the colony. The searchlight teams were also used to illuminate the cross-border checkpoints where the illegal immigrants were formally returned to the Chinese authorities.

Throughout the 1980s the annual cycle of peacetime activities of the GTR continued to revolve around the provision of administrative transport to the garrison and colony exercises, squadron training camps, parades, inspections, visits, skill-at-arms and sporting competitions. In 1981 there was a temporary increase in the size of The Brigade of Gurkhas to help it tackle the illegal immigrant problem in Hong Kong and to relieve the pressure of worldwide commitments on British units. This included a modest increase both in the GTR's manning levels in Hong Kong and in the number of soldiers serving with units in the United Kingdom. For the first time the GTR now began to train as a regiment as opposed to exercising by squadrons. 28 Squadron's fleet of Saracens was increased and there was a growing demand for the APCs for exercises and training by the colony's battalions. Until the early 1980s the regiment had only been able to send individuals and small detachments on overseas company exercises to such countries as Australia, Fiji and New Zealand. From 1984 it was itself allocated an overseas exercise and sent composite squadrons to train in Singapore, Malaysia and Brunei.

In 1983 the regiment celebrated its 25th anniversary with a Kasam Khane Parade, taken by the Colonel of the Regiment who was a former Commander GTR. By now the last of the soldiers who had transferred from the Gurkha battalions to the Gurkha ASC had gone on pension and for the first time the Gurkha Major, the regiment's senior Gurkha officer, was one who had enlisted directly into the Gurkha ASC. The year 1983 also saw one of the Queen's Gurkha Orderly Officers selected from the regiment, signifying that The Gurkha Transport Regiment had truly come of age. As with all Gurkha units, shooting played an important part in the lives of the GTR squadrons and in 1987 the Queen's Medal at Bisley was won by a soldier of the regiment.

By 1990 it had been nearly twenty-five years since the regiment had last seen active service. This, however, was soon to change, starting with the deployment of a GTR squadron to the Gulf in 1991. As the requirement for ambulance support expanded, 28 (Ambulance) Squadron GTR was raised in November 1990 to supplement the heavily committed RCT units, the majority of soldiers being found by 28 and 31 Squadrons. Within two weeks of being formed, the 200-strong unit moved to the United Kingdom to draw its mobilisation vehicles and equipment and begin training. At the beginning of January 1991 it deployed to Saudi Arabia as part of the Gurkha Ambulance Group which, in addition to the squadron, comprised members of five army bands, including The Band of The Brigade of Gurkhas (2 GR), employed in their secondary role as medical assistants. At the start of the land campaign the squadron was poised to operate the casualty evacuation chain with ambulance troops deployed to support each of the forward dressing stations with the armoured and artillery brigades and a coach troop supporting the field hospitals. During the 100-hour land battle the squadron moved 340 casualties – nearly all of them Iraqi prisoners. In April 1991 it returned to Hong Kong after an absence from the colony of four months.

Shortly after 28 (Ambulance) Squadron had returned from the Gulf the GTR was tasked with providing a squadron for a six-month emergency tour with the United Nations Peacekeeping Force in Cyprus (UNFICYP). The unit for this task had traditionally been provided by the RCT but, with the commitment of all its units to the Gulf War and post-conflict operations, the assistance of GTR was sought once again. Thus 34 (UNFICYP) Transport Squadron GTR was raised in June 1991 as a composite squadron of 130 all ranks from 28, 31 and 29 Squadrons and was deployed to Cyprus

(*Opposite*): Gurkhas of 1 RGR on parade at Church Crookham in Hampshire.

in July 1991. Based in Nicosia, it provided logistic support to the United Nations troops operating along the buffer zone between the Greek and Turkish Cypriot communities and provided assistance for another UN organisation, the United Nations High Commissioner for Refugees (UNHCR). In January 1992 the squadron completed its tour of duty and returned to Hong Kong.

Since 1977 the GTR had been the only regiment in The Brigade of Gurkhas not to have a royal title and this perceived inequality was increasingly felt by its Gurkha officers and soldiers. By 1992 the regiment had been a permanent unit of the brigade for over thirty years and, in view of its recent operational experience, a case was submitted for it to be granted a royal title. On 30 August 1992 Her Majesty The Queen approved the royal title of The Queen's Own Gurkha Transport Regiment (QOGTR). Six months later a ceremonial re-badging parade was held in the presence of the Commander British Forces Hong Kong. The parade also witnessed the formal disbandment of the Saracen APC troop as part of the drawdown of British forces in Hong Kong.

The future of The Brigade of Gurkhas post-1997 had been assured in Parliament in May 1989 but this was followed up by an announcement that it would be reduced in strength to 2,500 men following the British withdrawal from Hong Kong. In line with the other Gurkha Corps, the QOGTR was to be reduced to a small headquarters and one transport squadron to be stationed in the United Kingdom. It was also to retain a detachment in Brunei and establish a troop at the Army School of Mechanical Transport to train drivers for The Brigade of Gurkhas, a task previously performed by the Gurkha MT School.

In 1993 28 Squadron left Hong Kong for Britain to join 10 Transport Regiment Royal Logistic Corps (RLC), the RLC having been formed in April of that year by the amalgamation of the RCT, RAOC, Royal Pioneer Corps, Army Catering Corps and the Royal Engineers Postal Communications and Courier Service. Based in Colchester, it was equipped with the 15-tonne Demountable Rack Offloading and Pick Up System (DROPS) to undertake transport support to the UK Field Army. The following year 29 Squadron was transferred to the newly raised Hong Kong Logistic Support Regiment and, after thirty-five years' service, 31 Squadron was disbanded. The move of the Regimental Headquarters to the United Kingdom was completed in January 1995 when command of the QOGTR was passed to the Commanding Officer 10 Transport Regiment RLC. A detachment of the regiment continued to serve in Kong Hong providing transport support until the colony was finally handed over to China on 30 June 1997.

In November 1994 28 Squadron furnished the Tower of London Guard, this being the first occasion on which a Gurkha corps unit had undertaken public duties. Six months later, in April 1995, the squadron deployed as part of the British Logistics Battalion to the Former Republic of Yugoslavia for a tour with the United Nations Protection Force. This was the QOGTR's third operational tour in five years and the second time that it had worn the UN blue beret. The QOGTR was also the first formed Gurkha unit to be deployed to the Balkans. Based near the port of Split in Croatia on the Adriatic Coast, the squadron carried out routine resupply tasks, bulk fuel resupply and troop lifts in support of British units. Later in its tour it played a key role in supporting the UNHCR and assisting in the withdrawal of UN troops from the protected enclaves. In October 1995 the squadron returned to Colchester. At subsequent parades it was not unusual to see QOGTR soldiers wearing three campaign medals for the Gulf, the UN tour in Cyprus and now Bosnia.

The following year elements of 28 Squadron trained in the United States and in Cyprus and the first Kasam Khane Parade was held in the United Kingdom. In November 1996 half of 28 Squadron was once again deployed to Bosnia, where for the next three months it assisted in the draw-down of British units in Bosnia as the smaller NATO Stabilisation Force (SFOR) replaced the NATO Implementation Force (IFOR). At the end of their short tour elements of the squadron drove the 3,000 kilometres back to Colchester – one of the longest convoys ever undertaken by the regiment.

The QOGTR was now to have a respite from operations until the spring of 1999, although its versatility was again tested in April 1997 when 28 Squadron provided military aid to the civil powers by manning Green Goddess fire engines during the strike by the Essex Fire Brigade. In June 1997 the QOGTR Troop in Hong Kong was disbanded, as part of the final draw-down of the Hong Kong garrison, thus severing the regiment's 37-year continuous link with the colony. The following year the QOGTR celebrated the 40th anniversary of its formation with a ceremonial parade and Kasam Khane in the presence of the Colonel Commandant Brigade of Gurkhas, that appointment having replaced that of the Major General Brigade of Gurkhas in 1994. In April 1999 it deployed on its third operational tour to Bosnia where, based on the port of Split, it was employed in the general transport support role throughout the theatre of operations. Later in the summer a detachment from the squadron was also deployed to support operations in Kosovo.

Following on from the Labour government's Strategic Defence Review of 1998, the feasibility of forming a second QOGTR squadron now began to be examined with a view to the wider employment of Gurkhas within the RLC as well as helping to offset the army's continuing undermanning. A decision was eventually taken to convert a RLC stores squadron to a Gurkha unit and in November 2000 the first party of QOGTR soldiers was posted to 94 Stores Squadron, 9 Supply Regiment RLC for employment in the supply specialist trade. To reinforce the expanding role being taken on by the QOGTR, its title was changed, with royal approval, to The Queen's Own Gurkha Logistic Regiment (QOGLR) at a ceremonial parade held on 5 April 2001, that date being specifically selected to align the regiment's formation date with that of the RLC. Later that year 28 Squadron QOGLR deployed for its fourth operational tour to the Balkans, on that occasion to Kosovo.

By May 2002, 94 Stores Squadron QOGLR was fully manned, providing third line materiel support (less combat supplies) and replenishment vehicle support. The vision of Gurkhas being employed in the specialist storeman role, as reflected in the Tri-Partite Agreement of 1947 between Britain, India and Nepal, and for which recruits were initially selected for service with the RAOC, has come to fruition half a century later. Additionally, to reflect army policy of concentrating the trade of chef within the RLC, it was directed that all Gurkha cooks were to be rebadged as QOGLR in April 2002. Thus it is with increasing confidence that The Queen's Own Gurkha Logistics Regiment looks forward to a secure and expanding future.

GURKHA MILITARY POLICE

Gurkhas were first used in the military police role in the British Army with the formation in 1950 of 17 Gurkha Divisional Provost Company Royal Military Police, commanded by Maj J.S. Jackson who was later succeeded by Maj Alf Ritchie. In 1954 the first Gurkha officer, Lt (QGO) Deobahadur Rana, of the 2nd/6th Gurkha Rifles, was posted to the company.

Historically police work was not new to the Gurkhas. They had served in para-military police battalions on the frontiers of India and in Burma since the nineteenth century, while during the Second World War they had served with distinction in the Corps of Military Police (India) in all the theatres in which the Indian Army was present.

During 1948 and 1949 Gurkha NCOs were selected and transferred from the infantry regiments to undergo training in military police duties in Malaya as part of a wider aspiration of creating an all-arms Gurkha division. Together with a British element of the Royal Military Police (RMP), 17 Gurkha Divisional Provost Company became operational in Malaya on 1 June 1950. With its headquarters based in Kuala Lumpur, detachments of the company were stationed throughout the Malay Peninsula. During the Malayan Emergency campaign Gurkha military policemen assisted the civil police in the removal of illegal squatters, food control and searches for communist terrorists as well as carrying out routine traffic control, the provision of escorts to VIPs and crime detection. During the early days of its existence the company was also used on a number of operations in the infantry role and deployed into the jungle where it carried out patrols and manned ambushes.

In September 1955, along with the Gurkha squadrons of the Royal Engineers and Royal Signals, the Gurkha element of the Royal Military Police was incorporated into the order of battle of The Brigade of Gurkhas and designated the Gurkha Military Police (GMP). This subsequently led to the design and issue of a GMP cap badge and accoutrements.

By 1959 there had been a rapid expansion of the GMP as a result of a reduction in the number of RMP soldiers serving with 17 Gurkha Divisional Provost Company and the formation of two Gurkha brigade provost units. To meet this increase, additional soldiers had been transferred from the infantry regiments while, as an experiment, small drafts of newly trained soldiers were posted in directly from the Training Depot

The curved kukri knife is the world-famous symbol of the Gurkha soldier.

Brigade of Gurkhas. This was discontinued, as the trained soldier with four to seven years' service was considered to be better suited to the military police role than his younger and less mature counterpart. Further expansion followed at the beginning of the 1960s with the redesignation of the RMP Dog Company, based in Singapore, to 5 (Gurkha) Dog Company GMP and the raising of a third Gurkha brigade provost unit for service in Hong Kong.

The year 1962 was a watershed for the GMP. A brigade provost unit moved to the United Kingdom for a tour of duty, with other units of The Brigade of Gurkhas, as part of 51 Gurkha Infantry Brigade. That same year also saw the appointment of Maj (QGO) Narbir Thapa, formerly of the 2nd KEO Gurkha Rifles, as the GMP's first, and only, Gurkha Major. In the meantime 17 Gurkha Divisional Provost Company was disbanded and replaced by Headquarters and Training Establishment GMP to train and administer a growing GMP. In December of that year another brigade provost unit was deployed on operations following the outbreak of the Brunei Rebellion. Further deployments to Borneo by Gurkha brigade provost units and 5 (Gurkha) Dog Company GMP were to follow in 1963 and 1964 during the Confrontation.

The expansion of the GMP, commanded at this time by Maj David St John Newman, was, however, to be short-lived. In 1963, in anticipation of a cut in The

Brigade of Gurkhas, recruitment of military policemen was initially suspended and on 31 December 1964 the GMP was disbanded. On 1 January 1965 all serving Gurkha military policemen were re-badged as members of the infantry regiments of The Brigade of Gurkhas for service in an enlarged 5 (Gurkha) Dog Company which became an ERE pool unit under the command of Maj Peter O'Bree of the 6th QEO Gurkha Rifles, who eventually handed over to his second in command, Capt (GCO) Narbu Lama of the 2nd KEO Gurkha Rifles, in 1969. During this period the unit continued to be based in Singapore, guarding key installations and headquarters, until it was disbanded on 1 January 1970 as part of the run-down of The Brigade of Gurkhas.

THE STAFF BAND OF THE BRIGADE OF GURKHAS

Military bands have existed in Gurkha regiments in British service since the mid-nineteenth century. The Sirmoor Rifle Regiment, subsequently the 2nd KEO Gurkha Rifles, was the first to form a band in 1859, although it was not until 1877 that official sanction was given for Indian Army regiments to raise military bands. By the beginning of the First World War there were bands in all ten Gurkha regiments with some of those possessing two battalions featuring a band in each. During the 1930s, however, owing to cuts in military spending as a result of the world economic depression, a number of these were disbanded.

All the four Gurkha regiments which transferred to the British Army in 1948 had possessed military bands but none accompanied them; in the case of the 2nd KEO Gurkha Rifles all its bandsmen, being Indian domiciled, opted to remain with the Indian Army, as apparently did the members of the pipes and drums of the 6th, 7th and 10th Gurkha Rifles.

On joining the British Army each Gurkha regiment was therefore given the choice of raising either a regimental military band or pipes and drums for each of their two battalions. The 2nd KEO Gurkha Rifles opted for a military band, with a bugle section for each battalion, while the 6th, 7th and 10th Gurkha Rifles chose pipes and drums. In November 1949 the Army Council approved the raising of a major staff band for The Brigade of Gurkhas and a minor or regimental band for the 2nd KEO Gurkha Rifles. Band recruits were enlisted but because the Gurkha manpower ceiling could not be exceeded, the plan to raise a staff band was temporary shelved and all the recruits were made available for the regimental band of the 2nd KEO Gurkha Rifles.

In September 1955 authority was given to raise a major staff band for The Brigade of Gurkhas. It was eventually to comprise a British director of music, 68 Gurkha bandsmen and 20 band boys. When at full strength it was to be, among army bands at the time, second only in size to the Royal Artillery Band, Woolwich. The band was to be formed and trained at the Training Depot Brigade of Gurkhas in Malaya.

The first 30 potential Gurkha bandsmen for the staff band were posted in as a nucleus in November 1955 on completion of their recruit training. Following the arrival of instruments and a music library in January 1956, training started under the newly appointed Director of Music, Capt Bill Moore of the 6th Gurkha Rifles, formerly of The Somerset Light Infantry. He faced a daunting task as not one of the newly joined bandsmen had any notion of western music. Additionally the Gurkhas had only a rudimentary education and understood little English, while Capt Moore could speak only a little Gurkhali. Undismayed, the latter set to work with abundant energy. His enthusiasm soon infected the young Gurkhas, who were also eager to learn, and considerable progress was made within a short space of time. By the following year, after only nine months of training, it was considered that the staff band's musical and marching skills were sufficiently advanced for it to play on parade. Initially the music played was mainly by ear. Time was therefore set aside for its members to learn to read music in order to expand their musical repertoire.

Unfortunately in mid-1957 Capt Moore was struck down by pneumonia and died in the British Military Hospital at Taiping on 23 June. He was replaced in March 1958 by Lt Harry Burge, also of the 6th Gurkha Rifles and formerly of The East Yorkshire Regiment.

In 1959 the staff band was deemed to be sufficiently 'musically mobile' to go to Hong Kong for two months and perform regular band engagements. It then returned to Singapore and thereafter led a nomadic life, being attached to the various Gurkha

Musicians from The Band of The Brigade of Gurkhas pictured in Kabul, Afghanistan, during 2002.

Pipers of The Royal Gurkha Rifles.

The Pipes and Drums of 1 RGR in Kosovo.

units in the Far East. It was regarded very much as the workhorse for the units of The Brigade of Gurkhas, playing at unit parades, guards of honour for visiting dignitaries, the Queen's Birthday Parade and tattoos, as well as at dinner nights, cocktail parties and sports meetings.

Along with other units of the brigade, however, the staff band fell victim to the cuts announced following the end of the Borneo Confrontation campaign. In October 1966 it flew to Hong Kong for its last tour of duty. As part of the reduction in the size of The Brigade of Gurkhas, it was to be amalgamated with the regimental band of the 2nd KEO Gurkha Rifles. In early 1970 the staff band moved back to Singapore where, after only fifteen years in the British Army's Order of Battle, it underwent amalgamation on 15 May 1970, the combined band being redesignated The Band of The Brigade of Gurkhas (2 GR).

In 1994 following further reductions in the size of The Brigade of Gurkhas and the amalgamation of the four infantry regiments into The Royal Gurkha Rifles, the secondary title of (2 GR) was dropped from the band's designation.

CHAPTER 10

THE MODERN BRIGADE

During the early 1990s The Brigade of Gurkhas underwent a major transition as the British Army faced severe cutbacks and amalgamations as part of an extensive review following the Gulf War of 1991.

On 1 July 1994 the 2nd King Edward VII's Own Gurkha Rifles (The Sirmoor Rifles), 6th Queen Elizabeth's Own Gurkha Rifles, 7th Duke of Edinburgh's Own Gurkha Rifles and 10th Princess Mary's Own Gurkha Rifles were amalgamated to form one large regiment, The Royal Gurkha Rifles (RGR). Initially it comprised three battalions but shortly afterwards was reduced to two with the 1st Battalion (1 RGR) based in the United Kingdom, at Church Crookham in Hampshire, and the 2nd Battalion (2 RGR) in Brunei.

During 1995 company groups from The Royal Gurkha Rifles deployed to Bosnia as part of the Implementation Force (IFOR) along with detachments of The Queen's Gurkha Engineers, Queen's Gurkha Signals and Queen's Own Gurkha Transport Regiment.

The 1990s saw the British Army suffering from recruitment problems, particularly among infantry regiments. As a result three independent companies were formed by The Royal Gurkha Rifles, these being attached to regiments requiring reinforcement for operational reasons: the 1st Battalion The Royal Scots, the 1st Battalion The Princess of Wales's Royal Regiment (PWRR) and the 2nd Battalion The Parachute Regiment (2 PARA). In addition two further companies were formed to provide demonstration troops for the Royal Military Academy Sandhurst and the School of Infantry NCOs Tactics Wing at Brecon, redesignated the Infantry Training Centre Wales in 1995.

Throughout the mid- and late 1990s The Royal Gurkha Rifles saw active service in different parts of the world. In 1997 the reinforcement company attached to 1 PWRR deployed with the battalion to Zaire where it prepared to take part in an operation to evacuate hundreds of British nationals. The operation was eventually cancelled, however. A year later Gurkhas were back in the Balkans and in 1999 elements of 1 RGR were among the first troops into Kosovo where they deployed with 5 Airborne Brigade with the critical task of securing the airport; it was also a delicate task as Russian paratroops had arrived minutes beforehand.

During that same year 2 RGR was called on to mount a peace support operation in East Timor, flying from Brunei to northern Australia from where it mounted the operation. Operating under Australian command, the battalion was later commended for its performance.

Garja Lama VC, MM, visiting the 7th Gurkha Rifles at Church Crookham in 1993.

In 2000 members of C (Gurkha) Company 2 PARA, attached to 1 PARA, were among the first into Freetown in Sierra Leone to spearhead what was initially a national evacuation operation (NEO) to bring out British nationals trapped in the country. Thereafter the operation quickly changed format to that of a peace support operation (PSO) and the Gurkhas found themselves deployed in the country for six weeks with little more than the equipment they carried on their backs.

On 6 June 2000 1 RGR paraded for the last time at Queen Elizabeth Barracks at Church Crookham with the regiment's Colonel-in-Chief, His Royal Highness The Prince of Wales, taking the salute. He spent an afternoon with the battalion before it left for the new home of the UK-based Gurkha battalion at Sir John Moore Barracks at Shorncliffe in Kent.

Meanwhile two of the regiment's reinforcement companies deployed to the Balkans with 1 PWRR and The Royal Scots. During the following year 1 RGR moved to Brunei while 2 RGR arrived at Shorncliffe, undertaking a training package in Belize and supporting training commitments at Brecon, RMA Sandhurst and the Infantry Training Centre (ITC) at Catterick.

A member of 2 RGR pictured during a remembrance parade. The scarlet piping on the collar of his No. 2 Dress was inherited from the 2nd King Edward VII's Own Gurkha Rifles.

In 2001 C (Gurkha) Company 2 PARA took part in another operational deployment, this time in Macedonia to support the multi-national Task Force Harvest (TFH) operation monitoring the cease-fire and collecting weapons handed in by members of the KLA following international intervention to give Albanians greater participation in the affairs of the country.

Months later, in December 2001, as recounted in Chapter 8, C (Gurkha) Company received a warning order to deploy overseas once again, this time to Afghanistan where 2 PARA was among the British units forming part of the International Security Assistance Force (ISAF). By early 2002 the company was in Kabul where the Gurkhas quickly became a familiar if curious sight for the locals who could not quite understand why the Nepalese soldiers were in the British Army. Few, if any, of them were aware that the military forebears of today's Gurkhas had been in Kabul in the late 1800s.

C (Gurkha) Company 2 PARA drops during a battalion exercise. During its attachment to The Parachute Regiment, the company became highly regarded.

Members of The Royal Gurkha Rifles on exercise. These men are serving
with the Infantry Training Centre Wales at Brecon.

Gurkhas of 1 RGR on patrol in Kosovo. They were among the leading forces which arrived in the Balkans in June 1999.

RAF Chinook helicopters lift members of C (Gurkha) Company 2 PARA into Pristina, Kosovo, in June 1999.

Members of 1 RGR during the advance into Kosovo in June 1999.

The scene that met the Gurkhas as they arrived in Pristina. Serbian troops had set fire to hundreds of houses as they fled the country.

Gurkhas serving with 5 Airborne Brigade pictured in Kosovo in June 1999.

In March 2003, a company of 2 RGR was deployed to Sierra Leone as part of Operation Keeling. Its task was to enhance force protection at the UK base in Freetown.

A month earlier elements of The Queen's Own Gurkha Logistics Regiment, The Queen's Gurkha Signals and The Queen's Gurkha Engineers were deployed to the Middle East as part of Operation Telic, the UK's commitment to the Coalition operation to remove weapons of mass destruction from Saddam Hussein's arsenal. Vehicles were driven to Marchwood Military Port in January, the troops flying out to

Kuwait in February as part of 102 Logistics Brigade in order to provide vital support to British forces in Kuwait.

Subsequently, the Gurkha reinforcement company attached to the 1st Battalion Royal Irish Regiment deployed with it, as part of 16 Air Assault Brigade, to the Gulf where it subsequently took part in operations in Iraq.

Gurkhas chat with Russian paratroopers at Pristina airport in Kosovo after the race to be first to secure it.

A company group photograph of Gurkhas serving with 1 RGR in Pristina in 1999.

Members of 1 RGR and C (Gurkha) Company 2 PARA at Pristina airport together with Russian paratroops.

(*Above*): Members of 1 RGR patrol through a burned-out village in Kosovo.

(*Opposite*): A Gurkha manning an L7A1 GPMG during the deployment of 1 RGR in Kosovo.

Members of 2 RGR embarking aboard a C-130 transport aircraft before flying to East Timor as part of the UN forces deployed in 2000 to restore peace and stability to the country.

Gurkhas of 2 RGR on the streets of East Timor.

Members of 2 RGR on patrol in East Timor.

A Gurkha of 2 RGR stands guard alongside United
Nations vehicles at a roadblock in East Timor.

A Gurkha inspects a driver's papers at a roadblock in East
Timor.

(*Above*): Members of C (Gurkha) Company 2 PARA provide perimeter protection on the runway at Freetown in Sierra Leone.

(*Opposite*): Soldiers of 1RGR parade at Church Crookham for the final time on 16 June 2000, before moving to their new home at Shorncliffe, in Kent.

CHAPTER 11

RECRUITMENT AND TRAINING

Selection for The Brigade of Gurkhas is tough and it is truly a case of 'many come but few are chosen'. Recruiting takes place once a year and for each one of just over 200 places there are several thousand volunteers. To be more accurate, on average some 25,000 young Nepalese hillmen apply each year to join the brigade, a figure which cannot be matched by any other military formation in the world. To these young men, winning entry to the British Army's Brigade of Gurkhas is an honour and a source of great traditional family pride. The challenge of gaining a place, however, is a daunting one. On average only 230 Gurkhas are recruited each year, undergoing lengthy and rigorous training before joining their respective regiments or Corps units. For those who are successful, service with the British Army offers a well-paid career which will bring financial security and the ability to support their families, many of whom rely on the severely limited income from hill-farming, as well as a pension on retirement.

Sadly, those who are not selected often fear that their failure will bring shame on their families and as a result they do not return home. Instead some seek a job in the streets of Kathmandu while others drown their sorrows in alcohol. In the past a small number committed suicide by jumping from a bridge in Pokhara, before a safety net was placed under it to prevent further such tragedies. Other, more determined, individuals make their way to India to join the Indian Army's Gurkha Brigade, which to this day still includes the 1st, 3rd, 4th, 5th, 8th and 9th Gurkha Rifles in its order of battle.

The Gurkha homeland of Nepal is an independent kingdom, bounded to the north by Tibet, to the east by Sikkim and West Bengal and to the south and west by India. Apart from the area of the Terai along the southern border, the country is situated entirely in the Himalayas and contains some of the highest mountains in the world, including Everest. It depends on a predominantly rural economy with agriculture providing the main source of employment in the towns and villages that nestle in the shadows of some of the world's most breathtaking scenery. It is these areas in the foothills of the Himalayas that have traditionally been the recruiting grounds for The Brigade of Gurkhas with the Pahar and Hill regions providing the greatest numbers. The recruits come from two distinct religious and tribal groupings which, senior Gurkha officers say, can sometimes influence their character during their military career.

(*Above*): Young hill boys parade for the initial recruit selection.

(*Below*): In 1995 the Wilkinson Sword of Peace was awarded to the Gurkha Welfare Trust to mark its outstanding work in support of Gurkha soldiers and their families.

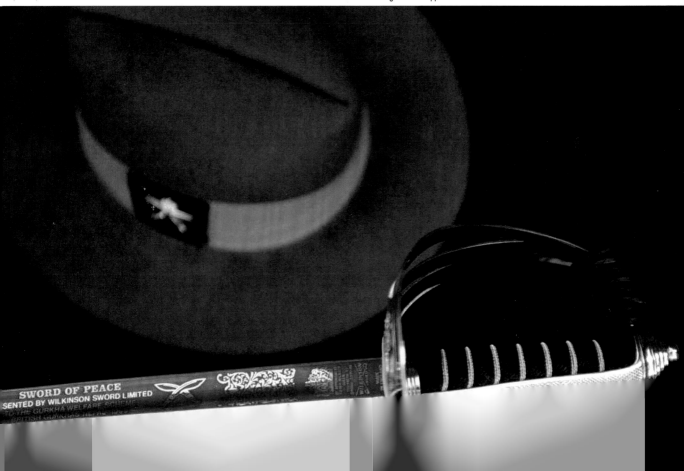

The headquarters of The Brigade of Gurkhas is in the Nepalese capital Kathmandu, which lies in the heart of Nepal. This is the main area of population and is home to an estimated one million people. British Gurkhas Nepal, or BGN as it is popularly known, is situated in Jawalakhel, Kathmandu. It exists to provide a line of communication to support the brigade worldwide and is responsible for recruiting and discharges, payment of pensions and the welfare of serving personnel and ex-servicemen. The brigade, directly and indirectly, is estimated to be the fourth biggest foreign currency earner for the Nepalese economy.

BGN comes under the direction of Headquarters Land Command in Britain. It is commanded by a full colonel who is also the British Defence Attaché in Kathmandu as well as being in overall command of the three Gurkha training posts of British Gurkhas Kathmandu, British Gurkhas Pokhara and British Gurkhas Itahari. British Gurkhas Kathmandu (BGK) is co-located with HQ BGN and is the focus for transit, in-service welfare, re-orientation, discharge, resettlement and payment of pensions.

Meanwhile to the west, close to Annapurna, there is a British Gurkha centre based in the remote town of Pokhara, which has a population of some 65,000 and takes about eight hours to reach by bus from Kathmandu. British Gurkhas Pokhara (BGP) is the centre that coordinates recruiting countrywide and is where the selection process is

Potential recruits pictured during the initial hill selection phase.

Recruits undergoing documentation procedures following selection at Pokhara.

conducted annually. Pensioners' records are held there and a Pension Paying Officer is based there as well, as is the headquarters of the Gurkha Welfare Scheme.

In the east of Nepal is British Gurkhas Itahari (BGI), a small centre housing a pension paying office and a movement detachment to facilitate BGN's operations in that part of the country.

The selection process begins months before the potential recruits arrive at Pokhara with a process known as Galla Selection. 'Galla' in Nepali means somebody who provides a commodity and the men who select the potential recruits in the hills are known as *galla wallahs*. These are ex-Gurkhas, normally retired senior NCOs, and each has an area where he is responsible for finding recruits. After a briefing from the recruiting officer in April, they will tour their respective areas between May and September, making their selection from the thousands of volunteers.

The young men selected by the *galla wallahs* then face Hill Selection, which takes place in the autumn. Six teams of retired Gurkha officers, along with serving Gurkha officers and NCOs, assess the applicants, who are brought in to selected locations in the hills. At this stage the selection process involves rudimentary medical, physical and education tests. Each *galla wallah* will bring in approximately 100 young men from whom only 10 to 15 will be chosen. On one occasion only 900 were selected from a total of over 20,000.

The next phase for the potential recruits is a move to Pokhara for Central Selection, which takes place in December and January. This is the most rigorous part of the process and involves a full medical by a doctor including a chest x-ray and a wide range of intensive physical and mental tests. Here, one of the first tasks of British officers is to establish the true age of each applicant – in the past many have been underage and have presented false evidence. In one well-known case a young boy tried on six occasions to achieve a place in The Brigade of Gurkhas, succeeding on his sixth attempt when the staff at Pokhara were satisfied that he had reached his eighteenth birthday.

The physical standards demanded of Gurkha recruits are extremely high and would daunt many potential recruits in Britain. The tests include 13 heaves to a chest bar and 25 sit-ups in one minute and then to carry on until unable to do so any further (one Gurkha is remembered for doing 400). The recruits must then run 1½ miles in 14 minutes, this being followed immediately by a further 1½ miles in 10 minutes. Finally they must run up and down an 1,800-ft steep hill, carrying 75lb, completing the test in 35 minutes.

Central Selection lasts for four and half days, at the end of which the recruiting officer has the difficult task of informing those who have not made the grade. Some are rejected owing to the fact that they are underweight, others because they are too young or are physically unfit for service. They are never told the reason for their failure but all are invited to return the following year to try again. All are given a cash allowance to meet the expense of getting back to their villages.

High in the hill villages, an ever-dwindling number of Second World War veterans still delight in telling stories about recruiting during Britain's time of dire need. As

(*Opposite*): Heavily camouflaged Gurkhas pictured during an exercise in Kent.

Gurkhas on a jungle warfare course in Brunei.

Recruits training with the kukri.

A Gurkha on exercise in Wales.

A Gurkha wearing Nuclear, Biological and Chemical Warfare clothing during an NBC exercise.

recounted in earlier chapters, the 20 regular battalions of the Indian Army were doubled, then almost trebled to a total of 55 before the war in the Far East ended in 1945.

In 2002 almost 25,000 young men from all over Nepal applied for a mere 275 places to join the British Army or the Gurkha Contingent of the Singapore Police Force (GCSPF). After the painstaking selection processes undertaken by the *galla wallahs* and Area Recruiting Officers (AROs) in various parts of Nepal, only 792 men were given gate passes to come to British Gurkha Camp Pokhara (BGP) for Central Selection. Of those, only some 200 or so would win places in The Brigade of Gurkhas. They are the fortunate ones who will sign up for service in the British Army, being attested at a simple ceremony in Pokhara; with a picture of Her Majesty The Queen in the background, they swear allegiance to the British Crown for an initial period of four years. At this juncture the recruits are introduced to British military uniform; for the majority this will be the first pair of boots they have ever owned.

Thereafter the recruits are flown to Britain, where they travel to the Infantry Training Centre at Catterick for the start of their training. Many have never travelled in a car, let alone an aircraft, and the transition needs a period of adjustment to life in the west. On arrival in the UK they are given cultural briefings about all aspects of life in Britain, ranging from food to the weather.

A colour sergeant of The Royal Gurkha Rifles in No. 2 Dress, holding his kukri.

Members of The Royal Gurkha Rifles march on parade, their rifles at the trail.

Gurkhas seen here serving with 24 Airmobile Brigade, which was later amalgamated with 5 Airborne Brigade to form 16 Air Assault Brigade.

Gurkhas of 2 RGR taking part in an endurance march during routine training in Brunei.

Gurkhas preparing for battle.

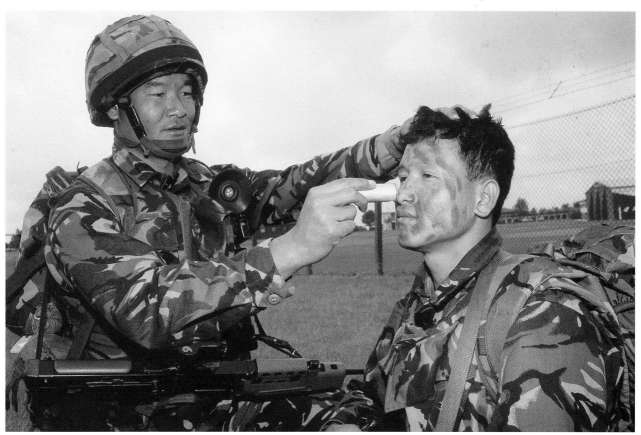

Gurkhas pictured during a jungle warfare lecture in which they are taught to live off the land.

A jungle warfare instructor in Belize. Many Gurkhas find themselves on training teams where they pass on their skills to other units.

A Gurkha jungle warfare instructor teaches personnel from British units how to trap and cook animals in the jungle.

Gurkhas of 2 RGR pictured during an endurance march.

A member of the UK-based Gurkha battalion, at that time part of 5 Airborne Brigade.

Until 1948 recruits for The Brigade of Gurkhas were trained at regimental centres in India. From August 1951 onwards all recruit training was conducted at the Training Depot Brigade of Gurkhas at Sungei Patani in northern Malaya. In 1971 the Depot moved to Hong Kong where as the Training Centre Brigade of Gurkhas, it was based at Malaya Lines at Sek Kong in the New Territories, where it remained until December 1994. At that point it was redesignated the Gurkha Training Wing (GTW) and moved to Britain, where it was located at Queen Elizabeth Barracks, in Church Crookham, Hampshire.

In December 1999 the GTW moved to Catterick, where it joined the 3rd Battalion, Infantry Training Centre. Redesignated Gurkha Company, it is based in Helles Barracks. The role of Gurkha Company is to mould a Nepalese youth into a Gurkha soldier trained to the highest standards of the British Army, who will live up to the traditions of The Brigade of Gurkhas. With a staff of 72 all ranks, the company currently has 231 recruits undergoing training, these being organised into two wings: A (Imphal) Wing and B (Meiktila) Wing.

At Catterick Gurkha soldiers are trained to be part of the modern British Army while retaining their proud heritage that is summed up in the Gurkha motto: *Khaphar hunnu bhanda marnu ramro chha* – 'It is better to die than to be a coward.'

(*Opposite*): HRH The Prince of Wales meets Gurkhas of 1 RGR during a visit to the battalion.

Gurkhas return to Nepal once every three years on five months' leave. They are also entitled to one married accompanied tour of between two and three years in their first fifteen years' service, and permanent accompanied service once they reach the rank of colour sergeant. At the end of their service they are discharged in Nepal under the provision of the Tri-Partite Agreement. On returning to their home country for the last time, all personnel attend a six-day reorientation course run by British Gurkhas Kathmandu. This includes lectures on local government, taxation and other issues which may have changed in their absence. They will be discharged after taking any leave due to them.

There are currently over 25,000 service pensioners and their widows in Nepal and BGN pays pension and remittances worth over £30 million annually. As mentioned earlier, there are three main payment offices in Kathmandu, Pokhara and Itahari, and about 55 per cent of ex-servicemen collect their pensions from them. Young British officers used to be sent out into the hills to pay pensions annually but now, in order to allow pensioners in the more remote areas to collect their pensions more easily and more frequently, payments are made quarterly from the Area Welfare Centres run by the Gurkha Welfare Scheme.

A Gurkha corporal of 2 RGR, armed with an L96A1 7.62mm sniper rifle.

FURTHER READING

Barber, Noel. *The War of the Running Dogs – The Malayan Emergency 1948–1960.* Collins, London, 1971.

Bidwell, Shelford. *The Chindit War – The Campaign in Burma 1944.* Book Club Associates, London, 1979.

Bowen, Hank. *Queen's Gurkha Sapper – The Story of The Royal Engineers (Gurkha), The Gurkha Engineers and The Queen's Gurkha Engineers 1948–1996.* Hank Bowen, 1998.

Cross, J.P. *A Face Like a Chicken's Backside – An Unconventional Soldier in South East Asia 1948–1971.* Greenhill Books, London, 1996.

Cross, John. *Jungle Warfare – Experiences and Encounters.* Guild Publishing, London, 1989.

Fergusson, Bernard. *Beyond The Chindwin – An Account of the Adventures of No. 5 Column of the Wingate Expedition into Burma 1943.* Collins, London, 1946.

Fergusson, Bernard. *The Wild Green Earth.* Collins, London, 1946.

Gould, Tony. *Imperial Warriors – Britain and The Gurkhas.* Granta Books, London, 1999.

James, Harold and Sheil-Small, Denis. *A Pride of Gurkhas – 2nd King Edward VII's Own Goorkhas (The Sirmoor Rifles) 1948–1971.* Leo Cooper, London, 1975.

Harclerode, Peter. *PARA! Fifty Years of The Parachute Regiment.* Arms & Armour, London, 1992.

Miller, Harry. *Jungle War in Malaya – The Campaign Against Communism 1948–60.* Arthur Barker, London, 1972.

Nicolson, Nigel. *Alex – The Life of Field Marshal The Earl Alexander of Tunis.* Weidenfeld & Nicolson, London, 1973.

Perowne, L.E.C.M. *Gurkha Sapper – The Story of The Gurkha Engineers 1948–1970.*

Praval, K.C. *India's Paratroopers – A History of The Parachute Regiment of India.* Leo Cooper, London, 1975.

Smith, E.D. *Britain's Brigade of Gurkhas.* Leo Cooper, London, 1984.

Smith, E.D. *Counter-Insurgency Operation 1: Malaya & Borneo.* Ian Allan, London, 1985.

Smith, E.D. *Valour – A History of The Gurkhas.* Spellmount, Staplehurst, 1997.

INDEX

Military Units

Armies: British 77, 78, 159, 198, 206, 208; British Eighth 27, 31, 33; British Fourteenth 63, 67, 156, 158; British Twenty-Fourth 44, 46, 49, 51; Chinese Fifth 50, 150; Indian 77, 159, 208; Indian National (INA) 44; Indonesian 99, 114, 117, 131; Japanese Fifteenth 44, 63, 67; Japanese Twenty-Fifth 42; Malayan Races Liberation (MRLA) 84, 85, 86, 88–9; US Fifth 33

Corps: British XXXIII 63; German Afrika Korps 27, 30, 31; I Burma 44, 50, 51; I Indian 22; II New Zealand 33, 34, 36; II Polish 38, 40; IV Indian 151; XV Indian 61–2, *see also* Gurkha Corps

Divisions: 1st Burma 44, 45, 49; 1st UK Armoured 39, 186, 195; 2nd Indian Airborne 159; 2nd Infantry 63; 2nd New Zealand 33, 35, 36, 40; 2nd South African 26, 27; 3rd Indian Infantry (Special Force) 52; 3rd (Lahore) 15, 19; 4th Indian 26, 27, 29, 30, 31, 33, 34, 35, 36, 38, 41, 42; 5th Indian 27, 62; 6th Indian 19; 7th Indian (Meerut) 15, 19, 62, 65; 8th Indian 33, 36; 10th Indian 24, 26, 38, 40, 42; 11th Indian 42, 43, 44; 17th Gurkha 78, 81, 90, 97, 102, 113, 155, 176, 177, 179, 187, 188, 189; 17th Indian 44, 45, 46, 47, 49, 51, 61, 65, 66, 68, 73, 151; 19th Indian 68, 69, 70, 71, 73; 20th Indian 66, 68, 73, 151, 155; 23rd Indian 61, 73, 76, 151; 26th Indian 62, 72, 158, 159; 34th US Infantry 35; 44th Indian Airborne 72, 156, 158, 159; 56th London 39; German 1st Fallschirmjägerdivision 34; German 4th Fallschirmjägerdivision 40; Japanese 15th 63, 152; Japanese 18th 'Chrysanthemum' 50, 53, 58; Japanese 31st 63, 65, 152; Japanese 33rd 44, 63; Japanese 53rd 55, 58; Japanese 55th 44; Turkish 35th 20

Brigades: 1 Malay 87; 2 Guards 82; 2 Infantry 184; 2 Malayan Federal 97; 3 Commando 87, 118, 169; 3 West African 54; 5 Airborne 165, 166, 213; 5 Indian Infantry 33, 35, 38, 41, 169; 6 Independent Parachute 159; 6 New Zealand 35; 7 Armoured 49, 51; 7 Indian Infantry 26, 27, 31, 33, 38, 41; 9 Indian Infantry 62; 10 Indian Infantry 27; 11 Indian Infantry 26, 27, 33, 38, 41; 14 Air Landing 156, 159; 14 Infantry 54; 16 Air Assault 166; 16 Indian Infantry 44, 45, 46, 53, 54; 17 Indian Infantry 36, 151; 18 Infantry 87; 23

Armoured 41; 26 Gurkha Infantry 78, 87, 90, 188, 189; 27 Infantry 176; 29 Indian Infantry 17, 18; 32 Indian Infantry 66; 36 Indian Infantry 72–3; 37 Indian Infantry 21, 22, 66; 42 Indian Infantry 22; 43 Gurkha Lorried Infantry 38, 39, 40, 41, 42; 48 Gurkha Infantry 69, 78, 87, 90, 179, 181, 188, 189; 48 Indian Infantry 44, 46, 47, 49, 50, 51; 49 Indian Infantry 151; 50 Indian Parachute 148, 149, 150–1, 151, 152, 154, 155, 156; 51 Gurkha Infantry 179, 180, 181, 189, 190, 191, 192, 207; 63 Gurkha Infantry 69, 78, 87, 90, 178, 179, 189; 63 Indian Infantry 49; 71 Indian Infantry 72–3; 77 Indian Parachute/Infantry 51, 52, 53, 54, 55, 57, 156, 158; 99 Gurkha Infantry 90, 102, 113, 178, 179, 188, 190, 198; 111 Infantry 53, 54, 58–9; Dehra Dun 15–16; Gurkha 24; Jullundur 17; Sirhind 16–17; US 5307th Composite Unit (Provisional) 60

Regiments: 1st Gurkha Light Infantry 5; 1st King George V's Own (KGO) Gurkha Rifles (Malaun Regiment) 5, 65, 234; 1st Royal Green Jackets (RGJ) 111; 2nd Federation Reconnaissance 126; 2nd King Edward VII's Own (KEO) Gurkha Rifles (Sirmoor Rifles) 9, 11, 74, 77, 78, 93, 207, 208, 212, 213; 2nd Prince of Wales's Own (PWO) Gurkha Rifles (Sirmoor Rifles) 7–8; 3rd Queen Alexandra's Own (QAO) Gurkha Rifles 9, 234; 4th Gurkha Rifles 9, 234; 4th Hussars 83; 4th Madras 155; 5th Royal Gurkha Rifles 10, 11, 65, 234; 6th Queen Elizabeth's Own (QEO) Gurkha Rifles (formerly 42nd Gurkha Rifles of Bengal Infantry) 12, 76, 77, 78, 82, 188, 201, 208, 209, 213; 6th Rajputana Rifles (Outram's) 159; 7th Baluch 155; 7th Duke of Edinburgh's Own (DEO) Gurkha Rifles 13, 14, 76, 77, 78, 119, 176, 188, 201, 208, 213; 8th Gurkha Rifles 13, 79, 234; 9th Gurkha Rifles (of Bengal Infantry) 13, 234; 10 Transport RLC 204; 10th Princess Mary's Own (PMO) Gurkha Rifles 14, 51, 76, 77, 78, 145, 161, 162, 188, 201, 208, 213; 11th Gurkha Rifles 22; 12th Indian Frontier Force 33, 159; 12th Royal Lancers 89; 13th Bengal Native Infantry 3; 13th King's 52; 14th Sikhs 17; 16th/5th Queen's Royal Lancers 201; 17th Dogra 154; 17th Gurkha Divisional Signal 188, 192; 20th King's Royal Hussars (KRH) 40; 21st Punjab 20; 21st SAS (Artists) (TA) 90;

22nd SAS 90, 136, 137, 161; 25th Dragoons 62; 30 Signal 195; 36 Engineer RE 185, 186; 40 Commando RM 109, 113, 114; 42 Commando RM 109, 112, 113, 117; 50th Gurkha Field Engineer RE 176–7, 178–9; 51st Field Engineer RE 177; 51st Highland Division Signal 188; 60th Rifles (later King's Royal Rifle Corps) 6,7; 66th Bengal Native Infantry 4–5; 69th Light Anti-Aircraft Royal Artillery 53; 72nd Highlanders (later Seaforth Highlanders) 10, 11; 92nd Highlanders (later Gordon Highlanders) 11; 93rd Field Battery RA 89; 149th Royal Tank 65; 160th Field Royal Artillery 53; Assam Light Infantry 11; Assam Rifles 63, 155; Buffs 22; Cameronians (Scottish Rifles) 59; Chinese 114th 57; Dorset 22; Durham Light Infantry 65; Essex 36; Fiji Infantry 90; Indian 9th Jat 51; Indian Parachute 156, 159; Japanese 16th 69; Japanese 112th 44; Japanese 128th 55; Japanese 143rd 44; King's 55; King's African 90; King's Own Royal (KORR) 59; King's Own Yorkshire Light Infantry (KOYLI) 114, 126; Lancashire Fusiliers 17, 56; Malay 81, 90; Nepalese Kalibahadur 153; Nigerian 54; Parachute 164, 165, 167; Princess of Wales's Royal Regiment (PWRR) 213; Queen's Gurkha Engineers 176–87; Queen's Gurkha Signals 187–96; Queen's Own Cameron Highlanders 27; Queen's Own Gurkha Logistics (QOGLR) 196–206; Queen's Own Highlanders (QOH) 113, 161; Queen's Own Royal Irish Hussars (QRIH) 108, 113, 114, 118; Rajputana Rifles 36; Royal Air Force (RAF) 133; Royal Australian 142; Royal Berkshire 65, 70; Royal Brunei Malay 113; Royal Fusiliers 36; Royal Gurkha Rifles (RGR) 166, 167, 195, 213; Royal Hampshire 22; Royal Irish Dragoons 3; Royal Leicestershire 17; Royal Malay (RMR) 113, 126; Royal New Zealand Artillery (RNZAR) 139; Royal New Zealand Infantry (RNZIR) 131; Royal Scots 213; Royal Signals 187, 196; Royal Sussex 35; Royal Warwickshire 18; Royal West Kent 63; Sarawak Rangers 113; Shere 151; Sirmoor Rifles 5–6, 7, 208; South Lancashire 18; South Staffordshire 55

Battalions: 1 PWRR 213, 214; 1st Paras/12th Indian Frontier Force 159; 1st/1 RGR 213, 214; 1st/1 Gurkha Rifles 5, 68; 1st/1st

KGO 15, 17; 1st/1st RGJ 111; 1st/2nd KEO Gurkha Rifles 21, 24, 26, 27, 30, 31, 33, 34, 36, 38, 77, 82, 84, 86, 87, 88, 92, 93, 102, 104, 108, 112, 113, 118, 119–20, 125, 131, 133, 161, 164; 1st/3rd QAO 44, 46, 65; 1st/4th Gurkha Rifles 9, 15, 16, 17, 18; 1st/4th PWO Gurkha Rifles 44, 46, 65, 66; 1st/5th Royal Gurkha Rifles 11, 17, 22, 33, 36, 37; 1st/6th QEO Gurkha Rifles 17, 18, 19, 68, 71, 85, 93, 94, 130, 189; 1st/7th DEO Gurkha Rifles 14, 22, 44, 45, 46, 61, 66, 97, 113, 127, 147, 165, 169, 176, 193; 1st/8th Gurkha Rifles 13, 21, 22, 62; 1st/9th Gurkha Rifles 15, 16, 21, 30, 31, 33, 35, 36, 38, 41; 1st/10th PMO Gurkha Rifles 22, 49, 61, 65, 82, 92, 116, 126, 127, 131, 162, 181; 1st/12th Frontier Force 33; 1st/Assam Rifles 151; 1st/Cameronians (Scottish Rifles) 59; 1st/Devonshires 82, 155; 1st/Gordon Highlanders 91; 1st/Indian Parachute 156; 1st/King's 55, 156; 1st/KOYLI 87, 114; 1st/Lancashire Fusiliers 56, 57; 1st/Nasiri Gurkhas 4–5, 6, 9; 1st/Queen's Own Highlanders 102, 104, 105, 108, 109, 113, 161; 1st/RNZIR 131; 1st/Royal Anglian 175; 1st/Royal Berkshires 65; 1st/Royal Fusiliers 36; 1st/Royal Green Jackets 113; 1st/Royal Gurkha Rifles (RGR) 165, 166; 1st/Royal Inniskilling Fusiliers 82; 1st/Royal Leicestershire 118; 1st/Royal

Scots 213; 1st/Seaforth Highlanders 82, 84; 1st/South Staffordshires 55, 56, 57, 156; 1st/West Yorkshires 66, 155; 1st/Worcestershires 89; 2 PARA 136, 137, 165, 166, 167, 172, 175, 213; 2nd/1st Gurkha Rifles 5; 2nd/1st KGO 42, 44; 2nd/2 RGR 213; 2nd/2nd KEO Gurkha Rifles 15, 16, 42, 44, 77, 78, 81, 82–3, 85, 89, 90, 93, 94, 129, 132, 137, 141, 142; 2nd/3rd QAO Gurkha Rifles 15, 16, 17, 22, 27, 38; 2nd/4th/PWO Gurkha Rifles 9, 21, 22, 27, 38; 2nd/5th Mahratta Light Infantry 27; 2nd/5th Royal Gurkha Rifles 11, 22, 44, 46, 65; 2nd/6th QEO Gurkha Rifles 22, 38, 39, 40, 41, 77, 117, 118, 206; 2nd/7th DEO Gurkha Rifles 14, 19, 20, 21, 23, 26, 27, 33, 36, 38, 41, 77, 91, 116, 176, 193; 2nd/8th Gurkha Rifles 13, 15, 27, 38, 39, 40, 41; 2nd/9th Gurkha Rifles 21, 42, 44; 2nd/10th PMO Gurkha Rifles 17, 18, 19, 26, 38, 39, 41, 114, 117, 128, 129, 142; 2nd/Burma Rifles 51; 2nd/Durham Light Infantry 65; 2nd/Gurkha Parachute 156; 2nd/KORR 59; 2nd/Nasiri Gurkhas 4–5, 6, 9; 2nd/QOCH 27, 33; 2nd/Royal Berkshire 70; 2nd/Royal Gurkha Rifles (RGR) 165, 175; 2nd/Royal Leicestershire 17; 3rd/1st KGO 68; 3rd/2nd KEO Gurkha Rifles 51, 52; 3rd/3rd QAO 66; 3rd/4th PWO Gurkha Rifles 53, 58, 59–60; 3rd/5th Gurkha Rifles 66; 3rd/6th

Gurkha Rifles 53, 55, 56, 57; 3rd/7th Gurkha Rifles 46, 150; 3rd/8th KEO Gurkha Rifles 66, 68; 3rd/9th Gurkha Rifles 53, 54, 55, 58; 3rd/10th Gurkha Rifles 61, 66, 73, 76; 3rd/Assam 63; 3rd/Gurkha Parachute 156, 158, 159; 3rd/RMR 126; 3rd/Royal Australian 142; 3rd/Royal Gurkha Rifles (RGR) 165; 4th Parachute/6th Rajputana Rifles (Outram's) 159; 4th/1st KGO Gurkha Rifles 62–3, 65; 4th/2nd KEO Gurkha Rifles 66, 68; 4th/4th PWO Gurkha Rifles 68, 70; 4th/5th Mahratta Light Infantry 151, 152, 153; 4th/5th Royal Gurkha Rifles 65; 4th/6th Royal Gurkha Rifles 68; 4th/8th Gurkha Rifles 62, 145; 4th/9th Gurkha Rifles 53, 54, 58, 60; 4th/10th Gurkha Rifles 68, 69; 4th/Gurkha Parachute 156, 159; 4th/Royal West Kent 63; 6th/Nigerian 54; 10th/Madras Infantry (Kubo Valley Military Police Battalion) 13–14; 13th/King's Regiment 51; 15th/Parachute 156; 14th Sikhs 17; 16th/Parachute 156; 151st/Parachute 148, 150; 152nd/Indian Parachute 148, 149, 151, 152–3, 154, 156; 153rd/Gurkha Parachute 148, 149, 150, 151, 152–3, 154–5, 156; 154th/Gurkha Parachute 150, 151, 156; 411th (Royal Bombay) Parachute Section Indian Engineers 148, 158; Kumaon 9; Sirmoor 4–7

General Index

Abbott, Lt Col B.E. 'Abbo' 148
Abdul Rahman, Tunku (Malayan Prime Minister) 95, 97, 99, 129, 147
Abernethy-Clark, Lt Bruce 179
Afghan War (1878–80) 9, 10
Afghanistan 10, 11, 15, 172, 175, 187, 215
Ah Fui (Malayan CT) 94–5
air support: 1st Air Commando Group (USAAF) 53, 56, 59; Fleet Air Arm 114, 131, 162, 191; Royal Air Force 50, 89, 91, 92, 102, 103, 104, 109, 142, 150, 153; Royal Australian Air Force (RAAF) 91; United States Army Air Force (USAAF) 53, 158–9
airborne units: British 41, 119, 129, 136, 161, 162, 164, 166, 167, 175; German 34, 40; Gurkha 148–56, 158–9, 161, 164, 165; Indian 148–56, 158–9; Indonesian 131; training 148, 161, 192
Aitasing Gurung, Capt (QGO), MM 118
Alexander, Gen Sir Harold (GOC Burma) 34, 46, 49, 50, 51
Alexander, Lt Col L.A. 51
Alison, J. 79
Allen, Maj John 179
Allenby, Gen Sir Edmund 22
Allmand, Capt Michael, VC 56, 57
Amarbahadur Gurung, Rfn 135
Amarbahadur Thapa, Rfn 121
Amoore, Lt Col Wyn 40

Anders, Gen Wladyslaw 38
Arakan campaign (1943–4) 61–3
Asahari, A.M. (TNKU) 100
Assam 51, 63, 150
Australian forces 42, 43, 44
Aylmer, Lt Gen Sir Fenton, VC 21

Baghatbahadur Rai, Lt (QGO) 142–3
Baghdad 19, 22
Bahasa Rana, Maj (QGO) 93
Baker, Maj John 184
Balkans 213, 214
Bangkok Accord 147, 165
Barisan Pemuda Sarawak (BPS) 127
Barton, Brig F.C. 'Billy', RM 118
Bashall, Lt Col James 167
Belbahadur Gurung, Rfn 121
Belize 165, 167, 185, 214
Benest, Lt Col David 165
Bengal–Assam railway 63
Bethell, Brig Richard (CRA) 76
Bhagatbahadur Rai, Lt (QGO) 143
Bhagtasing Gurung, Cpl 139, 140
Bharat Rai, Capt (QGO) 136
Bhim Sen Thapa (Nepalese Prime Minister) 1–2, 3, 4
Bhimbahadur Pun, WOII (CSM), DCM 86
Bhimbahadur Thapa, Rfn 125
Bhuwani Limbu, Lt (QGO) 166

Bhuwansing Limbu, Lt (QGO) 144
Birbahadur Gurung, Cpl, MM 135
Birbahadur Pun, L/Cpl, DCM 140, 142
Birbahadur Rai, Cpl 128
Birkabahadur Gurung, L/Cpl 141
Blaker, Maj F.G. 'Jim', VC 58
Blundell, Lt Col Peter 185, 186
Boatner, Brig Gen Hayward 60
Boisragon, Lt Col G.H., VC 11, 18
Bond, Lt Col George 150
Booth, Lt Col John 181
Borneo Communist Party (BCP) 127
Borneo conflict 82, 99, 100, 113, 119, 147, 161, 162, 163, 169, 178, 190, 192, 198, 207, 212
Bosnia 166, 186, 205, 213
Boucher, Maj Gen Charles 159
Bourne, Lt Gen Sir Geoffrey (GOC Malaya) 93
Bowen, Maj Hank 180
Bowring, Maj Terry 108
Boxer Rebellion (1900) 9
Branford, Maj Bill 178
Brereton, Flt Lt Bill, RAF 148
Brigade of Gurkhas 78, 93, 159, 164, 165, 176, 177, 181, 192, 198, 200, 201, 204, 206, 208, 213; British Gurkhas Nepal/Pokhara/Itahari (BGN/BGP/BGI) 236, 238; Emergency Commissioned Officers (ECOs) 24; Gurkha Commissioned Officers (GCOs) 78; Gurkha Independent Parachute Company 119, 129,

159, 161, 164, 165, 192; Gurkha Military
Police 206–8; Kasam Khane Parade 200, 202,
205; King's Gurkha Officers (KGOs) 78 ;
Queen's Gurkha Officers (QGOs) 93, 197;
Queen's Truncheon (Sirmoor Rifle Regiment)
7, 93; recruitment/selection/training 11, 13,
24, 63, 234, 236, 238, 242, 248; Staff Band
of The Brigade of Gurkhas 201, 202, 208–12;
Viceroy Commissioned Officers (VCOs) 24,
77; welfare and pensions 238, 250, *see also*
airborne units
Briggs, Gen Sir Harold/Briggs Plan 62, 90, 91
British forces 42, 44, 87, 96, 99, 109, 113, 136,
142; Army Catering Corps (ACC) 196;
Assault Pioneers 140, 143, 147;
Expeditionary Force (BEF) 15; Far East Land
Forces (FARELF) 102, 104; Jungle Warfare
Schools (JWS) 82, 119, 151, 161, 165; Royal
Army Ordnance Corps (RAOC) 196; Royal
Army Service Corps (RASC) 196, 197; Royal
Corps of Signals 188, 192, 206; Royal
Electrical and Mechanical Engineers (REME)
196; Royal Engineers 22, 176, 186, 187, 196,
206; Royal Marine commandos 118; Royal
Military Police (RMP) 196, 206; scout
battalion 11; Special Air Service (SAS)
118–19, 161, 162, *see also* Gurkha Corps
British Honourable East India Company 1
Brown, Maj R.D.P. 'Billy' 180
Brunei 98, 99, 100, 102, 119, 161, 165, 179,
180, 181, 185, 190, 193, 198–9, 207; Sultan
of 99, 100, 102, 112; TNKU (Tentera
Nasional Kalimantan Utara) 100, 102, 109,
111, 112, 113, 114, 116
Bulfield, Lt Col G.F.X. 40
Bullock, Capt Christopher 137, 138–9, 140, 141
Burge, Lt Harry 209
Burlison, Capt John 120
Burma campaign (1941–5) 13, 42, 44, 50, 54,
61, 67, 73, 76, 149, 156
Burma expeditionary force (1888–90) 9
Burmese Wars (1824–6, 1852, 1885) 11, 12
Burnett, Lt Col E.J.S. 'Bunny' 126
Burns, Lt Col 'Robbie' 185, 186
Butchard, Maj Harry 154

Cairo 27, 29
Callaghan, Lt Mike 162
Calvert, Brig 54, 55, 56
Cambodia 99
Cameron, Maj Ian 104, 105–6
Cane, Maj Peter 59
Carver, Lt Col John 177
Cassels, 2nd Lt James 108
Cassino, battle of 33–8
casualties: Brunei/Borneo 102, 111, 112, 121,
127, 132, 144, 147; 'friendly fire' 159;
Indonesian 127, 129, 130, 132, 133, 135,
137, 144, 147; Japanese 67, 69; Malaya 84,
86, 88, 90; WWI 15, 17, 21, 22, 23; WWII
35, 36, 39, 40, 41, 52, 55, 57–8, 65, 69, 76
Chabilal Rana, Sgt 139
Chamberlain, Gen Sir Neville 10
Chamling Anup, Rfn 172
Chandrabahadur Gurung, Rfn 120–1

Channer, Capt N.M., VC 5
Chapple, Wg Cdr J.H.D., RAF 148
Chesshyre, Maj Bill 184
Chiang Kai Shek, Generalissimo 45, 50, 80
Chin Peng (Ong Boon Hua) 79, 80, 84–5, 94
China, People's Liberation Army (PLA) 84
China/Chinese 9, 80, 117, 146, 177; in Hong
Kong 180–1; in Malaya 80, 83, 87, 95
Chindits 51, 52, 55, 58, 156
Chinese Communist Organisation (CCO) 113,
114, 130
Chinese forces 45, 50, 51, 55, 63
Christian, Ian 79
Christison, Lt Gen Sir Philip 61–2
Churchill, Winston (Prime Minister) 148
Clark, Gen Mark 33
Clements, Lt Col Johnny 118, 121, 124, 132,
135
Commonwealth forces 96, 136, 142, 147
Conference of the New Emerging Forces
(CONEFO) 146
Cook, Capt John, VC 10
Cooke, Lt Col S.A. 51
Couch, Maj Neil 193, 195
Cowan, Maj Gen D.T. 'Punch' 65
Cowan, Maj Gen/2nd Lt Sam 190–1
Cox, Maj George 187
Crawford, Maj Jim 186
Cronk, Maj Tony 179
Cross, Maj John 97–8, 119, 163, 164
Cutfield, Maj David 116
Cyprus 26, 27, 185, 192, 202, 204, 205

Dayton Peace Accord 166, 186
Dehra Dun, northern India 2, 5, 6, 13
Deobahadur Rana, Lt (QGO) 206
Deobahadur Thapa, Cpl 83
Deoparsad Gurung, Lt (QGO) 139
Dhanbahadur Gurung, Rfn 121
Dhanbahadur Rana, Rfn 44
Dhane Ghale, Cpl 134
Dharmalal Rai, Rfn 164
Dhojbir Limbu, Lt (QGO) 92
Dilbahadur Thapa, Rfn 134
Dillikumar Rai, Cpl 172
Dorman-Smith, Sir Reginald 49
Down, Maj Gen Eric 156
Drinkall, Capt Michael 35–6
Dujaila Redoubt attack 21
Dunne, Maj Murray 177

East India Company's Bengal Army 6
East Timor 214
Edward VII, King 7–8
Edwards, Lt Col Dick 73
Edwards, Lt Col John 181
Egypt 33
El Alamein, battle of (1943) 27
Elizabeth II, Queen 93, 193
Ellis, Lt Col Jeremy 195
Enfield rifle 6
Erskine-Tulloch, Maj Piers 141

Falklands War (1982) 169, 184–5, 193
Fatnassa Heights, battle of (1943) 31

Fergusson, Maj (Brig) Bernard 52, 53
Fielding, Capt Johnny 192
Fillingham, Lt Col Jim 115–16
First Sikh War (1846) 6
First World War 15, 22, 208
Fisher, John (British Resident, Sarawak) 102,
112, 119
Fisher, Maj 6
Fleming, Maj Jon 136
Fletcher, Gus (Special Branch) 94–5
Forbes, Maj Angus 165
Forster, Maj Tristam 166
Francis, Maj Dick 179
French forces 73
Freyberg, Lt Gen Sir Bernard, VC 33, 34
Fry, Maj Maurice 158, 159

gallantry awards: Distinguished Conduct Medal
(DCM) 87, 88, 142; Distinguished Service
Order (DSO) 87; Indian Order of Merit
(IOM) 10, 16; Military Cross (MC) 130, 132,
135, 142, 145; Military Medal (MM) 66,
116, 118, 130, 132, 135, 142; Victoria Cross
(VC) 5, 10, 11, 13, 17, 21, 22, 23, 31, 57, 58,
66, 145, 172
Gallipoli campaign 17–19
Gandhi, Mahatma 77
Ganju Lama, Rfn, VC, MM 66
Garwhal 1, 3, 9
Gent, Sir Edward 81
George V, King 5
Germany 189–90
Gilderson, Maj Simon 166
Gillespie, Maj Gen Rollo 1, 2, 3
Glennie, Brig Jack 104, 109
Gorringe, Lt Gen Sir G.E. 21
Gough, Brig Bill 148
Gracey, Maj Gen Douglas 73
Grant, Lt J.D., VC 13
Greece, National Guard 41
Greece, People's Liberation Army (ELAS) 41
Gregory, Lt Col/Maj Lionel 187, 188, 189
Griffiths, Lt Col 'Tadge' 189
Guides Infantry 7
Gulf War (1991) 202, 205
Gurkha Corps 176; Queen's Gurkha Engineers
Regiment 175–87, 198, 213 Queen's Gurkha
Signals 187–96, 198, 213; Queen's Own
Gurkha Logistics (QOGLR) 196–206; Queen's
Own Gurkha Transport Regiment 196, 213
Gurkhali language 24, 197, 209
Gurney, Sir Henry (Malayan High
Commissioner) 89, 90, 94, 96

Hakes, Capt Richard 172
Hakki Bey, Gen Ismail (Turkish Commander) 22
Hamilton, Gen Sir Ian 17
Hanaya, Lt Gen Tadashi 62
Hariparsad Gurung, WOII (CSM) 139, 140,
141, 142
Harising Bohra, Subedar Major 44
Harkasing Rai, Maj (GCO) 93–4
Harper, Lt Col Alec 58
Harrison, Tom 112, 113
Hastabahadur Pun, L/Cpl, MM 132

Havildar, Sgt Bahadur Thapa, IOM 16
Hawthorn, Maj Gen D.C. 73
Hazara Black Mountain Expedition (1891) 11
Hazel, Maj Tony 191
Hendicott, Lt Col Bob 186
Herring, Lt Col D.C. 54
Hill, Lt Col F.M. 'Paddy' 177
Hiroshima 73
Ho Chi Minh 73
Hong Kong 78, 165, 176, 177, 179, 180, 185, 186, 188, 192, 197, 198, 200, 205, 207; Chinese refugees/illegal immigrants 182, 201; handover to Chinese 186, 195; Royal Hong Kong Police 181, 184
Hope-Thomson, Brig M.R.J. 'Hope' 151, 154
Hopkinson, Maj Paul 150, 152
Horsford, Lt Col E.G. 'Slim' 117
Hutton, Lt Gen H.J. (GOC Burma) 44, 45, 46, 49

Imphal–Kohima battle (1943–4) 51, 60–3, 65, 66; airborne operations 152, 154, 155–6
India 41, 51, 76, 78, 156; North West Frontier 5, 9, 11, 15, 24, 187; Partition 77–8, 159
Indian forces 42, 44; airborne units 148–56, 158–9; Gurkha Brigade 14, 23, 234; Indian Corps 15–17; Jungle Warfare School, Raiwala 151
Indian Mutiny (1857–8) 4, 6–7, 9
Indochina 73
Indonesia/Indonesians 99–100, 113, 117, 119, 126, 128, 145, 147, 180
Indonesian Border Terrorists (IBT) 114, 115, 117, 119, 126, 127, 128
Indonesian Communist Party (PKI) 99, 145, 146
Indonesian forces 128, 131, 133, 164; 328th Raider Battalion 129; 518th Battalion 131; airborne units 128, 130, 131, 136, 137; Black Cobras 129; KKO 126, 127, 130; RPKAD para-commandos 128, 130, 136, 137, 163
intelligence-gathering units 149; Border Scouts 117, 119, 120–1, 124, 125, 161, 180; 'Sancol' (Burma) 155–6; SAS 19, 90, 118; Special Branch 101, 116, 118, 127, 137
International Security Assistance Force (ISAF) 172, 187
Irrawaddy campaign (1942) 50–1, 54, 59, 60, 67, 68
Italian forces 27
Italy 33, 42

Jackman, Capt Bruce, MC 133, 134, 135
Jackson, Lt Col Bill 178
Jackson, Maj J.S. 206
Jagatman Gurung, Rfn 135
Japanese forces 57, 62, 65, 73, 152
Java 73, 145
Jogiakarta, Sultan of 146
Johore 177, 178
Joy, Maj Michael 132–3

Kabul 10, 172, 215
Kalimantan 117, 126, 127, 136, 163, 165
Kalunga, battle of (1814) 2–3
Kandahar, battle of (1861) 11

Karamdhoj Sunwar, Lt (QGO) 128
Karnabahadur Thapa, Rfn, VC 22–3
Kent, Maj Pat 85
Kharakbahadur Thapa, Lt (QGO) 93
Kharbahadur Gurung, Rfn 83
Kharkabahadur Gurung, Rfn 121, 124
Kitchener, Lord Herbert (Secretary of State for War) 17
Kohima, battle for (1944) 60, 63, 65
Korea 146, 176, 200–1
Kosovo 187, 205, 213
Kuala Lumpar 79, 87, 119, 177, 187, 189, 206
Kulbir Thapa, Rfn, VC 17
Kurram Field Force 10–11
Kut, siege and surrender 21, 23

Lachhiman Gurung, Capt (KGO) 88
Lachhiman Gurung, Rfn, VC 145
Lalitbahadur Gurung, Lt (QGO), MM 118, 134
Lancashire Fusiliers 17
Langlands, Capt Johnny 104
Lauderdale, Maj Len 137
Lawes, Capt/Maj Johnny 79, 129–30
Lea, Maj Gen George 136
Lea, Maj Tony 102–3
Leathart, Capt Scott 84
Lee Kwan Yew (Prime Minister of Singapore) 99
Lentaigne, Brig W.D.A. 'Joe' 54, 58, 59
Lindsay, Lt Col Martin 148
Lloyd Williams, Maj Tony 102, 103
Loftus-Tottenham, Lt Col Freddy 148
Luce, Adm Sir David, RN 101

Macapagal, Diosdado (Philippines President) 129
McCall, Lt Alastair 105
Macdonald, Capt Johnny 104, 105
Macedonia 167, 215
MacGillivray, Sir Donald 93
McHardy, Lt Col W.G. 'Charlie' 104, 108
Mackie, Sgt Alastair 117
McLeod, Lt Hamish 182
McLune, Lt Bob 150
Makwanpore, battle of (1816) 3–4
Malaya 42, 43, 77, 78, 117, 161, 162, 163, 177, 179, 187, 196; Communist Terrorists (CT) 81–98, 176, 177; Emergency campaign 79, 82, 93, 94, 97, 136, 164, 178, 189, 190, 206; Federation Armed Forces 97; jungle postal network 84–5; Royal Malay Police 92; security forces strength 90–1; Special Constabulary 81
Malayan Communist Party (MCP) 79, 80, 81, 84
Malayan People's Anti-British Army (MPABA) organisation 79, 80, see also Communist Terrorists (CT)
Malayan People's Anti-Japanese Army (MPAJA) 79, 80
Malaysia, Federation of 80, 81, 95, 99, 113, 119, 120, 126, 128, 130, 165
Malik, Dr Adam 146, 147
Manbahadur Ale, Lt (QGO) 132
Mandalay 50, 68, 70
Manhahadur Pun, Sgt, DCM 87–8
Manners-Smith, Lt J., VC 11

Manuel, Capt Howard 141
Mareth Line (North Africa) 31
Masters, Capt John (RNZA), MC 138, 139, 140, 141, 142
Masters, Maj John 58
Maude, Lt Gen Sir Stanley 21
Maunsell, Capt Kit, MC 142, 143, 144, 145
Mayman, Maj Ian 128
Megiddo, battle of (1918) 23
Merrill, Brig Gen Frank 60
'Merrill's Marauders' (Burma campaign) 53
Mesopotamia campaign (1914–17) 19–22
Messervy, Gen Frank 62
Miller, Maj Douglas 179
Min Yuen (Malayan People's Movement) 80
Mogaung, battle for (1944) 55–7
Mole, Maj John 121–2, 124
Monro, 2nd Lt Donald 104
Monte Cassino, battle of (1944) 35
Montgomery, Gen Bernard 29–30
Moore, Capt Bill 209
Moore, Capt Jeremy, RM 109, 111
Morgan, Lt Col David 169
Morris, Brig J.R. 'Jumbo' 53, 54, 58, 59
'Morris Force' (Burma campaign) 53, 58, 60
Morris, Richard (British Resident, Sarawak) 101, 109
Mostyn, Maj David 111
Muljono, Maj 119, 124, 125
Mutaguchi, Gen Renya 63, 65, 67
Myers, Lt Col Peter 142, 145

Nagasaki 73
Naik (Cpl) Amarbahadur Khattri 36
Nainabahadur Rai, Rfn, MM 116
Nandaraj Gurung, Lt (QGO), MC 130
Nangle, Lt Col George 36
Narbir Thapa, Maj (QGO) 207
Narbu Lama, Capt (GCO) 125, 208
Nasution, Gen 145, 146
NATO Implementation/Stabilisation Forces (IFOR/SFOR) 205, 213
Neill, Lt Col/Capt D.F. 'Nick' 81–2, 83, 85, 129, 132, 138, 140, 141, 142
Nepal 1–4, 79, 186, 234, 250
Newland, Maj/Capt Jack 150, 158
Newman, Maj David St John 207
Nicholson, Brig Gen John 7
Niven, Capt Bruce 161
Nixon, Gen Sir John 19
North African campaign 26, 27, 42
North Vietnam 146
Nur-ud-Din, Gen (Turkish Commander) 20

O'Bree, Maj Peter 208
Ochterlony, Maj Gen David 1–2, 3, 4
O'Donnell, Maj Dan 167, 172
Oldfield, Lt Col Paul 195
Oldham, Lt Col Wilfred 67
O'Leary, Maj Dennis 127
operations: Bulldozer (Burma) 151; Chieftain (Malaya) 96; Claret (Borneo) 131, 132–3, 136, 137, 142, 145, 147, 162, 163; Dracula (Burma) 71–2, 158; Gyroscope (Malaya) 91–2; Kukri (Malaya, 1948) 83; Longcloth

(Burma) 52; Pursuit (Malaya) 89–90; Sickle (Malaya, 1948) 84; Smoke (Malaya) 85–6; Thursday (Burma) 53, 54, 60
Orgill, Lt Col A.W 26, 27

Pakistan 77, 78, 159
Palestine 23, 33
Panchabahadur Rai, Rfn 128
Parkinson, Maj Gen 33
Parkinson, Maj Ian 188
Parsons, Lt Col Hugh 150
Parsuram Gurung, Maj/Capt (KGO) 83, 188
Pasbahadur Gurung, Lt (QGO) 124
Patawari, Maj Andy 129
Paterson, Maj Hamish 190, 191
Patterson, Brig A.G. 'Pat' 113
Pearl Harbor (1941) 42
Pennell, Maj Mark 111
Perowne, Maj Gen Lance 188, 196
Persian Army 26
Phillips, Maj L.M. 'Phil' 129, 161, 162, 163
Police Field Force (PFF), Malaya/Sarawak 93, 102, 120, 126, 127, 129
Prince of Wales, HRH 214
Princess Royal, HRH 188, 193
prisoners of war 21, 27, 44
Purah Gorakh Regiment 1, 3
Purandjoh Rai, Lt (QGO) 128
Puransing Limbu, Lt (QGO) 143

Quantrill, Maj Peter 161

Rabilal Rai, Acting Unpaid L/Cpl 91
Radford, Maj Jimmy 177, 179
Ramadi, battle of (1917) 22
Rambahadur Limbu, L/Cpl, VC 143, 144
Ramparsad Gurung, L/Cpl, MM 141, 142
Ramparsad Pun, Rfn 139
Rangoon 44, 45, 49, 50, 71, 72, 158, 159
Ranjit Rai, Lt (QGO), MC 142, 143, 144
Rashid Ali 24, 26
Rawalpindi 9, 156, 187
Reid, Maj Charles 6
Resambahadur Thapa, Rfn, MM 130
Reshambahadur Thapa, L/Cpl 140
Rich, Maj Philip 180
Richards, Col Hugh 63
Richardson, Lt Col (Maj) Gordon, DSO 38, 82, 86
Rickets, Lt Col/Maj Tony 180, 181
Ridgeway, Lt R.K., VC 13
Ritchie, Lt Gen Neil 27
Ritchie, Maj Alf 206
Roach, Maj Gil 180, 181
Roberts, Lt David 180
Roberts, Maj Gen (FM) Frederick, VC 10, 11
Roberts, Maj Gen Ouvry 151
Roberts, Maj/Capt Jimmy 149–50, 154
Rolt, Capt Michael 148
Rommel, FM Erwin 27, 30
Royal Navy 21, 126, 147; HMS Albion 109; HMS Bulwark 131; HMS Cavalier 105; HMS Chawton 109; HMS Fiskerton 109; HMS Tiger 111
Rupsing Gurung, Sgt 134

Russo-Turkish War (1878) 9
Ryding, Capt Keith 192
Saifuddin, Sir Omar Ali (Sultan of Brunei) 99, 100, 102, 112
Saigon 73
Salonika 41
San Marino, advance on (1944) 38–9
Sangro, battle of (1943) 33
Sarawak 101, 113, 119, 128, 131, 133, 136, 147, 163, 165, 180, 198
Sarki Gurung, Rfn 83
Saudi Arabia 195, 202
Saunders, Maj John 155
Seagrim, Lt Col A.N. 'Knott' 116
Second World War 24, 77, 112
Segouli, Treaty of (1816) 4
Shakespear, Lt Col Gordon 102, 103
Shand, Lt Kynoch 154–5
Sharqat, battle of (1917) 22
Shell Petroleum Company (Brunei) 100, 104, 105, 108, 111, 147
Sheppard, Maj Alistair 186
Sherbikram Ale, L/Cpl, MM 132
Shere Thapa, WOII (CSM) 83
Sierra Leone 166, 214
Silajit Gurung, Maj (QGO) 195
Singapore 43, 78, 79, 99, 117, 119, 181, 192, 196, 198, 199, 200
Singbahadur Gurung, Cpl 164–5
Sittang Bridge, battle of (1942) 46–50
Siu Mah (MRLA) 88–9, 96
Skillicon, Flt Lt Brian, RAF 142
Slim, Maj Gen W.J. 'Bill' 24, 50, 63, 67, 71, 151, 156, 158
Smith, WOII Lawrence 137, 138–9, 141, 142
Smyth, Maj Gen John, VC 44, 46, 47
South East Asia 73, 76
South Vietnam 99
Spain, Maj Dudley 93
Special Force (Burma) 52–4, 58, 60
Special Operations Executive (SOE) 80; Ferret Force 82, 83; Force 136 79, 80, 82, 84, 112
Spencer, Maj J.H. 'Bill' 178
Stack, Maj Dermot 182
Stephens, Lt Col/Lt Mike 179, 184
Stephens, Lt David 103
Stilwell, Gen 'Vinegar Joe' 53, 55, 63
Stopford, Lt Gen Sir Montagu 63
Strawson, Lt Col John 113
Subedar Lalbahadur Thapa, VC 31
Subhas Chandra Bhose 44
Suez Canal 19
Suharto, Gen T.N.J. 145, 146, 147, 180
Sukarno, Ahmed (Indonesian President) 99, 100, 113, 114, 129, 145, 146, 147
Sukdeo Pun, Lt (QGO) 134
Sumatra 100, 117
Surendraman Gurung, Capt (QGO) 139, 141
Sweeny, Lt Col H.T. 'Todd' 111
Syambahadur Thapa, Rfn 135
Syria 33

Tarver, Lt Col G.L. 155
Taylor, Lt Simon 109
Tejbahadur Gurung, Cpl 120–1

Tejsing Gurung, Capt (VCO) 187
Tekbahadur Thapa, L/Cpl 139, 141
Templer, Gen Sir Gerald 90, 91, 93
Thailand 97, 99
Thapa, Balbahadur 3
Thapa, Gen Amarsing 2, 3
Thompson, Capt Nick 136
Thornber, Maj Jack 176
Thornton, Capt John 91
Tobruk, battles of (1941–2) 26–7, 33
Tofield, Cpl Christopher 134, 135
Tokyo summit talks (June 1964) 129, 130
Townshend, Maj Gen Charles 19, 20, 21
Truss, Capt Bill 85
Tuker, Lt Col Francis 'Gertie' 24, 26, 30, 31, 33, 34
Tulhabadur Pun, Rfn 57
Tunisia 31, 33

Umesh Pun, Lt 166
United Malays National Organisation (UMNO) 79–80, 95
United Nations 146
United Nations High Commissioner for Refugees (UNHCR) 204, 205
United Nations Honour Guard Company, South Korea 200–1
United Nations Implementation Force 186
United Nations Peacekeeping Force 202
United Nations Protection Force 204
United Nations Secretary General 127

Verdon, Capt Paddy 192
Verschoyle, Lt Dominic 179–80
Viet Minh 73
Vivian, Maj Graham 94–5
Von Arnim, Gen Hans (German C-in-C) 33

Walker, Arthur 79
Walker, Lt Mike 192
Walker, Maj Gen Walter 82, 102, 113, 114, 118, 119, 131, 132, 133, 136, 161, 162
Wallace, Lt Hugh 117–18
Watterton, Maj Bob 102, 103
Wavell, Gen Sir Archibald 43, 45, 49, 148
Wheeler, Lt Col L.G. 51
Wheeler, Maj G.C., VC 22
Williams, WOII John Williams (CSM) 136
Willoughby, Capt Digby, MC 124–5, 131, 132
Wilson, Maj Gen Archdale 6
Wimberley, Maj Neil 105, 108–9
Wingate, Maj Gen/Brig Orde 51, 53, 58, 59, 156
Wood, Gen 2
Woods, Lt Col E.G. 'Lakri' 83
Wright, Maj Mike 179
Wyldbore-Smith, Maj Gen Brian 101

Yakcharaj Limbu, Cpl 172
Young, Col Arthur 91
Young, Lt Frederick 3, 5
Young, Lt Max 190
Ypres Salient 15
Yugoslavia 204

Zaire 213